JAIIB

Legal & Regulatory Aspects of Bank

Latest Edition
Practice Kit

05 Tests

05 Mock Test

Based On Real Exam Pattern

✓ Thoroughly Revised and Updated

✓ Detailed Analysis of all MCQs

Title   : JAIIB Legal & Regulatory Aspects of Bank

Author Name   : Mr. Rohit Manglik

Published By   : EduGorilla Community Pvt. Ltd.

Publishers Address : 12/651, First Floor Opp. Arvindo Park, Near Jama Masjid,
Indira Nagar, Lucknow, Uttar Pradesh-226016, India

Copyright EduGorilla

Disclaimer EduGorilla

ROHIT MANGLIK
CEO, EduGorilla

Dear Applicants,

People say *"Success comes to those who work hard."* But I've seen people working hard for their exams day in and day out for marginal success. While others succeed in their examinations by putting in just half the work. So are they God Gifted? No! I believe that it's because they work *smart* and not just *hard*. Similarly, for your exams, you should strategize your preparation so as to increase the likelihood of success. Well with EduGorilla get ready to increase your *chances of selection* in your exam by *16x*.

EduGorilla helps you in not only working *hard* but also working in a *smart and strategic* manner. With EduGorilla's preparation package, you get a chance to make your exam preparation easy, and a fun learning path towards selection. Finding the right path to your preparations can be difficult if you don't know in which direction to head. Don't worry, we have you covered! EduGorilla will be your guide to success in your journey. With our Preparation Package, you can prepare strategically and beat the exam in just one attempt.

EduGorilla's Preparation Package includes-

- **Test Series**
- **Books**

Our preparation package is handcrafted as per the latest changes, expert opinions, and students' discretion. Thus, enabling you to get through each stage of the selection process for your exam.

Our Books are designed by the teachers and experts of the respective exam with a combined 150+ years of experience; to provide you with easy, efficient, and effective learning. Our books are smart, in the sense that not only do they give you the answers to the questions but also provide similar questions for practice.

EduGorilla's competent Test Series gives you real-time experience and confidence through which you can clear your offline or online exam in just one attempt. We currently host 83,000+ mock tests for 1,440+ competitive and academic exams.

Thus, EduGorilla misses no chance to assist you in your preparation and covers all stages of the exam, so that you don't have to look anywhere else.

We provide complete preparation packages for defense, banking, teaching, and other National & State-Level exams. Hence, it doesn't matter which exam you aspire to because you will reach your success.

ALL THE BEST !
Let EduGorilla be your Guide to Success.

Rohit Manglik,
Founder and CEO, EduGorilla

INTRODUCTION

EduGorilla focuses on guiding students to succeed in their examinations. With that in mind, our book, titled "JAIIB : Legal & Regulatory Aspects of Bank", has been drafted through the collective efforts of our distinguished experts with 150+ years of combined experience. This book consists of questions that are created following the latest changes in the syllabus and exam pattern. We compiled the book on the basis of questions that are most likely to appear in the JAIIB Exam. Through EduGorilla's "JAIIB : Legal & Regulatory Aspects of Bank" your chances of success will increase 16x.

EduGorilla does this through our Complete Preparation Package. This package consists of well-conceptualized and structured content in the form of questions that are tailor-made according to your needs and will help you practice for exams in a smart way by pinpointing all the necessary information. It also provides hints and solutions, along with a smart answer sheet for your self-evaluation. You can assess your shortcomings and work accordingly on areas that may require more of your attention.

EduGorilla promises to help you succeed in your examination and accomplish your dream goals. We believe in our aspirants and see them at the top of the merit list. And the first step towards the top is to start preparing with us. EduGorilla's "JAIIB : Legal & Regulatory Aspects of Bank" includes the following attributes.

➤ Well-Researched Content

➤ Top-Notch Quality

➤ Detailed Answers and Analysis

➤ Smart Answer Sheet

➤ Exam Relevant Questions

Therefore, EduGorilla fortifies your preparation and makes it durable enough to help you stand tall and beat the examination.

JAIIB Exam

Scan QR code for Eligibility, Exam Pattern, Syllabus and more.

Book ID: 0709

TABLE OF CONTENTS

Q.1 Shell bank refers to

A. the Foreign bank that does not have a branch in any country.

B. the financial institution that does not have a physical presence in any country.

C. the Indian bank that has a very small area covered.

D. All of the above

Q.2 Under the provisions of the Right to Information Act, a public authority means any authority established:

A. by or under the Constitution of India.

B. by any other law made by the Parliament or State Legislature.

C. by notification issued or order made by the appropriate government.

D. All of the above

Q.3 Under the Sale of Goods Act, if the sale is by a description of goods, the goods shall correspond with the description. If these do not correspond with the description,

A. the buyer has to buy the goods

B. the seller has to supply the goods as per contract

C. the buyer can reject the goods and claim back the payment

D. Any of these

Q.4 Under sub-section (9) of the Banking Regulation Act, a banking company can hold immovable property other than for its own use for a period of 7 years. But if the banking company fails to do so, RBI may extend this period by ___ years.

A. 3

B. 5

C. 7

D. any period on merits of the case

Q.5 Choose the correct statements:

{A} Foreign bank's paid-up capital and other funds should be minimum Rs. 15 lac in the form of deposit with RBI.

{B} Foreign bank's paid-up capital and other funds would be Rs. 20 lac if the place of business is Mumbai or Kolkata or both

{C} 20% of the foreign bank's profit is to be deposited with an Indian bank.

{D} Central government can relax this condition of its own.

A. {A}, {B}, {C} and {D}

B. {A}, {B} and {C}

C. {A} and {B}

D. {A} and {D}

Q.6 Which of the following instructions have been issued by RBI u/s 35A of BR Act.

{A} KYC Guidelines

{B} Clean Policy

{C} Fraud Reporting

{D} Ombudsman

A. {A}, {B}, {C} and {D}

B. {A}, {B} and {C}

C. {A}, {B} and {D}

D. {B}, {C} and {D}

Q.7 The date of the documents of a loan is January 25, 2006. The prescribed limitation period is three years. The suit can be filed latest by;

A. January 25, 2009.   **B.** January 24, 2009.

C. January 26, 2009.   **D.** January 27, 2009.

Q.8 A banking company cannot be acquired by Central Government under which of the following conditions?

A. Bank failed on more than one occasion to comply with RBI direction Under sub-section (21) and (35) of BR Act.

B. Bank is being managed in a manner detrimental to interest of depositors.

C. Acquisition is essential for safeguarding interest of the depositors.

D. Acquisition will benefit the shareholders and government both.

Q.9 As per Sale of Goods Act, the unpaid seller of goods in possession of the goods, is entitled to retain the possession of the goods until payment of the price is made, in which of the following cases?

A. If the goods have been sold without any stipulation as to credit.

B. If the goods have been sold on credit, but the term of credit has expired.

C. If the buyer becomes insolvent.

D. All of the above

Q.10 The objective of enacting Banking Regulation Act was to

A. regulate banking companies.

B. create banking system.

C. regulate acceptance of deposits from public.

D. All of the above

Q.11 For foreclosure of a mortgage, the limitation period is 12 years from the

A. date of the loan document.

B. date of mortgage.

C. date when the money secured by the mortgage becomes due.

D. Any of the above dates, whichever is earlier

Q.12 In which of the following situations is the limitation period not of three years?

A. Money payable for money lent

B. On a promissory note

C. On a mortgage

D. On arrears of rent

Q.13 Which of the following statements is correct?

A. Public sector banks have been created under a special

statute.

B. Banking companies are registered under BR Act.

C. Subsidiaries of state bank are companies registered under Companies Act.

D. Accepting deposits for safe custody falls under the definition of banking.

Q.14 For specific performance of a contract, what is the limitation period?

A. 1 year   **B.** 2 years   **C.** 3 years   **D.** 12 years

Q.15 Trading in shares of a bank at National Stock Exchange is regulated by

A. Company Law Board.

B. Security Exchange Board of India.

C. Controller of Capital Issue.

D. All of the above

Q.16 In which of the following cases shall the limitation period not get extended?

A. Borrower's agent deposited cash in the account within limitation period.

B. Borrower acknowledged the liability in his balance sheet within the limitation period.

C. Borrower acknowledged the liability by signing a letter after the limitation period.

D. All of the above

Q.17 Section 12 of Banking Regulation Act stipulates that the subscribed capital of a bank cannot be less than ___ % of its authorized capital and paid-up capital cannot be less than _____ % of the subscribed capital.

A. 10% , 50%   **B.** 25% , 25%

C. 50% , 50%   **D.** 50% , 10%

Q.18 As per provisions of Income Tax Act, 1961, the taxation of income of an assessee is not on which of the following bases?

A. his place of the source of income.

B. his residence

C. jurisdiction of the income tax authority.

D. None of the above

Q.19 Income tax is levied on the "income" of:

A. Total amount   **B.** Capital

C. Entity   **D.** Living being

Q.20 In a contract of sale,

{A} the seller transfers property in goods to the buyer for a price

{B} the seller agrees to transfer property in goods to the buyer for a price

{C} when the goods are transferred from the seller to the buyer, the contract becomes a sale

A. {A} and {C} are correct.

B. {A} and {B} are correct.

C. {B} and {C} are correct.

D. All are correct

Q.21 RBI can appoint a new director in a banking company in place of another director. The person so appointed shall continue to be in office

A. for 3 years.

B. till the date up to which his predecessor would have held office.

C. till the date up to which RBI issues another order.

D. till the date the Board reappoints him.

Q.22 Returns relating to shareholding of the Chairman, Managing Director or Chief Executive Officer of every banking company are to be sent to:

{A} RBI

{B} SEBI

{C} Registrar of Companies

A. {A}, {B} and {C} all

B. {B} and {C} only

C. {A} and {B} only

D. Neither {B} nor {C}

Q.23 X purchases a hot water bottle from Z, the retailer. On request of X, Z confirms that the bottle is meant to hold hot water. X is injured when hot water is put in the bottle and it bursts. Under the Sale of Goods Act, this is a

A. breach of condition.

B. breach of warranty.

C. breach of implied condition.

D. breach of implied warranty.

Q.24 NCCF was set up on and is administered under the Multi-State Cooperative Societies Act 2002.

A. 16 October 1965   **B.** 16 August 1965

C. 15 August 1965   **D.** 25 December 1965

Q.25 Banks are required to make deduction of tax at source but before that, they should have obtained

A. Permanent Account Number (PAN).

B. Tax Deduction Account Number (TAN).

C. Tax Identification Number (TIN).

D. All of the above

Q.26 Which of the following is not correct?

A. Section 21 of Banking Regulation Act authorizes RBI to issue guidelines on credit by banks.

B. Section 35-A of BR Act authorizes RBI to issue directives to banks in public interest.

C. Section 26 of BR Act stipulates submission of loan related statements by bank to RBI.

D. None of the above

Q.27 A borrower has an immovable property and he is not repaying the loan. The bank wants to recover the loan. Then, the bank can

A. take possession of the security for the loan.

B. manage the same or appoint any person to manage the same.

C. sell or lease or assign the right over the security.

D. All of the above

Q.28 Service tax is to be deposited by banks within

A. 5 days of close of the month.

B. 7 days of close of the month.

C. 5 days of close of the month in case of electronic deposit and 6 days in case of manual deposit.

D. 6 days of close of the month in case of electronic deposit and 5 days in case of manual deposit.

Q.29 If a bank fails to maintain CRR as per Section 42 (1) of RBI,

{A} RBI can charge penal interest of 3% OBR for the first fortnight

{B} 5% OBR is there for the next days

{C} and the shortfall persist for 3rd fortnight also, then every director, manager or secretary of the bank is punishable with fine

{D} RBI can impose a penalty for non-maintenance or non-reporting which is required to be paid within 30 days from date of demand

A. {A}, {B}, {C} and {D} are correct

B. {A}, {B} and {C} are correct

C. {A}, {B} and {D} are correct

D. {A}, {C} and {D} are correct

Q.30 Board for Financial Supervision of RBI,

{A} is a committee established under RBI (BFS) Regulations

{B} has jurisdiction over the banking companies, nationalized banks and State banks

{C} is established with a view to supervise and inspect banks

{D} holds a meeting every month

A. {A}, {B}, {C} and {D} are correct.

B. {A}, {B} and {C} are correct.

C. {B}, {C} and {D} are correct.

D. {A}, {C} and {D} are correct.

Q.31 Which of the following pairs does not match in the context of nomination provisions?

A. Nomination in locker - Section 45 ZE to ZF

B. Nomination in case of joint safe deposit of articles – only one nomination is allowed

C. Nomination in deposit – insolvent or minor can be nominee

D. Nomination in non-resident accounts – Permitted

Q.32 Under the Banking Ombudsman Scheme of RBI, the Ombudsman follows the procedure laid in the provision of

A. Banking Regulation Act.

B. Arbitration and Conciliation Act.

C. RBI Act.

D. All of the above

Q.33 RBI can cancel the registration of a Securitization Company, without giving opportunity to such company in certain circumstances. Which of these is not one among them?

A. Company ceases to carry on business of securitization.

B. Company ceases to hold any investment from qualified institutional buyers.

C. Company fails to comply with directions of RBI.

D. Cancellation without giving opportunity cannot be done, as it is illegal.

Q.34 Cenvat credit can be availed of in respect of tax paid on

A. certain specified services.

B. certain specified input services.

C. all input services.

D. all services.

Q.35 If the provisions of Transfer of Property Act and SARFAESI Act relating to an immovable property are different

A. provisions of Transfer of Property Act would prevail.

B. provisions of SARFAESI Act would prevail.

C. provisions of Transfer of Property Act or SARFAESI Act would prevail at the discretion of the creditor.

D. provisions of Transfer of Property Act or SARFAESI Act would prevail at the discretion of the debtor.

Q.36 Lok Adalt is organized by:

A. State authority or district authority.

B. Supreme court legal services committee.

C. High court legal services committee.

D. All of the above

Q.37 Which of the following statements is not correct in relation to a Securitization Company under SARFAESI Act?

A. It is a company registered with Registrar of Companies.

B. It requires registration with Reserve bank for conducting securitization business.

C. It can set up separate trusts, for separate securitization transactions.

D. None of the above

Q.38 If a case is referred to Lok Adalat and there is no settlement of

A. the case shall be dismissed.

B. the case shall be decided in due course of time.

C. the case shall be remitted back to the court that referred the matter to Lok Adalat.

D. Any of the above, at discretion of the Lok Adalat.

Q.39 A normal Lok Adalat (other than organized by DRT) can entertain disputes involving:

A. up to Rs. 20 lakh.   **B.** up to Rs. 15 lakh.

C. up to Rs. 10 lakh.   **D.** up to Rs. 5 lakh.

Q.40 When a securitization company issues a security receipt that is purchased by qualified institutional buyers

A. it requires registration with Registrar of Companies.

B. it requires registration with Central Registry.

C. it requires registration with Registrar of Assurances.

D. it does not require any registration.

Q.41 To ensure that the banks are maintaining SLR, RBI calls for a monthly return from banks, which is to be submitted by banks within ___ of close of the month.

A. 7 days   **B.** 10 days   **C.** 15 days   **D.** 20 days

Q.42 Disputes arising in cases under SARFAESI Act can be referred to which of the following?

A. Lok Adalat

B. District Courts and High Courts

C. DRT

D. Any of the above

Q.43 What is the full form of FEMA?
A. Federal Exchange Management Act
B. Foreign Exchange Management Act
C. Financial Exchange Management Act
D. Financial Exchange and Monetary Act

Q.44 A transaction that results in change in asset or liability position outside India of a person resident in India or position in India of a person resident abroad is called
A. current account transaction.
B. balance of payment.
C. capital account transaction.
D. trade balance.

Q.45 The additional directors in a company appointed by the Board of Directors by passing a resolution can remain in office
A. as per the term fixed in their appointment by the board.
B. up to the date of the next annual general meeting.
C. for one year at the maximum.
D. for 6 months at the maximum.

Q.46 If the court where the suit is field is closed on the date of expiry of limitation, the suit
A. can be filed a day before.
B. cannot be filed at all.
C. can be filed on the first day of re-opening of the court.
D. can be filed at the discretion of the court.

Q.47 Section 43A of the Banking Regulation Act deals with
A. notification of rules for the preservation of records.
B. rules governing nomination.
C. voluntary winding up of a banking company.
D. preferential payments on liquidation of a bank.

Q.48 The Banking Laws (Application to Cooperative Societies) Act, 1965 extends certain provisions of:
{A} Companies Act, 1956
{B} Banking Regulation Act
A. {A} and {B} both
B. {A} only
C. {B} only
D. None of the above

Q.49 A popular bank makes payment to Y, of a bearer crossed cheque across the counter. The cheque is drawn in favour of X. In this case
A. the bank is liable to the drawer for a wrongful payment.
B. being a bearer cheque, the bank can make a cash payment to anyone.
C. the bank is liable to X, the true owner.
D. the bank is liable both to the drawer and the true owner.

Q.50 As per Sale of Goods Act, the seller of goods is deemed to be unpaid seller, when the _____ has/have not been paid.
A. interest   **B.** price   **C.** penalty   **D.** damages

Q.51 Which of the following are not a current account transaction?
A. Payments due as interests on loans
B. Export and import of goods account services

C. Expenses incurred in connection with travel abroad
D. None of the above

Q.52 The general superintendence and direction of the RBI is entrusted with
A. 3 Finance Ministry representatives.
B. 2 Finance Ministry representatives.
C. a panel of Finance Ministry representatives.
D. 1 Finance Ministry representative.

Q.53 NCCF was set up on 16 October 1965 and is administered under the
A. Multi-State Cooperative Societies Act of 2002.
B. Multi-State Cooperative Societies Act of 1965.
C. Multi-State Cooperative Societies Act of 1964.
D. Multi-State Cooperative Societies Act of 1960.

Q.54 Under the provisions of Section 22 of the RBI Act:
A. RBI regulates the banks.
B. RBI conducts government business.
C. RBI is the sole authority to issue and manage currency in India.
D. RBI issues note refund rules.

Q.55 As per FEMA 1999, an office or a branch or an agency in India that is owned and controlled by a person resident outside India, falls under the category of
A. non-resident persons.
B. a person resident in India.
C. foreigners.
D. foreign companies.

Q.56 Which of the following pairs is incorrectly matched?
A. Clean bill - where the bill is not supported by any document of title to goods
B. Supply bill - where the bill is drawn on the basis of transaction with the government
C. Accommodation bill - a bill which is drawn without any consideration or without any sale or purchase of goods
D. Foreign bill - a bill which is drawn in India and payable in India only

Q.57 When foreign exchange is brought to India and sold to an authorized person, as per FEMA 1999, it is called
A. repatriation.
B. repatriation from India.
C. repatriation to India.
D. expatriation.

Q.58 Liability of partners in a partnership business is _______.
A. limited
B. unlimited
C. limited and unlimited
D. None of these

Q.59 A pledge is bailment of goods to secure a loan. The goods are delivered by the owner to the creditor. These parties as per Section 172 of Indian Contract Act are called
A. bailor and bailee.
B. bailee and bailor.

C. pledger and pledgee.

D. pawner and pawnee.

Q.60 Which of the following is not correct with regard to a deferred payment guarantee?

A. guarantee is issued normally for purchase of capital assets on long term credit from the supplier.

B. guarantee is issued in lieu of term loan and appraisal is also done like a term loan.

C. difference between TL and such guarantee is of outlay of funds.

D. this is a payment guarantee issued to your importer for deferred or timely receiving of the goods.

Q.61 Principle : A citizen is expected to take reasonable duty of care while driving on the road and not to cause injuries to any person.

Facts : X, the owner of a car, asked his friend Y to drive the car to his office. As the car was near his (X's) office, it hit a pedestrian P on account 'Y's negligent driving and injured him seriously. P sued X for damages.

The standard of care generally used in cases of negligence is the ________________.

A. skill and care of a professional person

B. care taken by an intelligent and prudent man

C. foresight of a prudent man

D. skill and foresight of an ordinary person of prudence and competence

Q.62 Bank X gives a bank guarantee on behalf of one of its customers against some payment to be deposited by the customer in a pending court case. Such a guarantee can be classified as:

{A} financial guarantee

{B} performance guarantee

{C} deferred payment guarantee

{D} statutory guarantee

A. {A} or {D}

B. {A} only

C. {D} only

D. {B} or {C}

Q.63 As per FEMA 1999, the term foreign exchange does not include which of the following?

A. Amount payable in foreign currency.

B. DD drawn in Indian currency but payable in foreign currency.

C. DD drawn abroad but payable in Indian currency.

D. None of the above

Q.64 For a securitization company, which of the following conditions is applicable for their capital and capital adequacy ratio?

A. minimum capital of Rs. 200 cr and capital adequacy ratio of 15% of the financial assets acquired by the company

B. minimum capital of Rs. 100 cr and capital adequacy ratio of 15% of the financial assets acquired by the company

C. minimum capital of Rs. 100 cr and capital adequacy ratio of 10% of the financial assets acquired by the company

D. minimum capital of Rs. 200 cr and capital adequacy ratio of 10% of the financial assets acquired by the company

Q.65 To enable the beneficiary to rely on the authenticity and genuineness of the LC, the letter of credit is received by the beneficiary:

A. through advising bank.

B. directly from the issuing bank.

C. from negotiating bank, which is to make payment also.

D. through confirming bank to make sure that payment would be definitely received.

Q.66 In an LC, the documents are to be negotiated in the beginning of September, which means that documents can be presented for negotiation during:

A. first week.

B. first two days.

C. 1st to 10th of the month.

D. 1st to 15th of the month.

Q.67 A security interest created under the SARFAESI Act requiring registration with Central Registry with a period of:

A. 15 days. **B.** 30 days. **C.** 45 days. **D.** 60 days.

Q.68 If a bill of exchange is dishonored,

{A} the drawer is liable to the holder

{B} the drawer's liability is secondary if it is accepted

{C} the drawer's liability is primary when it has not been accepted

{D} the drawee is liable whether he accepts the bill or not in all circumstances

A. {A}, {B} and {C} only

B. {A}, {B} and {D} only

C. {B}, {C} and {D} only

D. {A}, {B}, {C} and {D}

Q.69 If there is a contravention of provisions of FEMA 1999 by a person and the amount is not quantifiable, a penalty can be levied:

A. up to Rs. 2 lakh.

B. up to the amount involved in such contravention.

C. up to two times of amount involved in such contravention.

D. up to thrice the amount involved in such contravention.

Q.70 Under the Prevention of Money Laundering Act, 2002, banks are required to maintain a record of cash transactions of the value of:

A. Rs. 50000 and above

B. Rs. 1 lakh and above

C. Rs. 10 lakh and above

D. Above Rs. 10 lakh

Q.71 For opening an account of a company, under the Prevention of Money Laundering Act, 2002, which of the following documents is not mandatory?

A. Officially valid document in respect of a person to operate the account.

B. Certificate of Incorporation and Resolution from Board of Directors.

C. Memorandum of Association and Articles of Association.

D. None of the above

Q.72 Section 49-A of the Banking Regulation Act makes provisions for which of the following?

{A} Declaration of bank rate

{B} Restrictions on the type of business that the banks cannot undertake

{C} No person other than a bank is authorized to accept deposits withdrawable by cheque

{D} Acceptance of deposits by banks

A. Only {A}
B. Only {A} and {C}
C. Only {C}
D. Only {B}

Q.73 When the sellers sell the goods to the government or public sector undertakings, the transaction is covered through:

A. bills discounting
B. bills purchasing
C. supply bills
D. documentary bills

Q.74 If a banking company is found to be not complying with the requirement of the Prevention of Money Laundering Act, 2002, the Director can impose a fine of:

A. Rs. 10000.
B. Rs. 20000.
C. a minimum of Rs. 10000 and maximum Rs. 1 lakh.
D. a minimum of Rs. 10000 and maximum of Rs. 5 lakh.

Q.75 Which kind of assistance is provided by EXIM Bank to Indian companies?

A. Direct loans to exporters
B. Technology services
C. Consultancy services
D. All the above

Q.76 Director under Prevention of Money Laundering Act 2002 is appointed by:

A. Reserve bank of India.
B. Financial Intelligence Unit, India.
C. Government of India.
D. Security and Exchange Board of India.

Q.77 CIP stands for:

A. Consumer Identification Procedure.
B. Customer Identification Parameters.
C. Customer Identification Planning.
D. Customer Identification Procedure.

Q.78 Consider the following statements:

1. Fiscal deficit shows the net borrowing of the government.

2. Revenue deficit is not a part of the fiscal deficit.

Which of the above statements are correct:

A. 1 only
B. 2 only
C. Both 1 and 2
D. Niether 1 nor 2

Q.79 A banking company cannot hold shares in any company whether as pledgee, mortgagee or absolute owner of an amount exceeding ____ of the paid-up capital of that company or ____ of its own paid-up capital and reserves, whichever is less.

A. 20%, 25%
B. 20%, 30%
C. 25%, 25%
D. 30%, 30%

Q.80 Which of the following is not correct regarding the Loan system of credit delivery?

A. Interest on loan portion and cash credit portion of limit can be different.
B. Security is common for the Loan portion and Cash credit portion.
C. Demand Loans can be paid in a lump sum or in installments.
D. None of these

Q.81 Under the Contract Act, a minor is considered a person who is:

A. 17 years old.
B. 18 years old.
C. Less than 17 years of age.
D. Both (A) and (C)

Q.82 If the service provider fails to comply with the order of a District Forum under the Consumer Protection Act, punishment can be:

A. fine up to Rs. 10000 and imprisonment up to 3 years.
B. fine up to Rs. 10000 and imprisonment up to 2 years.
C. fine up to Rs. 5000 and imprisonment up to 3 years.
D. fine up to Rs. 1000 and imprisonment up to 1 year.

Q.83 When a bill is discounted through bank, which of the following conditions is correct?

A. The bank will not get the title of the holder in due course.
B. The bank will become the payee.
C. The bank will receive the amount after deducting the interest charged by the bank at the time of discounting the bill.
D. The bank will become the drawer.

Q.84 Under SARFAESI Act, the Central Registrar shall register all of the following types of transactions, except:

A. securitization of financial assets.
B. reconstruction of financial assets.
C. creation of security assets.
D. sale of financial assets.

Q.85 Under provisions of Right to Information Act, the person requesting for information has to pay the prescribed fee, which can be in the form of all of the following, except

A. cash against proper receipt.
B. cheque from the account of the information seeker.
C. demand draft or bankers' cheque.
D. indian postal order.

Q.86 Which of the following is not a type of mortgage?

A. Simple mortgage
B. Equitable mortgage
C. English mortgage
D. Absolute mortgage

Q.87 The National Agricultural Cooperative Marketing Federation (NAFED), established in

A. 1965.
B. 1955.
C. 1970.
D. 1958.

Q.88 The constitutional validity of Securitisation and Reconstruction of Financial Assets and Enforcement of Security Interest Act was questioned before the Supreme Court in which of the following cases?

A. Transcore vs Union of India

B. Mardia Chemicals vs Union of India

C. Mardurai Chemicals vs Union of India

D. Marshal Chemicals vs ICICI Bank

Q.89 Bank B failed to file an appeal against DRT order to DRAT within the mandatory 45 day period. Which of the following remedies is available?

A. The bank has no option except to follow the decree passed by DRT.

B. The bank can make a request to DRT to extend the period, which it can consider.

C. The bank can request DRAT explaining the circumstances and if satisfied, DRAT may permit the bank.

D. The bank can request a high court which has the authority to permit the bank

Q.90 When is it necessary for a bank to form a consortium for lending a borrower though RBI has waived the requirement for the same?

A. When credit facilities are more than 15% of the capital fund of the financing bank in the case of single borrowers.

B. When credit facilities are more than 40% of the capital fund of the financing bank in case of a group.

C. When financing an infrastructure project.

D. Only A and B.

Q.91 Spurious goods and services mean:

A. goods and services which are claimed to be genuine but are not so.

B. goods or services which are genuine and claimed to be genuine.

C. counterfeit products.

D. All of the above

Q.92 Essential features of a of bailment are ......

A. Contract

B. Delivery of possession

C. Purpose / return of specific goods

D. All of the above

Q.93 If appeal is to be made by the liable party to the next court, under Consumer Protection Act, it can be made within ___ days of _____ by depositing ___ of the amount of decree, with varying maximum amount.

A. 15, date of order, 50%

B. 30, date of order, 50%

C. 30, date of order, 75%

D. 30, date of receipt of order, 50%

Q.94 To create an agency, the consideration required is:

A. 25290

B. 26000

C. 50000

D. No consideration at all

Q.95 Association, Agreement, Business, sharing of profits, and sum up the features of a partnership:

A. consideration

B. mutual agency

C. liability

D. interest

Q.96 Lien of the unpaid seller is terminated when:

A. the buyer gets possession of the goods.

B. the seller gets possession of the goods.

C. the buyer leaves possession of the goods.

D. None of the above

Q.97 Implied authority of the partner can be used by him in which of the following circumstances?

A. Withdraw a suit pending in a court

B. Acquire a transfer of immovable property on behalf of the firm

C. Open bank account on behalf of the firm in his own name

D. Appoint agent with the consent of the other partners

Q.98 In winding up proceedings the depositors shall ...... for the amounts shown in the books of the bank standing to their credit.

A. be deemed to have filed a claim

B. have to file a claim

C. have no claim

D. None of the above

Q.99 Income earned by a shareholder on a company shareholding is called:

A. Interest

B. Discount

C. Dividend

D. None

Q.100 Which of the following mortgages does not require registration with the Registrar of Assurances?

A. Equitable mortgage

B. English mortgage

C. Usufructuary mortgag

D. Simple mortgage

Q.101 Under provisions of Prevention of Money Laundering Act 2002, who appoints the director for tracking money laundering:

A. Reserve Bank of India.

B. Central Bureau of Investigation.

C. Central government.

D. Each State government concerned.

Q.102 As per RBI guidelines, a bank must lend through a consortium when credit facilities are more than:

A. Rs. 5 crore

B. Rs. 50 crore

C. Rs. 100 crore

D. None of the above

Q.103 The High court shall order the winding up of a banking company if the banking company is unable to ....

A. pay its debts.

B. file returns in time.

C. eliminate non-performing assets.

D. None of the above

Q.104 Liability of the surety is ________ that of the principal debtor.

A. coextensive with

B. primary to

C. secondary to

D. None of these

Q.105 When the LC specifies the Bank that is to negotiate the bills drawn under the LC, then the bank is also called……

A. Confirming Bank
B. Reimbursing Bank
C. Nominated Bank
D. None of the above

Q.106 Acceptance of deposits by non-banking financial bodies and companies is regulated by which of the following?

A. SEBI & RBI
B. RBI & government
C. Registrar of companies & SEBI
D. Stock exchange & SEBI

Q.107 Reimbursing Bank is the Bank

A. that reimburses the seller.
B. that reimburses the Negotiating/Paying or Confirming Bank.
C. that reimburse the buyer on the goods being found defective.
D. None of the above

Q.108 There is an implied condition on the part of the seller that he has a right to _________ the goods.

A. use
B. sell
C. retain
D. resell

Q.109 In ___________ the ownership of goods is yet to pass from the seller to the buyer.

A. agreement to sell
B. contract of sale
C. contract of future goods
D. contract of specific goods

Q.110 There is no _______ as to the quality or fitness of goods for any particular purpose.

A. implied condition
B. implied warranty
C. express condition
D. express warranty

Q.111 Right to Information includes the right to …… (i) inspect works, documents, records, (ii) take notes, extracts or certified copies of documents or records, (iii) obtain information in form of printouts, diskettes, floppies, tapes, video cassettes or in any other electronic mode or through printouts.

A. Only (i) and (ii)
B. Only (i) and (iii)
C. Only (ii) and (iii)
D. (i), (ii) and (iii)

Q.112 If a securitization company fails to comply with RBI guidelines, under the SARFAESI Act, who can impose penalties and up to what extent?

A. RBI, fine up to Rs. 5 lakh, and if the default continues, Rs. 10000 per day.
B. SEBI, fine up to Rs. 5 lakh.
C. RBI, fine up to Rs. 1 lakh.
D. SEBI, fine up to Rs. 5 lakh, and if the default continues, Rs. 10000 per day.

Q.113 Goods mean:

A. every kind of movable property including actionable claims excluding money.
B. every kind of movable property including actionable claims and money.
C. every kind of movable property excluding actionable claims and including money.
D. every kind of movable property excluding actionable claims and money.

Q.114 How much minimum margin should be kept by banks while issuing guarantees on behalf of stockbrokers or brokers in commodity exchange?

A. 50% of which cash margin should be a minimum of 25%
B. 25% with no sub-limit for a cash margin
C. 100% of which cash margin should be minimum 50%
D. 50% with no sub-limit for a cash margin

Q.115 Which of the following rights is not available to the unpaid seller where the property has passed on to the buyer?

A. A lien on goods for the price while he is in possession of the goods
B. In case of insolvency of the buyer, a right of stopping the goods in transit after he has parted with the possession of them
C. A right of resale
D. None of the above

Q.116 What are the minimum and maximum number of partners in a Limited Liability Partnership?

A. Minimum 2 and maximum no limit
B. Minimum 2 and maximum of 50
C. Minimum 2 and maximum of 20
D. Minimum 2 and maximum of 10

Q.117 The minimum number of directors required in a public company is _______.

A. 3
B. 7
C. 12
D. 2

Q.118 Alternate directors are appointed by the _________

A. board of Directors.
B. promoter.
C. underwriters.
D. shareholders.

Q.119 If a person commits offence under Prevention of Money Laundering Act, 2002, he shall be liable for imprisonment up to:

A. three years.
B. five years.
C. five to ten years.
D. three to seven years.

Q.120 'Certificate of commencement of business' is issued in the case of ……

A. Association of persons.
B. Public Limited company.
C. Private Limited Company.
D. Company Ltd. by Guarantee.

// Smart Answer Sheet //

Correct   Indicates percentage of students who answered questions correctly.

Skipped   Indicates percentage of students who skipped questions.

Q.	Ans.	Correct / Skipped	Q.	Ans.	Correct / Skipped	Q.	Ans.	Correct / Skipped	Q.	Ans.	Correct / Skipped	Q.	Ans.	Correct / Skipped
1	B	40.43 % / 20.21 %	17	C	21.4 % / 38.05 %	33	D	31.99 % / 19.14 %	49	C	16.41 % / 37.69 %	65	A	12.37 % / 35.07 %
2	D	47.09 % / 35.07 %	18	C	25.92 % / 36.27 %	34	B	21.05 % / 37.81 %	50	B	41.5 % / 34.96 %	66	C	25.21 % / 34.96 %
3	C	39.36 % / 29.25 %	19	C	43.88 % / 7.84 %	35	B	23.19 % / 32.34 %	51	D	18.67 % / 30.44 %	67	B	40.07 % / 36.98 %
4	B	21.88 % / 37.45 %	20	D	41.02 % / 27.47 %	36	D	30.2 % / 31.51 %	52	B	18.79 % / 28.18 %	68	A	22.59 % / 38.17 %
5	C	11.18 % / 37.45 %	21	B	21.4 % / 25.33 %	37	D	11.53 % / 37.34 %	53	A	16.88 % / 38.41 %	69	A	16.05 % / 38.41 %
6	C	12.25 % / 34.12 %	22	D	11.53 % / 36.39 %	38	C	31.39 % / 34.96 %	54	C	40.31 % / 34.6 %	70	D	13.79 % / 36.51 %
7	A	17.95 % / 36.98 %	23	A	20.81 % / 15.46 %	39	A	39.0 % / 37.22 %	55	B	14.15 % / 32.7 %	71	D	40.43 % / 21.04 %
8	D	17.0 % / 36.51 %	24	A	20.81 % / 38.29 %	40	D	14.03 % / 36.51 %	56	D	37.46 % / 37.93 %	72	C	30.68 % / 28.42 %
9	D	35.08 % / 38.52 %	25	B	14.86 % / 36.86 %	41	D	12.6 % / 26.16 %	57	C	31.75 % / 37.57 %	73	C	24.02 % / 37.34 %
10	A	13.08 % / 34.96 %	26	C	27.47 % / 37.33 %	42	C	33.06 % / 36.38 %	58	B	30.68 % / 34.6 %	74	C	32.46 % / 35.2 %
11	C	29.37 % / 31.75 %	27	D	48.28 % / 23.78 %	43	B	63.38 % / 29.72 %	59	D	25.09 % / 32.22 %	75	D	36.15 % / 36.86 %
12	C	24.85 % / 36.03 %	28	D	11.06 % / 38.29 %	44	C	26.16 % / 37.45 %	60	D	27.11 % / 28.89 %	76	C	20.69 % / 33.65 %
13	A	22.35 % / 26.88 %	29	B	17.72 % / 26.16 %	45	B	21.88 % / 26.99 %	61	D	30.2 % / 38.29 %	77	D	35.67 % / 37.22 %
14	C	29.25 % / 36.15 %	30	A	34.72 % / 34.48 %	46	C	36.15 % / 36.74 %	62	C	15.93 % / 35.44 %	78	A	15.34 % / 35.79 %
15	B	58.26 % / 30.09 %	31	B	23.54 % / 32.58 %	47	D	17.0 % / 33.06 %	63	D	22.12 % / 32.58 %	79	D	33.06 % / 21.99 %
16	C	22.83 % / 31.39 %	32	B	12.84 % / 31.04 %	48	C	16.29 % / 37.34 %	64	B	24.85 % / 38.17 %	80	D	17.95 % / 31.28 %

Q.	Ans.	Correct / Skipped
81	D	52.68 % / 25.44 %
82	A	30.44 % / 35.32 %
83	B	11.06 % / 38.64 %
84	D	29.25 % / 33.65 %
85	B	20.1 % / 38.05 %
86	D	47.8 % / 35.67 %
87	D	9.99 % / 38.76 %
88	B	31.15 % / 36.98 %

Q.	Ans.	Correct / Skipped
89	C	32.1 % / 38.29 %
90	D	36.15 % / 37.57 %
91	A	24.73 % / 37.81 %
92	D	41.62 % / 37.21 %
93	B	28.18 % / 26.99 %
94	D	31.15 % / 37.46 %
95	B	26.63 % / 32.94 %
96	A	28.54 % / 34.12 %

Q.	Ans.	Correct / Skipped
97	D	24.61 % / 38.29 %
98	A	30.8 % / 36.03 %
99	C	57.79 % / 32.94 %
100	A	26.16 % / 31.99 %
101	C	22.47 % / 36.98 %
102	D	13.08 % / 37.22 %
103	A	34.84 % / 37.81 %
104	A	23.9 % / 34.01 %

Q.	Ans.	Correct / Skipped
105	C	21.52 % / 37.34 %
106	B	37.93 % / 36.98 %
107	B	46.25 % / 30.92 %
108	B	29.13 % / 37.58 %
109	A	28.89 % / 25.81 %
110	A	26.87 % / 36.03 %
111	D	47.09 % / 22.59 %
112	A	39.6 % / 37.69 %

Q.	Ans.	Correct / Skipped
113	D	27.71 % / 23.66 %
114	A	16.05 % / 37.81 %
115	D	9.27 % / 33.66 %
116	A	20.69 % / 36.98 %
117	A	38.29 % / 23.18 %
118	A	44.59 % / 35.67 %
119	D	38.29 % / 23.07 %
120	B	25.09 % / 28.89 %

Performance Analysis

Avg. Score (%)	26.0%
Toppers Score (%)	98.0%
Your Score	

//Hints and Solutions//

1. Shell bank means a bank that has no physical presence in the country in which it is incorporated and licensed, and which is unaffiliated with a regulated financial group that is subject to effective consolidated supervision. Physical presence means meaningful mind and management located within a country.

Hence, the correct option is (B).

2. Public authorities are the repository of information which the citizen has right to have under the Right to Information Act, **2005.** As defined in the Act, a " Public authority" is any authority or body or institution of self-government established or constituted by or under the Constitution or by any other law made by the Parliament or a State Legislature or by a notification issued or order made by the Central Government or a State Government.

Hence, the correct option is (D).

3. Where there is a contract for the sale of goods by description, there is an implied condition that the goods shall correspond with the description and, if the sale is by sample as well as by description, it is not sufficient that the bulk of the goods correspond with the sample if the goods do not also correspond with the description. Therefore, in that condition, the buyer can reject the goods and can claim back the payment.

Hence, the correct option is (C)

4. No banking company shall hold any immovable property howsoever acquired, except such as is required for its own use, for any period exceeding seven years from the acquisition or from the commencement of Banking Regulation Act.

Provided further that the Reserve Bank may in any particular case extend the aforesaid period of seven years by such period not exceeding five years where it is satisfied that such extension would be in the interests of the depositors of the banking company.

Hence, the correct option is (B).

5. Under sub-section (2) of section 11 of the BR Act, a foreign bank operating in India has to deposit and keep deposited with the Reserve Bank, an amount of Rs. 15 lac and if it has a place of business in Mumbai or Kolkata or both, Rs. 20 lac. The amount has to be kept in cash, unencumbered approved securities or partially in both.

Hence, the correct option is (C).

6. RBI had announced 'Clean Note Policy' in January 1999, for withdrawing soiled notes from circulation. Under sub-section and pumping fresh notes into circulation (35)A BR Act. Also, RBI notified the Banking Ombudsman Scheme 2006 (on Dec 26, 2005) u/s (35)A BR Act. KYC Guidelines were also introduced u/s (35)A BR Act.

Hence, the correct option is (C).

7. If a suit is based on multiple causes of action, the period of limitation will begin to run from the date when the right to sue first accrues successive violation of the right will not give rise to the fresh cause and the suit will be liable to be dismissed if it is beyond the period of limitation counted from the day when the right to sue first accrued.

Thus, if the limitation period is of 3 years and it started on January 25, 2006, we need to count it from the exact date for successive three years. Thus, it will be till January 25, 2009.

Hence, the correct option is (A).

8. The Reserve Bank shall, if it has been directed by the Central Government to cause an inspection to be made, and may, in any other case, report to the Central Government on any inspection made under this section, and the Central Government if it is of opinion after considering the report that the affairs of the banking company are being conducted to the detriment of the interests of its depositors.

Hence, the correct option is (D).

9. Subject to the provisions of this Act, the unpaid seller of goods who is in possession of them is entitled to retain possession of them until payment or tender of the price.

(A) where the goods have been sold without any stipulation as to credit

(B) where the goods have been sold on credit, but the term of credit has expired

(C) where the buyer becomes insolvent.

Hence, the correct option is (D).

10. The Banking Regulation Act, 1949 is a legislation in India that regulates all banking firms in India. The Act provides a framework using which commercial banking in India is supervised and regulated.

Hence, the correct option is (A).

11. Article 63(a) of Indian limitation act, 1963 provides a limitation period, in case of foreclosure of mortgaged property. The limitation period for filing a suit for sale of mortgaged property is twelve years from the date when the mortgage debt becomes due.

Hence, the correct option is (C).

12.

- Mortgages are also known as "liens against property" or "claims on property."
- With a fixed-rate mortgage, the borrower pays the same interest rate for the life of the loan.
- A burgeoning share of the lender market includes non-banks.

Hence, the correct option is (C).

13. Companies like a Non-Banking Financial Company (NBFC) are the companies registered under the Companies Act, 1956 not BR Act.

Subsidiary banks are defined in the State Bank of India (Subsidiary Banks) Act, 1959 and not Companies Act.

Accepting deposits for safe custody falls under banking regulation act.

Hence, the correct option is (A).

14. The period of limitation for a suit for specific performance of a contract is three years and the time of limitation starts to run from the date fixed for the performance, or, if no such date is fixed, when the plaintiff has notice that performance is refused.

Hence, the correct option is (C).

15. The Securities and Exchange Board of India (SEBI) is the regulatory authority established under the SEBI Act, 1992 and is the principal regulator for Stock Exchanges in India. Thus, trading in shares of a bank at National Stock Exchange is regulated by this authority.

Hence, the correct option is (B).

16. The acknowledgement binds only those persons who have signed it. Thus, if borrower has acknowledged the liability by signing a letter after the limitation period, the limitation period shall not get extended.

Hence, the correct option is (C).

17. Under section 12 of Banking Regulation Act, no banking company shall carry on business in India, unless it satisfies the condition that the subscribed capital of the company is not less than one-half of the authorised capital and the paid-up capital is not less than one-half of the subscribed capital.

Hence, the correct option is (C).

18. Levy of tax is separate on each of the persons. The levy is governed by the Indian Income Tax Act, 1961 and the taxation of individual's income is dependent on income tax authority.

An Assessing officer shall exercise his jurisdiction over persons who carry business in his area of jurisdiction.

Hence, the correct option is (C).

19. Income tax is levied on the "income" of the entity.

Income Tax Act, 1961:

- In consultation with the Ministry of Law, the Income Tax Act, 1961 was passed and it has been brought into force from 1 April 1962.
- It is a comprehensive statute that focuses on the various rules and regulations that govern taxation in the country.
- It provides for levying, administering, collecting, and recovering income tax for the Indian government.
- Income tax is a tax paid directly to the government on basis of income or profit.
- Tax can be direct or indirect.
- Direct tax is the income tax paid directly to the government and is levied on the income of an entity or an individual.

Hence, the correct option is (C).

20. Property means the general property in goods, and not merely a special property and seller means a person who sells or agrees to sell goods to the buyer for a price. When the goods are transferred from the seller to the buyer, the contract becomes a sale as "contract of sale" includes anagreement to sell as well as a sale. Thus, all the given statements are true.

Hence, the correct option is (D).

21. Every director elected under 'election of new directors', shall hold office until the date up to which his predecessor would have held office, if the election had not been held.

Hence, the correct option is (B).

22. Every Chairman, Managing Director or Chief Executive Officer, by whatever name called, of a banking company shall furnish to the Reserve Bank through that banking company returns containing full particulars of the extent and value of his holding of shares.

Hence, the correct option is (D).

23. A condition is a stipulation essential to the main purpose of the contract, the breach of which gives rise to a right to treat the contract as repudiated. X demanded the bottle to be able to withhold the hot water, but it did not and thus, it didn't stand by the condition.

Hence, the correct option is (A).

24. The NCCF, a national level consumer origination, was set up in 1965 under the provisions of the Bombay Co-operative Societies Act, 1925 as extended to the U.T. of Delhi. It is now deemed to be registered under the provisions of the Multi-State Cooperative Societies Act, 2002.

Hence, the correct option is (A).

25. Tax Deduction Account Number or Tax Collection Account Number is a 10-digit alphanumeric number issued by the Income Tax Department (we will refer to it as TAN). TAN is to be obtained by all persons who are responsible for deducting tax at source (TDS) or who are required to collect tax at source.

Hence, the correct option is (B).

26. Every banking company shall, within thirty days after the close of each calendar year, submit a return in the prescribed form and manner to the Reserve Bank as at the end of such calendar year of all accounts which have not been operated upon for ten years.

Hence, the correct option is (C).

27. The Securitisation and Reconstruction of Financial Assets and Enforcement of Security Interest Act, 2002 (also known as the SARFAESI Act) is an Indian law. It allows banks and other financial institutions to auction residential or commercial properties to recover loans. Bank may take recourse to one or more of the above measures.

Hence, the correct option is (D).

28. The due date for payment of service tax is 6th day of the month following the relevant month/quarter, if electronically paid and in other cases, 5th day of the month following the relevant month/quarter. It is provided under section 75 of the Finance Act, 1994 that in case of delayed payments (after due date), the assessee is required to pay simple interest at the rate prescribed.

Hence, the correct option is (D).

29. (A) In case of default in maintenance of CRR requirement on a daily basis, penal interest will be recovered for that day at the rate of three per cent per annum above the Bank Rate on the amount by which the amount actually maintained falls short of the prescribed minimum on that day.

(B) If the shortfall continues on the succeeding day(s), penal interest will be recovered at the rate of five per cent per annum above the Bank Rate.

(C) In cases of default in maintenance of CRR on average basis during a fortnight, penal interest will be recovered as envisaged in sub-section (3) of section 42 of Reserve Bank of India Act, 1934.

Hence, the correct option is (B).

30. The Board of Financial Supervision (BFS) was constituted in November 1994 as a committee of the Central Board of Directors. Its objective is to undertake consolidated supervision of the financial sector comprising commercial banks, financial institutions and non-banking finance companies. The RBI carries out its functions related to financial supervision under the guidance of BFS. The Board normally holds meeting every month.

Hence, the correct option is (A).

31. The nomination to be made by the depositor or, as the case may be, all the depositors together in respect of a deposit held by a co-operative bank to the credit of one or more individuals. Where the locker is hired from a co-operative bank by two or more individuals jointly, the nomination is to be made by such hirers. Thus, it is not limited to only one hirer.

Hence, the correct option is (B).

32. The Banking Ombudsman, assuming the charge of an arbitrator, shall follow the procedure as laid down under the Scheme read with the provisions of the Arbitration and Conciliation Act, 1996.

Hence, the correct option is (B).

33. A securitization company or reconstruction company aggrieved by the order of cancellation of certificate of registration may prefer an appeal, within a period of thirty days from the date on which such order of cancellation is communicated to it, to the Central Government provided that before rejecting an appeal, such company shall be given a reasonable opportunity of being heard as cancellation without giving opportunity is not licit.

Hence, the correct option is (D).

34. Excise duty paid on input goods, service tax paid on input services and excise duty paid on capital goods make them eligible for Cenvat Credit.

Hence, the correct option is (B).

35. The provisions of the SARFAESI Act will prevail in case of any conflict and inconsistency of any provision therein with any provisions of the Transfer of Property Act and the CPC.

Hence, the correct option is (B).

36. The state authority or district authority, supreme court legal services committee, high court legal services committee and taluk legal services committee can organize Lok Adalts.

Hence, the correct option is (D).

37. It is an Act to regulate securitization and reconstruction of financial assets, enforcement of security interest, and for matters connected therewith or incidental thereto. It need not to be registered with the Companies Act.

Hence, the correct option is (D).

38. If no settlement is there, the case shall be remitted back to the court which referred the matter to Lok Adalt. In case of the potential court case, Lok Adalat shall advise the parties to seek a remedy in court.

Hence, the correct option is (C).

39. RBI, during April 2001, advised banks and financial institutions that cases involving an amount up to Rs. 20 lac (RBI enhanced it from Rs. 5 lac, Aug 03, 2004).

Hence, the correct option is (A).

40. "Security receipt" means a receipt or other security, issued by a securitization company or reconstruction company to any qualified institutional buyer pursuant to a scheme, evidencing the purchase or acquisition by the holder thereof, of an undivided right, title or interest in the financial asset involved in securitization. Thus, in that case, it does not require any registration.

Hence, the correct option is (D).

41. For ensuring compliance with the provisions, a banking company shall furnish to RBI, not later than 20 days after the close of the month, a monthly return, showing particulars of its Liquid Assets maintained and its Demand and Time Liabilities at close of business of each alternate Friday during the month.

Hence, the correct option is (D).

42. The SARFAESI Act provides stringent powers to the Banks and Financial Institutions whereby, the secured asset of the borrower is auctioned without the intervention of the DRT. The law under Section 17 of the SARFAESI Act gives a period of 45 days from the date of the receipt of the possession notice under Section 13(2) of the Act the Borrower can file an appeal before the Debt Recovery Tribunal.

Hence, the correct option is (C).

43. The Foreign Exchange Management Act, 1999 (FEMA) is an Act of the Parliament of India "to consolidate and amend the law relating to foreign exchange with the objective of facilitating external trade and payments and for promoting the orderly development and maintenance of foreign exchange market in India".

Hence, the correct option is (B)

44. Capital account transaction is defined as a transaction which alters the assets or liabilities, including contingent liabilities, outside India of persons resident in India. In other words, it includes those transactions which are undertaken by a resident of India such that his/her assets or liabilities outside India are altered (either increased or decreased).

Hence, the correct option is (C).

45. Additional Directors are appointed by the Board between the two annual general meetings subject to the provisions of the Articles of Association of a company. Additional Directors shall hold office only up to the date of the next annual general meeting of the company.

Hence, the correct option is (B).

46. Where the period of limitation prescribed for any suit, appeal or application expires on a day when the court is closed, the suit, appeal or application may be instituted, preferred or made on the day that the court re-opens.

Hence, the correct option is (C).

47. Section 43A of Banking Regulation Act deals with preferential payments to depositors on liquidation of a bank.

After payments have been made first to depositors in the savings bank account and then to the other depositors in accordance with the foregoing provisions, the remaining assets of the banking company available for payment to general creditors shall be utilised for payment on a pro-rata basis of the debts of the general creditors and of the further sums, if any, due to the depositors and after making adequate provision for payment on a pro-rata basis as aforesaid of the debts of the general creditors, the official liquidator shall, as and when the assets of the company are collected in cash, make a payment on a pro-rata basis as aforesaid, of the further sums, if any, which may remain due to the depositors referred to in clause (a) and clause (b) of sub-section (2).

Hence, the correct option is (D).

48. The Banking Regulation Act,1949 is a legislation in India that regulates all banking firms in India.

Companies Act enables companies to be formed by registration, and set out the responsibilities of companies, their directors and secretaries.

Hence, the correct option is (C).

49. Bank is always liable to the person whomsoever the check is favourable to, not the bearer. Thus, in the given case, the bank is liable to X.

Hence, the correct option is (C).

50. The seller of goods is deemed to be an "unpaid seller", when the whole of the price has not been paid or tendered or when a bill of exchange or other negotiable instrument has been received as conditional payment, and the condition on which it was received has not been fulfilled by reason of the dishonour of the instrument.

Hence, the correct option is (B).

51. 'Current account transaction' is a transaction other than a capital account transaction and such transaction includes payments due in connection with foreign trade, interest on loans and foreign travel, education and medical care of parents, spouse and children.

Hence, the correct option is (D).

52. RBI is entrusted with the 21-member Central Board of Directors: the Governor, 4 Deputy Governors, 2 Finance Ministry representatives, and 10 government-nominated directors to represent important elements from India's economy, and 4 directors to represent local boards.

Hence, the correct option is (B).

53. The NCCF is the National level Consumer Cooperative organization in the country. The NCCF was set up on 16th October 1965 and is administered under the Multi-State Cooperative Societies Act.

Hence, the correct option is (A).

54. Section 22 of the RBI Act 1934 makes provided that RBI has the sole right to issue bank notes of all denominations. Thus, Reserve Bank is responsible for the design, production and overall management of the nation's currency, with the goal of ensuring an adequate supply of clean and genuine notes.

Hence, the correct option is (C).

55. An office or branch or an agency in India that is owned and controlled by a person resident outside India, falls under the category of persons resident in India.

Hence, the correct option is (B).

56. Foreign bill is a payment drawn up in one country that is payable in another country. An example of a foreign bill of exchange is an agreement drawn up between two countries for trading purposes.

Hence, the correct option is (D).

57. "Repatriation to India" means bringing into India the realised foreign exchange and the selling of such foreign exchange to an authorised person in India in exchange for rupees, or the holding of realised amount in an account with an authorised person in India to the extent notified by the Reserve Bank.

Hence, the correct option is (C).

58. In a general partnership, each partner has unlimited personal liability. Partnership rules usually dictate that whatever debts are incurred by the business, it is the legal responsibility of all partners to pay them off.

Hence, the correct option is (B).

59. As per Section 172 of Indian Contract Act, the bailment of goods as security for payment of a debt or performance of a promise is called "pledge". The bailor is in this case called the "pawner". The bailee is called the "pawnee".

Hence, the correct option is (D).

60. Deferred Payment Guarantee: Under this type of the guarantee, the banker guarantees payment of installments over a period of time. This type of the guarantee is required when the customer on credit purchases goods/machinery and payment is to be made in installments on specified dates.

Hence, the correct option is (D).

61. Negligence, in general, is legally defined as "the standard of conduct to which one must conform and is that of a reasonable man under like circumstances".

In tort law, a duty of care is a legal obligation which is imposed on an individual requiring adherence to a standard of reasonable care while performing any acts that could foresee ably harm others. It is the first element that must be established to proceed with an action in negligence. When it is claimed that a person has negligently performed a task involving the exercise of special skills, the test for carelessness is whether the defendant carried out the work as carefully as a reasonably competent person possessing those skills would have. Hence, the standard of care generally used in cases of negligence is the skill and foresight of an ordinary person of prudence and competence.

Hence, the correct option is (D).

62. In case the bank guarantees on behalf of one of its customers against some payment to be deposited by the customer in a pending court case, such guarantees are classified under statutory guarantees.

Hence, the correct option is (C).

63. The legal framework for administration of exchange control in India is provided by the Foreign Exchange Management Act, 1999. Under the Act, freedom has been granted for buying and selling of foreign exchange for undertaking current account transactions.

Hence, the correct option is (D).

64. Every Securitization Company or Reconstruction Company shall maintain, on an ongoing basis, a capital adequacy ratio, which shall not be less than fifteen percent of its total risk weighted assets and minimum capital of Rs. 100 cr.

Hence, the correct option is (B).

65. Advising bank advises the letter of credit to the exporter at the request of the issuing bank. Advising banks act upon issuing bank's request advising the letters of credit to the beneficiaries. Once the letter of credit is issued, it must be conveyed to the importer.

Hence, the correct option is (A).

66. Documents can be presented for negotiation during first 10 days of the month.

Negotiation letter of credit means a letter of credit in which the credit engagement from insurer runs to drawers and endorsers, and bonafide holders under a standard negotiation clause. It extends the credit engagement to parties other than the person with whom the account party is doing business.

Hence, the correct option is (C).

67. "Central Registry" means the registry set up or cause to be set up under sub-section (1) of section 20. The particulars of every

transaction of securitization, asset reconstruction, or creation of security interest shall be filed, with the Central Registrar in the manner and on payment of such fee as may be prescribed, within thirty days after the date of such transaction or creation of security, by the securitization company or reconstruction company or the secured creditor.

Hence, the correct option is (B).

68. It was held that until the bill has been accepted, the drawer is the principal debtor and after acceptance, the drawee or acceptor is the principal debtor and the drawer becomes secondarily liable. Hence, the correct option is (A).

69. If any person contravenes any provision of this Act or contravenes any rule, regulation, notification, direction or order issued in exercise of the powers under this Act, or contravenes any condition subject to which an authorization is issued by the Reserve Bank, he shall, upon adjudication, be liable to a penalty up to thrice the sum involved in such contravention where such amount is quantifiable, or up to two lakh rupees where the amount is not quantifiable, and where such contravention is a continuing one, a further penalty which may extend to five thousand rupees for every day after the first day during which the contravention continues.
Hence, the correct option is (A).

70. As per Rule 3 of the Rules notified by Notification No. 9/2005, every banking company, financial institution, and intermediary shall maintain a record of all cash transactions of the value of more than Rs. 10 lakh or its equivalent in foreign currency.

Hence, the correct option is (D).

71. For opening an account of a company, under the Prevention of Money Laundering Act, 2002, all the documents listed in the options are required.

Prevention of Money Laundering Act, 2002 is an Act of the Parliament of India enacted by the NDA government to prevent money-laundering and to provide for confiscation of property derived from money-laundering. PMLA and the Rules notified there came into force with effect from July 1, 2005.

Hence, the correct option is (D).

72. Section 49-A of Banking Regulation Act, 1949 states that no person, other than a banking company, the Reserve Bank, the State Bank of India or any other 21 banking institution [firm or another person that are notified by the Central Government in this behalf on the recommendation of the Reserve Bank] shall accept from the public, deposits of money withdrawable by cheque.

Hence, the correct option is (C).

73. A supply bill authorizes the expenditure of funds on government activities for the whole or part of the financial year. It is introduced by the government as part of parliament's involvement in the raising and spending of public funds.

Hence, the correct option is (C).

74. If the Director, in the course of any inquiry, finds that a banking company, financial institution or an intermediary or any of its officers has failed to comply with the provisions contained in section 12, then, without prejudice to any other action that may be taken under any other provisions of this Act, he may, by an order, levy a fine on such banking company or financial institution or intermediary which shall not be less than ten thousand rupees but may extend to one lakh rupees for each failure.

Hence, the correct option is (C).

75. The financial assistance provided by the EXIM Bank widely includes the following:

- Direct financial assistance.
- Foreign investment finance.
- Term loaning options for export production and export development.
- Pre-shipping credit.
- Buyer's credit.
- Lines of credit.
- Reloaning facility.
- Export bills rediscounting.

Hence, the correct option is (D).

76. The Adjudicating Authority is the authority appointed by the central government through a notification to exercise jurisdiction, powers, and authority conferred under PMLA. It decides whether any of the property attached or seized is involved in money laundering.

Hence, the correct option is (C).

77. Customer identification means identifying the customer and verifying his/her identity by using reliable, independent source documents, data or information.

Hence, the correct option is (D).

78. "Fiscal deficit shows the net borrowing of the government." Only this statement is correct.

- Fiscal deficit is the difference between the government's total expenditure and its total receipts excluding borrowing.
- Gross fiscal deficit = Total expenditure - (Revenue receipts + Non-debt creating capital receipts)
- The fiscal deficit will have to be financed through borrowing. Thus, it indicates the total borrowing requirements of the government from all sources.
- Net borrowing at home includes that directly borrowed from the public through debt instruments (for example, the various small savings schemes) and indirectly from commercial banks through Statutory Liquidity Ratio (SLR).
- The gross fiscal deficit is a key variable in judging the financial health of the public sector and the stability of the economy.
- From the way gross fiscal deficit is measured as given above, it can be seen that revenue deficit is a part of

fiscal deficit (Fiscal Deficit = Revenue Deficit + Capital Expenditure - non-debt creating capital receipts).

- A large share of revenue deficit in fiscal deficit indicated that a large part of borrowing is being used to meet its consumption expenditure needs rather than investment. So, the revenue deficit is part of the fiscal deficit. Therefore, statement 2 is incorrect.

Hence, the correct option is (A).

79. Sub-section (2) of the Section 19 of the Banking Regulation Act, 1949 provides that no banking company shall hold shares in any company, whether as pledgee, mortgagee or absolute owner, of any amount exceeding 30 per cent of the paid-up share capital of that company or 30 per cent of its own paid-up share capital and reserves.

Hence, the correct option is (D).

80. The draft on guidelines on Loan System for Delivery of Bank Credit released by RBI on December 6, 2018, states that the new guidelines on 'Loan System for Delivery of Bank Credit' for borrowers having an aggregate fund-based working capital limit of ₹1500 million and above from the banking system will be effective from April 1, 2019. The above guidance is applicable to both existing as well as new relationships. The present 40 percent loan component will be revised to 60 percent, with effect from July 1, 2019.

Hence, the correct option is (D).

81. Minors (those under the age of 18, in most states) lack the capacity to make a contract. So a minor who signs a contract can either honor the deal or void the contract. There are a few exceptions, however. For example, in most states, a minor cannot void a contract for necessities like food, clothing, and lodging.

Hence, the correct option is (D).

82. If any person fails or omits to comply with the order of a Forum, he may be punished with imprisonment up to three years (section 27 of the Act) or with fine of Rs. 2000, which may extend to Rs. 10000 or both.

Hence, the correct option is (A).

83. The bank will get the title of the holder in due course, the bank will become the payee and not the drawer. The bank will receive the full payment, no amount as interest will be deducted.

Hence, the correct option is (B).

84. The Central Government has issued the Securitization and Reconstruction of Financial Assets and Enforcement of Security Interest (Central Registry) Rules, 2011 and prescribed the forms to be used for the purpose of filing information for registration in respect of transactions of securitization, asset reconstruction of financial assets and security interest over the property. Thus, it doesn't deal with the sale of financial assets.

Hence, the correct option is (D).

85. The person requesting the information has to pay the prescribed fee, which cannot be in the form of a cheque, be it from the account of the information seeker.

Hence, the correct option is (B).

86. An absolute mortgage is not a type of mortgage.

Simple mortgage- If the mortgagor fails to repay the loan, the lender has the right to sell the property and recover the amount from its sale. This mortgage system is called a simple mortgage. In this system, the possession remains with the mortgagor (borrower).

Equitable mortgage- In an equitable mortgage, the owner has to transfer his title deed to the lender, thereby creating a charge on the property. The owner also orally confirms the intent of creating a charge on the property. An equitable mortgage is also known as an implied or constructive mortgage.

English mortgage- The Transfer of Property Act defines an English mortgage, as where the mortgagor binds himself to repay the mortgage money on a certain date and transfers the mortgaged property absolutely to the mortgagee but subject to a proviso that he will retransfer it to the mortgagor upon payment of the mortgage money.

Hence, the correct option is (D).

87. National Agricultural Cooperative Marketing Federation of India Ltd (NAFED) is an apex organization of marketing cooperatives for agricultural produce in India, under the Ministry of Agriculture, Government of India. It was founded on the birthday of Mahatma Gandhi on 2 October 1958 to promote the trade of agricultural produce and forest resources across the nation. It is registered under the Multi-State Co-operative Societies Act. NAFED is now one of the largest procurement as well as marketing agencies for agricultural products in India. With its headquarters in New Delhi, NAFED has four regional offices at Delhi, Mumbai, Chennai, and Kolkata, apart from 28 zonal offices in capitals of states and important cities.

Hence, the correct option is (D).

88. Effective implementation of the SARFAESI Act was delayed by more than two years because several writ petitions were filed in the High Courts. The matter was finally decided by this Court in Mardia Chemicals vs Union of India (2004) 4 SCC311 and the validity of the SARFAESI Act was upheld except the condition of deposit of 75% amount enshrined in Section 17(2).

Hence, the correct option is (B).

89. If bank B failed to file an appeal against DRT order to DRAT within the period then the bank can request DRAT explaining the circumstances and if satisfied, DRAT may permit the bank.

Hence, the correct option is (C).

90. For meeting escalations in capital expenditure to be incurred under the rehabilitation program, banks/financial institutions may provide, where considered necessary, appropriate additional financial assistance up to 15 percent of the estimated cost of rehabilitation by way of contingency loan assistance. Interest on this contingency assistance may be charged at the concessional rate allowed for working capital assistance.

Banks should undertake proper scrutiny of the relevant loan applications, and satisfy themselves, among other things, about the genuineness of the purpose, the quantum of the financial assistance required, the creditworthiness of the borrower, his repayment capacity, etc. and also observe the usual safeguards, such as, obtaining periodical stock statements, carrying out periodical inspections, determining drawing power strictly on the basis of the stock held, maintaining a margin of not less than 40 to 50 percent, etc. They should also ensure that materials used up in the construction work are not included in the stock statements for the purpose of determining the drawing power.

Hence, the correct option is (D).

91. As per The Consumer Protection Act, 1986 " spurious goods and services" mean such goods and services which are claimed to be genuine but are actually not so.

Hence, the correct option is (A).

92.

- There should be a contract: A bailment is based on a contract, i.e., it is created by a contract.
- Delivery of goods by one person to another: In bailment, there must be delivery of goods by one person to another.
- The goods are delivered for certain purpose
- The same goods must be returned

Hence, the correct option is (D).

93. If an appeal is to be made by the liable party to the next court, under Consumer Protection Act, it can be made within thirty days of the date of the order by depositing half of the amount of decree, with varying maximum amount.

The Consumer Protection Act overhauls the administration and settlement of consumer disputes in India. It provides for strict penalties, including jail terms for adulteration and for misleading advertisements. Ensure fair, competitive, and responsible markets that work well for consumers and promote ethical business practices. To promote and protect the economic interests of consumers.

Hence, the correct option is (B).

94. Consideration is not mandatory. There is no legal requirement of consideration, to support the relationship between the principal and agent. One who is legally competent to contract is eligible to employ an agent, i.e. he should have attained the age of 18 years and of sound mind.

Hence, the correct option is (D).

95.

- Two or More Persons: There must be at least two persons to form a partnership.
- Agreement
- Lawful Business
- Sharing of Profits
- Mutual Agency (i.e., Principal-Agent Relationship)
- No Separate Legal Existence
- Unlimited Liability

Hence, the correct option is (B).

96. The unpaid seller of goods loses his lien or right of retention thereon –

(a) when he delivers the goods to a carrier or other bailee or custodier for the purpose of transmission to the buyer without reserving the right of disposal of the goods

(b) when the buyer or his agent lawfully obtains possession of the goods

(c) by waiver thereof.

Hence, the correct option is (A).

97. Implied authority, also known as "usual authority", is the authority of an agent acting on behalf of another person or entity. The person acting with implied authority does what is reasonably necessary in order to effectively perform his duties. The acts undertaken surrounding the use of implied authority depend on the circumstances and the case.

Thus, in case of implied authority of the partner, one can appoint agent with the consent of the other partners.

Hence, the correct option is (D).

98. Booked depositors' credits to be deemed proved.— In any proceeding for the winding up of a banking company, every depositor of the banking company shall be deemed to have filed his claim for the amount shown in the books of the banking company as standing to his credit and, notwithstanding anything to the contrary contained in 2[section 474 of the Companies Act, 1956 (1 of 1956), the High Court shall presume such claims to have been proved unless the official liquidator shows that there is the reason for doubting its correctness.

Hence, the correct option is (A).

99. A dividend is a compensation paid to shareholders who have invested in the equity of a business, typically extracted from the net income of the company.

Hence, the correct option is (C).

100. In an equitable mortgage, the owner has to transfer his title deed to the lender, thereby creating a charge on the property. The owner also orally confirms the intent of creating a charge on the property. An equitable mortgage is also known as an implied or constructive mortgage.

Hence, the correct option is (A).

101. (1) This Act may be called the Pruention of Money Laundering Act, 2002

(2) It extends to the whole of India.

(3) It shall come into force on such date as the Central Government may, by notification in the Official Gazette, appoint, and different dates may be appointed for different provisions of this Act and any reference in any such provision to the commencement of this Act shall be construed as a reference to the coming into force of that provision.

Hence, the correct option is (C).

102. 50 crates and above from more than one bank) or voluntary (fund based credit limits below Rs. 50 crores from more than one

bank) in nature. However, the share of a bank as a member of the consortium should be a minimum of 5 percent of the fund based credit limits or Rs. 1 crore whichever is more.

Hence, the correct option is (D).

103. In case the bank is unable to do so, winding up has to be done in order to realize all the debts of its creditors and depositors. An official liquidator is appointed to carry on this purpose according to the provisions of this Act and he shall pay off the debts of all the claimants accordingly.

Hence, the correct option is (A).

104. The liability of the surety is co-extensive with that of the principal debtor unless it is otherwise provided by the contract. The provision that the surety's liability is coextensive with that of the principal debtor means that his liability is exactly the same as that of the principal debtor.

Hence, the correct option is (A).

105. The term nominated bank refers to the financial institution that receives payment on behalf of a beneficiary to a letter of credit. Nominated banks are typically used to facilitate the receipt of payment when goods or services are provided to the importer.

A letter of credit (LC), also known as a documentary credit or banker's commercial credit, or letter of undertaking (Lou), is a payment mechanism used in international trade to provide an economic guarantee from a creditworthy bank to an exporter of goods. Letters of credit are used extensively in the financing of international trade, where the reliability of contracting parties cannot be readily and easily determined. Its economic effect is to introduce a bank as an underwriter, where it assumes the counterparty risk of the buyer paying the seller for goods.

Hence, the correct option is (C).

106. Banks, including co-operative banks, can accept deposits. Non-bank finance companies, which have been issued a Certificate of Registration by RBI with a specific license to accept deposits, are entitled to accept the public deposits. The Reserve Bank regulates the deposit acceptance only of banks, cooperative banks, and NBFCs.

Hence, the correct option is (B).

107. Reimbursing Bank is one of the parties involved in an LC. The reimbursing bank is the party authorized to honor the reimbursement claim of negotiation/ payment/ acceptance. Reimbursing Bank is the settlement bank between the issuing bank and the nominated bank or the confirming bank.

Hence, the correct option is (B).

108. An implied condition on the part of the seller is that, in the case of a sale, he has a right to sell the goods and that, in the case of an agreement to sell, he will have a right to sell the goods at the time when the property is to pass.

Hence, the correct option is (B).

109. Where under a contract of sale the property in the goods is transferred from the seller to the buyer, the contract is called a sale, but where the transfer of the property in the goods is to take place at a future time or subject to some condition thereafter to be fulfilled, the contract is called an agreement to sell.

Hence, the correct option is (A).

110. There is no implied condition as to the quality or fitness for any particular purpose of goods supplied under a contract of sale. In other words, the buyer must satisfy himself with the quality as well as the suitability of the goods.

Hence, the correct option is (A).

111. "Right to Information" means the right to information accessible under this Act which is held by or under the control of any public authority and includes the right to inspection of work, documents, records, taking notes, extracts or certified copies of documents or records, taking certified samples of material obtaining information in the form of diskettes, floppies, tapes, video cassettes or in any other electronic mode or through printouts where such information is stored in a computer or in any other device.

Hence, the correct option is (D).

112. If any securitization company or reconstruction company fails to comply with any direction issued by the Reserve Bank under Section 12, such company and every officer of the company who is in default shall be punishable with a fine which may extend to Rs. 5 lakh rupees. In the case of a continuing offense, with an additional fine which may extend to Rs. 10 thousand for every day during which the default continues.

Hence, the correct option is (A).

113. 'Goods' is defined as per Section 2 (7) of the 'Act' as. "Every kind of movable property other than actionable claims and money and includes stock and shares, growing crops, grass, and things attached to or forming part of the land which are agreed to be severed before sale or under the contract of sale."

Hence, the correct option is (D).

114. To protect the bank's credit exposure to the highly volatile commodities markets, the RBI has directed banks to obtain from brokers a minimum margin of 50%, 25% of which would be in cash, while issuing guarantees on behalf of them to the multi-commodity exchanges such as NCDEX, MCX, and NMCE.

Hence, the correct option is (A).

115. Subject to the provisions of Sale of Goods Act, 1930 and of any law for the time being in force, notwithstanding that the property in the goods may have passed on to the buyer, the unpaid seller of goods, as such, has by implication of law —

(a) a lien on the goods for the price while he is in possession of them

(b) in case of the insolvency of the buyer, a right of stopping the goods in transit after he has parted with the possession of them

(c) a right of resale as limited by this Act.

Hence, the correct option is (D).

116. Limited Liability Partnership Act 2008 (the Act) is the governing Act for incorporation of an LLP. The Act mandates a minimum of two partners to create an LLP but there is no limit regarding the maximum number of partners.

Hence, the correct option is (A).

117. The 1956 Act prescribed a minimum of 2 directors for a private and 3 for a public company respectively to constitute a Board. This criterion has been retained by the new Act, but the maximum limit of directors on the Board has now been raised from 12 to 15.

Hence, the correct option is (A).

118. The Board of Directors of a company may, if so authorized by its articles or by a resolution passed by the company in general meeting, appoint a person, not being a person holding any alternate directorship for any other director in the company, to act as an alternate director for a director during his absence for a period of not less than three months.

Hence, the correct option is (A).

119. Persons found guilty of an offense of money laundering are punishable with imprisonment for a term which shall not be less than three years but may extend up to seven years and shall also be liable to fine.

Hence, the correct option is (D).

120. Prior to Companies Act, 2013, a private company or public company not having share capital was not required to obtain the certificate of commencement of business, only a public limited company having share capital was required to obtain the certificate of commencement of business.

Hence, the correct option is (B).

Q.1 Under Prevention of Money Laundering Act, 2002, banks are required to maintain record of cash transactions of the value of

A. Rs.50000 and above.

B. Rs.1 lakh and above.

C. Rs.5 lakhs and above.

D. Rs.10 lakhs and above.

Q.2 Section 49-A of Banking Regulation Act makes provisions for which of the following?

(a) Declaration of bank rate.

(b) Restrictions on the type of business that the banks cannot undertake.

(c) No person other than a bank is authorized to accept deposits withdrawable by cheque.

(d) Acceptance of deposits by banks.

A. Only (a)

B. Only (a) and (c)

C. Only (c)

D. Only (b)

Q.3 Banks can undertake permitted business activities u/s 6 (1) of the Banking Regulation Act such as

(a) buying or selling of bullion.

(b) undertaking and executing trusts.

(c) undertaking the administration of estates as executors and trustees.

(d) providing safe deposit vaults.

A. (a), (b) and (c) only

B. (b), (c) and (d) only

C. (a), (c) and (d) only

D. All of the above

Q.4 A bank has to file a suit on the basis of a promissory note dated September 22, 2006. The bank made the demand for payment on November 10, 2006. The suit can be filed latest by__________ .

A. November 09, 2009

B. September 22, 2009

C. September 21, 2009

D. November 10, 2009

Q.5 RBI can make an application to the High Court for winding up of a banking company if

(a) government directs RBI to do so.

(b) the company fails to maintain minimum paid-up capital and reserves as per Sec 11 of BR Act.

(c) RBI has prohibited the bank to accept fresh deposits u/s 35-4 of BR Act.

(d) the bank has failed to remain entitled to carry on banking activities.

A. Only (a), (b) and (d)

B. Only (a), (c) and (d)

C. (b), (c) and (d)

D. All of the above

Q.6 The 'fit and proper' criterion is used by companies

A. while conducting the shareholders' meeting.

B. while appointing directors.

C. while appointing the managing director.

D. passing resolutions by the board members.

Q.7 Section 45s of RBI Act relates to which of the following?

A. Prohibits unincorporated association of persons from accepting deposits from the public

B. Prohibits banks from accepting deposits from public

C. Allows government companies to accept deposits from public

D. Restricts the banks to pay counter interest

Q.8 If a securitisation company fails to comply with RBI guidelines, under the SARFAESI Act, who can impose penalties and up to what extent?

A. RBI, fine up to Rs. 5 lakhs and if the default continues, Rs.10000 per day

B. SEBI, fine up to Rs.5 lakhs

C. RBI, fine up to Rs.1 lakh

D. SEBI, fine up to Rs.5 lakhs, and if the default continues, Rs.10000 per day

Q.9 Which of the following is incorrectly matched?

A. Section-8 of Banking Regulation Act: prohibitions for a banking company for trading activities

B. Section-9 of Banking Regulation Act, 1949: holding immovable property for a period exceeding 7 years, except for its own use

C. Section 10(1) of Banking Regulation Act, 1949 : banking company shall employ or be managed by a managing agent

D. Section 5(0) of Banking Regulation Act, 1949: Central Government has the authority to specify the activities that can be undertaken by a bank

Q.10 Regional rural banks are

A. cooperative societies.

B. companies created under the Companies Act.

C. body corporates created under a special statute.

D. public sector undertakings of the Central Government.

Q.11 The major objective of the formation of RBI by enacting the RBI Act, 1934 was to

(a) regulate the issue of banknotes.

(b) keep reserves for securing monetary stability in India.

(c) operate the currency and credit system of India.

(d) keep control over the capital market and foreign exchange markets.

A. Only (a), (b) and (c)

B. Only (b), (c) and (d)

C. Only (a), (c) and (d)

D. All of the above

Q.12 Section 6(1)(o) of the Banking Regulation Act deals with which of the following aspects?

A. RBI powers to recommend amalgamation of a bank

B. Central Government authority to notify other forms of business of a banking company

C. Central Government authority to order merger of a bank

D. RBI powers to supersede the management of a bank

Q.13 The part of the capital which will be called up only in the event of winding up of the company is called _____ capital.

A. issued　　**B.** paid-up　　**C.** reserve　　**D.** uncalled

Q.14 For banking business, the banking companies are licensed by which of the following?

(a) RBI

(b) Company Law Board

(c) Registrar of Companies

(d) Security and Exchange Board of India

A. Only (a)　　　　　　**B.** Only (a), (b) and (c)

C. Only (a) and (d)　　**D.** All of the above

Q.15 RBI can issue a direction to banks u/s 21 and u/s 35-A of Banking Regulation Act for

(a) Section 21 in the public interest.

(b) Section 35-A in the public interest.

(c) Section 21 relating to loans.

(d) Section 35-A relating to loans.

A. Only (a) and (b)　　**B.** Only (a) and (d)

C. Only (b) and (c)　　**D.** Only (c) and (d)

Q.16 If a borrower has been outside India for some time, for the purpose of calculation of limitation, that period shall be

A. included.

B. included if bank could not prove his absence.

C. excluded.

D. excluded if the bank could prove his absence.

Q.17 RBI issues instructions on rate of interest to banks. The provisions u/s 21A of Banking Regulation Act relate to

A. maximum interest rate ceiling imposed by RBI.

B. method for fixing BPLR.

C. rate of interest fixed by banks as per RBI guidelines are not subject to scrutiny by courts.

D. cases of NPA accounts in which interest can be debited only when it is recovered.

Q.18 Bank B sanctioned a term loan to XYZ, repayable in 28 quarterly installments. The party did not pay few due installments and the bank wants to file suit. Which of the following is the most appropriate answer?

A. Bank can file the suit within 3 years for the entire amount.

B. Bank can file the suit within 3 years for installments not paid from the due date of respective installments.

C. Bank can file the suit within 3 years for installments not paid from the due date of respective installments and also the balance amount, if the agreement provides for that.

D. Bank can file suit for the due amount and for the balance amount bank will have to wait.

Q.19 Which of the following shows Liquidation of NPAs?

A. Factoring of NPAs

B. Securitization of NPAs

C. Reconstruction of NPAs

D. None of the above

Q.20 Income earned by a shareholder on a company shareholding is called

A. interest.　　　　　**B.** discount.

C. dividend.　　　　　**D.** None of the Above

Q.21 For an Indian bank, as per Section-11 of the Banking Regulation Act, the minimum paid-up capital and reserves should be

(a) Rs.5 lakhs, if the bank is having business in more than one state.

(b) Rs.10 lakhs, if the business is in more than one state and includes Mumbai or Kolkata or both.

(c) Rs.2 lakhs, if the place of business is in the state and does not include Mumbai or Kolkata.

A. Only (a), (b) and (c)　　**B.** Only (a) and (b)

C. Only (b) and (c)　　　　**D.** All of the above

Q.22 In computing the period of limitation, the day from which such period is to be reckoned shall be

A. excluded.　　　　　**B.** included.

C. taken into account.　**D.** None of the above

Q.23 The banking companies have to furnish _____ copies of the balance sheet and Profit & Loss account as returns to the Reserve Bank within _____ months from the end of the period to which they refer.

A. 2 copies, 6 months　　**B.** 3 copies, 4 months

C. 2 copies, 3 months　　**D.** 3 copies, 3 months

Q.24 Banks are required to obtain licence from RBI for commencing operation due to which of the following reasons?

A. To make the provision of Banking Regulation Act applicable

B. To prevent indiscriminate formation of banking companies

C. To regulate the formation of a banking company

D. All of the above

Q.25 Which of the following pairs is incorrectly matched?

A. Nationalised banks - Banking Companies Act, 1969

B. State Bank of India - SBI Act, 1955

C. State Bank Associate Banks - State Bank (Subsidiary Banks) Act, 1955

D. RRBs - RRB Act, 1976

Q.26 The benefits provided by an employer to its employees attract payment of tax. It is called

A. income tax.　　　　**B.** perquisites tax.

C. fringe benefit tax.　**D.** super-benefit tax.

Q.27 Where a bank has been charging interest rate from a borrower at a rate prescribed by RBI, such rates of interest cannot be questioned in a court of law under the provisions of which of the following?

A. RBI directives

B. Section 16 of Usurious Loans Act

C. Section 21(A) of Banking Regulation Act

D. Usurious Loans Act, 1918

Q.28 The provisions of the SARFAESI Act are not applicable in case of a loan account in which the amount due is

A. 20% or less of the principal amount.

B. less than 20% of the principal amount.

C. 20% or less of the principal amount and interest.

D. less than 20% of the principal amount and interest.

Q.29 What is the type of banking where banks operate only from a single branch called as?

A. Narrow banking

B. Shadow banking

C. Unit banking

D. None of the above

Q.30 The name of a bank can be included in the 2nd schedule of the RBI Act to make it a scheduled bank if it is a/an

(a) State Cooperative Bank.

(b) the company defined u/s 3 of the Companies Act.

(c) institution notified by the Central Government on this behalf.

(d) the company incorporated outside India under foreign law.

A. Only (a), (c) and (d)

B. Only (a), (b) and (c)

C. Only (b) and (c)

D. All of the above

Q.31 The Lok Adalat is constituted under provisions of which of the following acts?

A. Constitution of Lok Adalt Act

B. SARFAESI Act

C. Legal Services Authority Act

D. Recovery of Debts due to Bank and FI Act

Q.32 Which of the following statements is incorrect?

A. Winding up means closing a company and settling the accounts.

B. Moratorium means a legal authority to a debtor to postpone payment of dues for a specified time.

C. Amalgamation means breaking a company into two or more parts for the betterment of the company.

D. None of the above

Q.33 The SARFAESI Act provisions are applicable in which of the following cases?

A. Creation of security interest in any vessel

B. Creation of security interest in any aircraft

C. Creation of security interest in land

D. None of the above

Q.34 Who performs the functions and exercises the powers of supervision and inspection of banks under RBI Act and BR Act?

A. SEBI

B. BFS

C. Board of Governors

D. Inspection Department of RBI

Q.35 Action under provisions of SARFAESI Act cannot be initiated by which of the following?

A. Commercial Banks

B. Financial Banks

C. Regional Rural Banks

D. Securitisation and reconstruction companies

Q.36 Which of the following statements is not correct with regard to publication of accounts and balance sheet of a bank?

A. The publication has to be in a newspaper in circulation at the place where the principal office of the banking company is located

B. The publication should be within 6 months from the end of the period to which the account and balance sheet relate

C. The publication can only be in a newspaper that is published every day

D. The publication is undertaken u/s 31 of BR Act

Q.37 Majority of share capital in RBI is held by which of the following?

A. Public

B. Central Government

C. RBI

D. Financial institutions

Q.38 Which of the following is/are correct regarding FEMA, 1999?

A. It replaced FERA, 1973

B. It extends to the whole of India

C. It applies to branches of banks outside India also

D. All of the above

Q.39 Which of the following Act has been enacted in India on account of initiative of UN Commission on International Trade law?

A. Prevention of Money Laundering Act

B. Information Technology Act

C. Right to Information Act

D. None of these

Q.40 Where a bank is wound up, the holder of a cheque (issued by a customer of the bank having sufficient funds), becomes

A. trustee.

B. beneficiary.

C. debtor.

D. creditor.

Q.41 Which of the following statements are correct regarding the cash reserve that is maintained by banks with RBI u/s 42 of the RBI Act?

(a) It is called the cash reserve ratio.

(b) It is maintained at a minimum of 3% and a maximum of 20% of NDTLs.

(c) No interest is paid by RBI on this amount.

(d) It is maintained as a fortnightly average balance with RBI.

A. Only (a), (c) and (d)

B. Only (a), (b) and (c)

C. Only (a), (b) and (d)

D. All of the above

Q.42 U/s 26 of Banking Regulation Act, the banks submit to RBI, a return on ______ basis, within ____ from close of the said period, relating to ______.

A. half-yearly, one month, inoperative deposits

B. yearly, 30 days, unclaimed deposits

C. yearly, 15 days, inoperative deposits

D. half-yearly, 30 days, unclaimed deposits

Q.43 Banks submit various returns to RBI under RBI Act or BR Act. Which of the following is not one of such returns?

A. Monthly return of liquid assets u/s 24(3) of BR Act

B. Quarterly return of NPA advances u/s 42 of RBI Act

C. Return of unclaimed deposits u/s 26 of BR Act

D. Fortnightly return on cash reserves u/s 42 of RBI Act

Q.44 Which of the following statements are correct regarding the acceptance of deposits by banks?

(a) Banks can refuse to accept deposits from undesirable persons.

(b) For opening an account, an introductory reference is not mandatory.

(c) For the opening of an account, identification is essential.

(d) Banks can accept deposits of money only.

A. Only (a), (b) and (c)
B. Only (b), (c) and (d)
C. Only (a), (c) and (d)
D. All of the above

Q.45 Which of the following Act recognizes the electronic signatures and records equal to physical signatures and records?

A. Information Technology Act
B. Negotiable Instrument Act
C. Indian Evidence Act
D. All of the above

Q.46 Which of the following statements is incorrect regarding the balance sheet of a bank?

A. For the public sector, it is prepared as per the 3rd Schedule of BR Act
B. For banking companies (private banks), it is prepared as per part I of Schedule VI of the Companies Act
C. It is prepared on the last day of the financial year
D. The provisions for the preparation of the balance sheet are contained in Section 29 of the BR Act

Q.47 Under FEMA, the term authorized person means:

A. Authorized dealers, money changers, all banks
B. Authorized dealers and all banks
C. Authorized dealers and money changers
D. All the above

Q.48 Under the right to Information Act, the information that can be accessed should be held by or under the control of

A. government authority.
B. public authority.
C. public or private authority.
D. government authority, public authority, or private authority.

Q.49 Which of the following agreements with minors is/are not valid?

A. Agreement for the benefits of minor
B. Agreement for supply of necessities
C. Agreement for enjoying luxuries
D. All of the above

Q.50 Which of the following Sections of the Companies' Act 1956 relates to the maintenance of proper books of accounts?

A. Section-211
B. Section-217
C. Section-209
D. Section-205

Q.51 Which of the following statements is false?

A. Licence from RBI is essential to open a bank under Section 22 of BR Act
B. Every banking company has to use the word bank as part of its name
C. No company, other than a banking company, can use the word bank or banker as part of its name
D. A firm or group of individuals can use the words banking company as part of their name or for the purpose of business by giving public notice

Q.52 Which of the following conditions should be fulfilled for a bank to get protection against the conversion of a cheque?

(a) The collection should be for a customer.

(b) The collection should be of a crossed cheque, crossed before falling into the hands of the collecting bank.

(c) The collection should be in good faith.

(d) The collection should be without negligence.

A. Only (a) and (d)
B. Only (a) and (c)
C. Only (a), (c) and (d)
D. All of the above

Q.53 The Transfer of Property Act contains provisions relating to the transfer of

A. actionable claims.
B. movable assets.
C. goods.
D. None of the above

Q.54 A bank is under obligation to make payment of cheque issued by its customer under Negotiable Instruments Act, 1881. Which of the following conditions is incorrect regarding the payment of the cheque?

A. The parties must be certain
B. The funds must be properly available for payment of the said cheque
C. The signatures of the customer should be as per the records of the bank
D. The cheque should be drawn in one ink, one handwriting, and one script

Q.55 A floating charge is a/an

A. charge on all floating assets of the company.
B. charge at the time or before the company is floated.
C. equitable charge on all assets of the company.
D. None of the above

Q.56 Which of the following is a correct statement?

A. Protection available to a bank for the conversion is as per Section 10 of the NI Act
B. Protection against conversion for demand draft is as per Section 131 of the NI Act
C. Bank gets protection for conversion as per Section 131 in case of cheque and Section 131-A for demand draft, as per the Banking Regulation Act
D. Conversion means unauthorized interference in the property of a third party

Q.57 Which of the following is the objective of the Foreign Exchange Management Act (FEMA), 1999?

A. To conserve foreign exchange
B. To manage foreign exchange
C. To facilitate external trade and promote orderly development of forex markets in India
D. All of the above

Q.58 Which of the following is incorrect in the context of the letter of credit?

A. The party on whose request LC is issued is called the beneficiary

B. The bank that makes the payment to the beneficiary against documents and claims payment from the issuing bank is called the negotiating bank.

C. The bank that has the final liability on LC, if documents are received in order, is called the issuing bank

D. The bank with which credit is available is called the nominated bank

Q.59 Which of the following is incorrect in the case of a contract of indemnity and guarantee?

A. In indemnity, the loss is to be made good as soon as it occurs

B. In the case of guarantee, surety's liability is secondary and principal debtor's liability is primary

C. An indemnity is for the reimbursement of loss

D. A guarantee is for bearing the loss that is caused due to the action of the principal debtor or any other party

Q.60 A bank guarantee has been issued by the bank in lieu of the customer being required to deposit cash security. Such a guarantee is called

A. cash guarantee.

B. financial guarantee.

C. performance guarantee.

D. deferred payment guarantee.

Q.61 The sale becomes absolute in case of mortgage by conditional sale, when

A. borrower makes payment of the due amount.

B. borrower fails to make payment of the due amount.

C. loan is re-structured.

D. limitation expires.

Q.62 Under RTI Act 2005, the information can be taken in the form of

A. diskettes or floppies.

B. tapes or video cassettes.

C. printouts or in any other electronic form.

D. All of the above

Q.63 XYZ created equitable mortgage in favour of Bank A on January 14, 2007 (not registered), a simple mortgage with Bank B on January 28, 2007 (and registered on March 12, 2007) and a simple mortgage with Bank C on February 10, 2007 (and registered on February 28, 2007). The priority of mortgage in this case would be in which of the following orders?

A. Bank C, Bank B and Bank A

B. Bank B, Bank C and Bank A

C. Bank B, Bank A and Bank C

D. Bank A, Bank B and Bank C

Q.64 Where forged notes or counterfeit currency has been used as genuine, record of such transactions is required to be maintained if the amount of such transaction is

A. Rs. 50000 or above.

B. Rs. 1 lakh or above.

C. Rs. 10 lakhs or above.

D. irrespective of the amount.

Q.65 Which of the following cannot be deemed to be a contingent credit facility?

A. Letter of credit

B. Bank guarantee

C. Co-acceptance

D. Overdraft which is not availed

Q.66 Which of the following is incorrect in the case of hypothecation?

A. It is defined as per the SARFAESI Act

B. The ownership remains with the borrower

C. The possession remains with the creditor

D. The creditor has the right to demand possession

Q.67 Which of the following is incorrect in the context of partnership firms?

A. The partnership is registered with the Registrar of Firms and not the partnership deeds

B. Registration of partnership firms is not compulsory

C. Registered firms have certain advantages over unregistered firms

D. Non-registration of the firm adversely affects the capacity of the partners to carry on the business

Q.68 Which of the following can prescribe the nature of records to be maintained by a bank under the Prevention of Money Laundering Act, 2002?

A. RBI and the State Government

B. Central Government and State Government

C. SEBI and RBI

D. SEBI and the State Government

Q.69 If a person seeks information from a public authority

A. he has to give reasons for seeking the information.

B. he is not liable to give reasons for seeking the information.

C. if reason is given, it can help in quick disposal of the request for information.

D. information cannot be provided by the public authority without knowing the reasons for seeking information.

Q.70 Which of the following is a charge which is created by a company on its present or future assets and is not attached to a particular asset?

A. Exclusive charge   **B.** Pari-passu charge

C. Floating charge   **D.** Fixed charge

Q.71 If a company does not want to include in its name the words 'limited', it can do so u/s 25 of Companies Act, 1956 after obtaining a license from

A. SEBI.

B. company law board.

C. registrar of company.

D. regional director.

Q.72 Which of the following acts has not been amended to bring it in tune with the Information Technology Act, 1999?

A. Indian Penal Code, 1860

B. Indian Evidence Act and Bankers' Book Evidence Act

C. RBI Act, 1934

D. Companies Act, 1956

Q.73 When a person wants to file a case under the SARFAESI Act, it will approach _____ and for appeal, it will go to_______.

A. district court, high court
B. high court, supreme court
C. debt recovery tribunal, debt recovery appellate tribunal
D. debt recovery tribunal, high court

Q.74 SARFAESI Act has been declared valid by Supreme Court but it struck down Section _____ of the Act in the case of _____ vs _____, which provided for a deposit of 75% of the amount due to the bank before approaching DRT?

A. 13, mardia chemicals, ICICI bank ltd
B. 17(2), mardia chemicals, the union of India, and others
C. 13, mardia chemicals, the union of India and others
D. 17, mardia chemicals, union bank of India

Q.75 SARFAESI Act, 2002 is applicable to housing finance companies whose names are notified by

A. Reserve Bank.
B. National Housing Bank.
C. Central Government.
D. State Government Concerned.

Q.76 An un-registered partnership firm

(a) can not file sue for enforcement of contracts entered into by it with the third party.

(b) cannot file sue on its own partners.

(c) other parties can file suit against the unregistered firm.

A. Only (b) and (c)   **B.** Only (a) and (c)
C. Only (a) and (b)   **D.** All of the above

Q.77 A private company has two shareholders who are also the directors of the company. They die in an accident. The

A. company will be run by their legal heirs.
B. company will invite the public to be shareholders who will choose new directors.
C. company will still exist.
D. the advice of the company law board will be sought.

Q.78 Under the RTI Act, 2005, information can be accessed under the control of a public authority. For this purpose, the public authority means any authority established by

A. or under the Constitution.
B. any other law made by the Parliament of India or by the State Legislature.
C. any notification issued or order made by the appropriate Government.
D. All of the above

Q.79 Under the RTI Act, 2005, the period for providing the information is

A. 5 days.   **B.** 1 week.   **C.** 21 days.   **D.** 30 days.

Q.80 Which of the following is correct?

(a) A company can commence its business without obtaining a Certificate of Commencement of business if it is a private company.

(b) A company can commence its business without obtaining a Certificate of Commencement of business if it is a company without any share capital.

(c) A company can commence its business after obtaining a Certificate of Commencement of business u/s 125 if it is a public company.

A. Only (a) and (c)   **B.** Only (a) and (b)
C. Only (b) and (c)   **D.** All of the above

Q.81 _____ Governs the transactions through cheques.

A. RBI Act, 1934
B. Negotiable Instruments Act, 1881
C. Banking Regulation Act, 1949
D. Indian Contract Act, 1872

Q.82 Which of the following is correct?

(a) Certificate of Incorporation is the birth certificate of a company.

(b) Certificate of Incorporation is conclusive evidence of the creation of a company.

(c) On the basis of Certificate of Incorporation, the bank can open an account without any other introduction.

(d) Certificate of Commencement is required both by the public and private companies.

A. Only (b), (c), and (d)
B. Only (a), (b), and (c)
C. Only (a), (c), and (d)
D. All of the above

Q.83 The lease for a purpose, other than for agricultural and manufacturing purposes, is deemed to be a lease from _____ and it can be terminated by giving _____ notice.

A. year to year, 2 months
B. year to year, 3 months
C. month to month, 30 days
D. month to month, 15 days

Q.84 Which of the following statements are correct according to the sentence?

Where a company creates a charge on its assets and fails to get the charge particulars filed and registered

(a) any person interested in the charge can file and get it registered.

(b) if the charge is not filed and registered, the creditor becomes an unsecured creditor in the event of liquidation of the company.

(c) if the charge remains unregistered, the loan becomes due immediately.

(d) it is the responsibility of the company to file the charge within the given time period.

A. Only (b), (c), and (d)
B. Only (a), (c), and (d)
C. Only (a), (b), and (c)
D. All of the above

Q.85 Which of these are correct for hypothecation as per the SARFAESI Act?

(a) It is a charge on movable assets.

(b) It is in favour of the secured creditor.

(c) It is without the delivery of possession.

(d) It gives the right to the creditor to sell the assets.

A. Only (b), (c), and (d)

B. Only (a), (b), and (c)

C. Only (a), (b), and (d)

D. All of the above

Q.86 Which of the following are correct regarding the SARFAESI Act, 2002?

(a) It is applicable in entire India, including Jammu & Kashmir.

(b) It provides for the sale of security without court intervention subject to fulfillment.

(c) It provides for setting up of Central Registry for registration of securitization transactions.

(d) It covers all types of loan accounts.

A. Only (a), (b) and (d)

B. Only (a), (b) and (c)

C. Only (a), (c), and (d)

D. All of the above

Q.87 In Mardia Chemicals vs Union of India and others case, the Supreme Court had decided that

A. SARFAESI Act is fully invalid.

B. condition of deposit of 75% amount by the borrower before approaching DRT against possession notice by banks, is invalid.

C. condition of deposit of 75% amount by the borrower before approaching DRAT, against the decision of DRT, is invalid.

D. condition of 60 days notices before possession is correct.

Q.88 The Prevention of Money Laundering Act, 2002 was enacted with which of the following objectives?

A. To prevent money laundering

B. To provide for confiscation of property derived from money laundering

C. To prevent the use of the banking system for money laundering

D. All of the above

Q.89 Which of the following facts is incorrect regarding a securitization company?

A. It is a company registered under the Companies Act

B. It has to obtain registration with SEBI for undertaking securitization

C. It can set up a separate trust for different schemes of securitization

D. Its minimum paid-up capital is Rs.100 crores and net worth is at least 15% of the acquired assets

Q.90 Before the enforcement of security interest (sale of a security), the creditor, to show his intention to take possession, is required to obtain possession of the security by giving a

A. a reasonable period of notice.

B. notice of 15 days.

C. notice of 30 days.

D. notice of 60 days.

Q.91 Which of the following is incorrect regarding the lease of immovable property?

A. The transferor is called the lessor

B. The transferor is called the lessee

C. The price in a lease is called the lease rental

D. None of the above

Q.92 As per the Prevention of Money Laundering Act, 2002, the banks are required to maintain a record of the specified transaction for a period of

A. 20 years.

B. 10 years.

C. 5 - 8 years.

D. 5 years.

Q.93 Where a company has been financed by a consortium of banks, the decision to take possession and sell the security under SARFAESI Act is to be taken by

A. the banks having 75% share by value on the record date, in the consortium.

B. all the major banks financing the company.

C. the lead bank in the consortium.

D. the banks having 60% share by value on the record date, in the consortium.

Q.94 Which of the following transactions does not require registration with the Central registry under provisions of the SARFAESI Act?

A. Securitization

B. Reconstruction

C. Creation of security interest

D. None of the above

Q.95 A customer files a complaint with the Ombudsman, which was rejected. Which of the following remedies is available to the customer?

A. The grounds of rejection cannot be appealed against by the customer

B. Customer can only file suit in a court of law

C. Customer can request for review

D. Grounds of rejection can be appealed against within 30 days

Q.96 Registration of a partnership firm under provisions of Indian Partnership Act, 1932 can be with the

A. registrar of firms in the area in which the business of the firms is conducted.

B. registrar of firms of the area in which the registered office of the firm is located.

C. registrar of companies in the area in which the business of the firm is conducted.

D. registrar of companies in the area in which the registered office of the firm is located.

Q.97 Under provisions of the Transfer of Property Act, subject to agreement between parties, a property can be sold without the intervention of court if it is located at

A. any place.

B. only Chennai, Mumbai, and Kolkata.

C. only towns notified by the State Government.

D. only Chennai, Mumbai, and Kolkata or towns notified by the state government.

Q.98 What is the maximum maturity period of funds/instruments in the money market?

A. 1 day   **B.** 7 days   **C.** 14 days   **D.** 364 days

Q.99 A suit has been filed by Bank-B in DRT located at place Z. Now the bank wants to transfer this case to another DRT located at place Y. It can be permitted by the

A. high court.

B. president of the DRT with the consent of the president of the other DRT.

C. chairperson of DRAT having jurisdiction over both DRTs.

D. chairperson of DRAT irrespective of jurisdiction over both DRTs.

Q.100 Recovery of debt. due to banks and Financial Institutions Act, 1993 Section 2 (g) provides a definition of 'debt'. It does not include any liability

A. inclusive of interest which is secured.

B. inclusive of interest which is not secured.

C. payable under a decree or order of a civil court.

D. recoverable by the bank from its employee who committed fraud.

Q.101 Which of the following is the period for DRT decision on the application filed by the bank?

A. It must be decided within 90 days from the date of the first hearing

B. DRT to make effort to dispose of the application within a maximum of 180 days from the date of receipt of the application

C. It is binding on DRT to decide the matter within 180 days from the date of its receipt

D. DRT is not bound to abide by any time limit

Q.102 If any false information is provided to the Registrar of Firms in connection with the registration of a firm, the penalty is imprisonment

A. up to 1 month or fine or both.

B. up to 2 months or fine or both.

C. up to 3 months or fine or both.

D. up to 6 months or fine or both.

Q.103 _______may apply to the High Court for winding up of a banking company under Section 38 of the BR Act.

A. Registrar of companies

B. Reserve Bank

C. Central Government

D. None of the above

Q.104 For the purpose of application of Bankers' Book Evidence Act, the bankers' books include

(a) records kept as a back-up.

(b) records available as disaster recovery.

(c) records on microfilm.

(d) records in physical form.

A. Only (d)

B. Only (c) and (d)

C. Only (a), (c), and (d)

D. All of the above

Q.105 The regulation and control of NBFCs are done by which of the following Act?

A. Companies Act 1956

B. RBI act 1934

C. BR Act of 1949

D. None of the above

Q.106 Which of the following is correct in the context of the Consumer Protection Act?

A. A complaint can be filed by the consumer himself, as on his behalf no consumer association can file the complaint

B. Retailers who buy goods to sell to other consumers can file the complaint

C. The consumer courts are quasi-judicial in nature

D. Consumer Protection Act has been enacted to protect the manufacturers and service providers from the consumers

Q.107 ___ involves the promotion of corporate fairness, transparency, and accountability in the interest of all stakeholders.

A. Risk management

B. Corporate risk management

C. Corporate strategies

D. Corporate governance

Q.108 In a mortgage suit, the preliminary decree becomes the final decree when the

A. the request is made by the bank as a creditor.

B. borrower fails to pay the decretal amount.

C. the court takes a decision on the basis of its discretion.

D. the request comes from the bank and the borrower.

Q.109 Under the Companies Act, which of the following powers can be exercised by the Board of directors

______________.

A. power to sell any of the companies undertakings

B. power to make calls

C. power to borrow in excess of paid-up capital

D. power to appoint an auditor

Q.110 Which of the following options is correct according to the sentence?

A contract is valid if the consideration is lawful when at the desire of the promisor, the promisee

(a) has done or abstained from doing something.

(b) does or abstains from doing something.

(c) promises to do or abstains from doing something.

A. Only (a) and (c)   **B.** Only (a) and (b)

C. Only (b) and (c)   **D.** All of the above

Q.111 For actions of a partner in a limited liability partnership

A. all the partners become automatically liable.

B. the LLP does become liable.

C. other partners do not become liable for one.

D. None of the above

Q.112 If a bank refuses to make payment of a cheque wrongfully, the bank is liable to compensate the_______, in case he suffers any loss.

A. holder   **B.** payee   **C.** endorsee   **D.** drawer

Q.113 The difference between the value of a nation's visible exports and visible imports is called _________.

A. balance of trade

B. balance of payments

C. balance of the current account

D. balance of the capital account

Q.114 A lease for agricultural or manufacturing purpose can be terminated by the lessor or lessee by giving ___________ notice to one another.

A. 6 months   **B.** 15 days

C. 10 days   **D.** None of these

Q.115 When the transfer of the property in the goods is to take place at a contract is called _________.

A. contract of sale

B. agreement to sell

C. contract of future goods

D. contract of specific goods

Q.116 At least _________ of the total number of directors of a public company are to be persons whose period of office is liable to determination by retirement of directors by rotation.

A. 2   **B.** 3   **C.** 7   **D.** $\frac{2}{3}$

Q.117 A lease for an agricultural or manufacturing purpose is deemed to be a lease for

A. year to year.   **B.** month to month.

C. week to week.   **D.** an infinite period.

Q.118 Right to Information means the right to

A. inspection of work, documents, and records.

B. taking notes, extracts, or certified copies of documents or records.

C. taking certified samples of materials.

D. All of the above

Q.119 Public authority means a/an

A. authority established by the Government.

B. authority established by law.

C. non-Government organization.

D. authority or body or institution of self-government established by Constitution.

Q.120 Loan Delivery System was recommended by the Committee headed by

A. Rashid Jilani.   **B.** N. Vaghul.

C. K. Kannan.   **D.** C. Rangarajan.

// Smart Answer Sheet //

Correct   Indicates percentage of students who answered questions correctly.

Skipped   Indicates percentage of students who skipped questions.

Q.	Ans.	Correct / Skipped	Q.	Ans.	Correct / Skipped	Q.	Ans.	Correct / Skipped	Q.	Ans.	Correct / Skipped	Q.	Ans.	Correct / Skipped
1	D	54.07 % / 16.48 %	17	C	30.77 % / 39.78 %	33	D	16.48 % / 23.3 %	49	C	18.9 % / 39.34 %	65	D	24.4 % / 37.58 %
2	C	32.97 % / 36.48 %	18	C	36.7 % / 38.25 %	34	B	18.02 % / 37.8 %	50	C	37.8 % / 35.61 %	66	C	30.77 % / 35.82 %
3	D	39.78 % / 32.09 %	19	B	32.53 % / 15.38 %	35	C	26.15 % / 34.07 %	51	D	54.29 % / 32.96 %	67	D	22.42 % / 38.24 %
4	C	12.09 % / 38.46 %	20	C	61.76 % / 30.55 %	36	C	30.33 % / 34.51 %	52	C	20.44 % / 32.31 %	68	C	24.18 % / 38.24 %
5	D	30.11 % / 38.46 %	21	B	33.41 % / 29.89 %	37	B	47.03 % / 38.24 %	53	A	21.32 % / 38.24 %	69	B	26.15 % / 39.12 %
6	B	20.88 % / 36.7 %	22	A	21.1 % / 38.68 %	38	D	53.41 % / 35.82 %	54	D	40.44 % / 36.04 %	70	C	24.18 % / 39.12 %
7	A	34.07 % / 38.68 %	23	D	37.8 % / 20.88 %	39	B	16.7 % / 38.03 %	55	C	24.4 % / 34.5 %	71	D	11.43 % / 23.73 %
8	A	46.37 % / 38.47 %	24	B	5.05 % / 38.03 %	40	D	23.74 % / 37.8 %	56	D	8.13 % / 39.34 %	72	D	12.09 % / 32.09 %
9	C	19.78 % / 40.44 %	25	A	25.49 % / 38.47 %	41	A	16.48 % / 29.01 %	57	C	4.18 % / 38.68 %	73	C	44.62 % / 38.68 %
10	C	32.97 % / 35.82 %	26	C	21.54 % / 38.02 %	42	B	37.36 % / 38.46 %	58	A	20.44 % / 37.14 %	74	B	25.93 % / 36.49 %
11	A	27.69 % / 34.07 %	27	C	46.59 % / 27.26 %	43	B	28.13 % / 32.97 %	59	D	23.52 % / 35.16 %	75	C	11.65 % / 37.36 %
12	B	25.71 % / 39.13 %	28	D	22.64 % / 39.56 %	44	D	19.56 % / 38.9 %	60	B	43.74 % / 31.86 %	76	B	9.45 % / 35.82 %
13	C	31.65 % / 30.33 %	29	C	18.24 % / 29.01 %	45	A	38.24 % / 29.89 %	61	B	35.16 % / 38.69 %	77	C	21.54 % / 39.12 %
14	A	42.86 % / 37.58 %	30	D	18.46 % / 36.49 %	46	B	18.02 % / 39.56 %	62	D	54.95 % / 35.82 %	78	D	48.35 % / 36.05 %
15	C	25.93 % / 34.07 %	31	C	28.35 % / 34.29 %	47	C	15.82 % / 34.51 %	63	D	18.68 % / 36.48 %	79	D	50.77 % / 24.83 %
16	C	18.9 % / 32.97 %	32	C	51.65 % / 32.97 %	48	B	17.14 % / 38.46 %	64	D	38.02 % / 38.24 %	80	B	7.25 % / 33.41 %

Q.	Ans.	Correct / Skipped
81	B	36.92 % / 30.77 %
82	B	23.52 % / 36.48 %
83	D	10.11 % / 37.8 %
84	D	25.71 % / 38.25 %
85	B	8.57 % / 38.9 %
86	B	31.87 % / 36.92 %
87	B	25.71 % / 38.25 %
88	D	52.09 % / 38.02 %

Q.	Ans.	Correct / Skipped
89	B	19.78 % / 39.78 %
90	D	18.9 % / 38.24 %
91	C	9.45 % / 38.46 %
92	B	32.53 % / 38.02 %
93	D	23.96 % / 29.89 %
94	D	22.2 % / 38.24 %
95	D	45.05 % / 35.61 %
96	A	7.91 % / 36.71 %

Q.	Ans.	Correct / Skipped
97	D	21.54 % / 38.68 %
98	D	39.12 % / 36.7 %
99	C	29.89 % / 36.48 %
100	D	32.09 % / 33.84 %
101	B	23.3 % / 39.56 %
102	C	26.37 % / 38.9 %
103	B	32.97 % / 38.02 %
104	D	40.0 % / 36.04 %

Q.	Ans.	Correct / Skipped
105	B	15.38 % / 38.69 %
106	C	23.52 % / 38.46 %
107	D	38.02 % / 32.31 %
108	B	21.76 % / 38.46 %
109	B	19.78 % / 30.33 %
110	D	32.31 % / 37.58 %
111	C	33.85 % / 25.05 %
112	D	28.35 % / 37.58 %

Q.	Ans.	Correct / Skipped
113	A	48.35 % / 27.03 %
114	A	29.23 % / 38.24 %
115	B	21.1 % / 36.04 %
116	D	36.92 % / 38.24 %
117	A	57.58 % / 27.26 %
118	D	48.57 % / 37.58 %
119	D	39.34 % / 27.03 %
120	A	19.78 % / 33.19 %

Performance Analysis

Performance Analysis	
Avg. Score (%)	27.0%
Toppers Score (%)	98.0%
Your Score	

//Hints and Solutions//

1. The Prevention of Money-laundering Act, 2002 and the Rules there under require every intermediary to furnish details of the following cash transactions:

(A) All cash transactions of the value of more than rupees 10 lakhs or its equivalent in foreign currency.

(B) All series of cash transactions integrally connected to each other which have been valued below rupees 10 lakhs or it's equivalent in foreign currency where such series of transactions have taken place within a month.

Hence, the correct option is (D).

2. Section 49-A of Banking Regulation Act, 1949 states that no person, other than a banking company, the Reserve Bank, the State Bank of India or any other 21 banking institution [firm or other person that are notified by the Central Government in this behalf on the recommendation of the Reserve Bank] shall accept from the public, deposits of money withdrawable by cheque.
Hence, the correct option is (C).

3. Section 6(1) in BANKING REGULATION ACT, 1949 permits:

The buying, selling and dealing in bullion and specie, undertaking and executing trusts, undertaking the administration of estates as executor, trustee or otherwise and the providing of safe deposit vaults.

It provides that a banking company in addition to the business of banking engage in one or more of the following forms of business. Section 16 of the Banking Regulation Act, 1949, a person is prohibited to be appointed as director of more than one banking company.

Hence, the correct option is (D).

4. On the basis of a promissory note, one can file a suit for recovery of money latest by the completion of third year. The given promissory note is dated September 22, 2006. Thus, suit can be filed latest by September 21, 2009.
Hence, the correct option is (C).

5. The Reserve Bank may make an application under this section for the winding up of a banking company if the banking company has failed to comply with the requirements specified in Section 11 or has by reason of the provisions of Section 22 become disentitled to carry on banking business in India or has been prohibited from receiving fresh deposits by an order under clause (a) of Sub-section (4) of Section 35 or under clause (b) of Sub-section (3A) or Section 42 of the Reserve Bank of India Act, 1934. If the company has failed to comply with any requirement of the Act other than the requirements laid down in Section 11, has continued such failure, after notice in writing of such failure or contravention has been conveyed to the banking company.
Hence, the correct option is (D).

6. This criterion is used by the nomination committee before an appointment of a person as director or after a person is appointed as a director on a continuing basis.

The "fit and proper" criteria (or "fit and proper test") make reference to requirements for evaluating managers, directors, and shareholders. Particularly, the ability to fulfill their duties ("fitness"), as well as their integrity and suitability ("propriety"), are examined.

Hence, the correct option is (B).

7. Section 45s of RBI Act relates to 'deposits not to be accepted in certain cases'. Under this, no person, being an individual or a firm or an unincorporated association of individuals, shall accept any deposit.
Hence, the correct option is (A).

8. If any securitization company or reconstruction company fails to comply with any direction issued by the Reserve Bank under Section 12, such company and every officer of the company who is in default shall be punishable with a fine which may extend to Rs. 5 lakhs rupees. In the case of a continuing offense, with an additional fine which may extend to Rs. 10 thousand for every day during which the default continues.
Hence, the correct option is (A).

9. Section 10(1) in BANKING REGULATION ACT, 1949
No banking company
(a) shall employ or be managed by a managing agent,
(b) shall employ or continue the employment of any person
(i) who is, or at any time has been, adjudicated insolvent, or has suspended payment or has compounded with his creditors, or who is, or has been, convicted by a criminal court of an offense involving moral turpitude,
(ii) whose remuneration or part of whose remuneration takes the form of commission or of a share in the profits of the company.
Hence, the correct option is (C).

10. The public sector banks, namely, State Bank and its subsidiaries, the Nationalized banks, and the regional rural banks are statutory corporations(or body corporate) established under special statutes.

Regional Rural Banks (RRBs) are Indian Scheduled Commercial Banks (Government Banks) operating at the regional level in the different states of India. They have been created with a view of serving primarily the rural areas of India with basic banking and financial services.

Hence, the correct option is (C).

11. Section 45 of the RBI Act

45-IE. Supersession of Board of directors of the non-banking financial company (other than Government Company). Bank to regulate or prohibit the issue of prospectus or advertisement soliciting deposits of money.

The primary objective for the RBI would be to regulate the various banking functions for India in the money market. Thus, they focus mainly on issuing new notes.

The RBI was established with the aim of being a banker's bank and also the bank for the government. Its task was to promote the economic growth of the country through various frameworks and economic policies of the government.

Hence, the correct option is (A).

12. Section 6(1)(o) of the Banking Regulation Act, 1949, provides that a banking company in addition to the business

of banking engage in one or more of the following forms of business. Section 21 provides that RBI has the power to control advances by banking companies.
Hence, the correct option is (B).

13. A company may reserve a portion of its uncalled capital to be called only in the event of winding up of the company. Such an uncalled amount is called the 'Reserve Capital' of the company. It is available only for the creditors on winding up of the company.

Hence, the correct option is (C).

14. For banking business, the banking companies are licensed by the Reserve Bank of India. Under the Banking Regulation Act, 1949, no company shall carry on banking business in India unless it holds a license issued on that behalf by the Reserve Bank.
Hence, the correct option is (A).

15. RBI can issue a direction to banks u/s 21 and u/s 35-A of Banking Regulation Act for-

Section 35(A) of the Banking Regulation Act says that the RBI in the public interest and to "to prevent the affairs of any banking company being conducted in a manner detrimental to the interests of the depositors or in a manner prejudicial to the interests of the banking company, or to secure the proper management of any banking company generally" can issue directions to these entities.

Section 21 of the Act allows RBI to control loans and advances extended by banking companies. RBI may issue directions in respect of the following items to banking companies and every banking company has to necessarily comply with its directions:

- To specify the purposes for which advances may or may not be made.

- The margins to be maintained in respect of secured advances

- The maximum amount of advances that can be made to a particular company, firm, association of persons, or individual having regard to the paid-up capital, reserves, and deposits of a banking company.

- The maximum amount of guarantee that can be made by banking on behalf of a particular company, firm, association of persons, or individual having regard to the paid-up capital, reserves, and deposits of a banking company.

- The rate of interest and other terms and conditions on which advances may be made or guarantees may be given.

Hence, the correct option is (C).

16. Under Limitation Act, 1963, in computing the period of limitation for any suit, the time during which the defendant has been absent from India and from the territories outside India under the administration of the Central Government, shall be excluded.
Hence, the correct option is (C).

17. Section 21-A of Banking Regulation Act relates to rate of interest that is fixed by banks, as per RBI guidelines, are not subject to scrutiny by courts.
A transaction between a banking company and its debtor shall

not be reopened by any court on the ground that the rate of interest charged by the banking company in respect of such transaction is excessive.
Hence, the correct option is (C).

18. Any bank can file a suit within 3 years for installments not paid from the due date of respective installments and also the balance amount if the agreement provides for that.

Filing a suit means presenting a formal document called a Petition or Complaint with a court that initiates a lawsuit. In the petition, the Plaintiff (person filing the petition) alleges a Cause of Action against a Defendant for which they seek economic relief.

Hence, the correct option is (C).

19. Securitization of NPAs is a process where non-liquidated financial assets (dues from a borrower) are converted into marketable securities (security receipts), that can be sold to investors.
Hence, the correct option is (B).

20. The term 'Dividend', as generally understood, refers to the return(s) earned by a shareholder for investing in a company by buying its shares. Such dividend is tax-free for the recipient as companies paying dividends already pay Dividend Distribution Tax when they pay out the dividend
Hence, the correct option is (C).

21. For an Indian bank, as per Section-11 of Banking Regulation Act, the aggregate value of its paid-up capital and reserves shall not be less than if it has places of business in more than one state, Rs.5 lakhs, and if any such place or places of business is or are situated in the city of Bombay or Kolkata or both, Rs.10 lakhs.

If it has all its places of business in one state, none of which is situated in the city of Bombay or Kolkata, Rs.1 lakh in respect of its principal place of business, plus Rs.10 thousand in respect of each of its other places of business situated in the same district in which it has its principal place of business, plus Rs.25 thousand in respect of each place of business situated elsewhere in the state, otherwise in the same district.
Hence, the correct option is (B).

22. Under Limitation Act, 1963, in computing the period of limitation for any suit, appeal, or application, the day from which such period is to be reckoned, shall be excluded.
Hence, the correct option is (A).

23. The banking companies have to furnish three copies of the balance sheet and Profit & Loss account as returns to the Reserve Bank within three months from the end of the period to which they refer. The Reserve Bank can extend the period for submission by a further period not exceeding three months.

Section 220(1) of the Companies Act, 1956 requires a company to submit three copies of the balance sheet and the profit and loss account along with the auditor's report to the Registrar of Companies. However, section 32(1) of the BR Act requires the banking companies to send three copies of the balance sheet, the profit and loss account and auditor's report to the registrar as submitted to RBI as per provisions of Section 31 of BR Act. The copies so sent to the registrar must be dealt with in all respects as if they were filed in accordance with Section 220(1) of the Companies Act, 1956.

Hence, the correct option is (D).

24. It is to ensure that only those banks are continuing which were operating on sound lines and to prevent indiscriminate formation of banking companies.
Hence, the correct option is (B).

25. Banks that were nationalized in 1969 and 1980 draw power from the Banking Companies (Acquisition and Transfer of Undertakings) Act of 1969 and 1980. They are known as nationalized banks.
Hence, the correct option is (A).

26. The fringe benefits tax (FBT) was the tax applied to most, although not all, fringe benefits in India. A new tax was imposed on employers by India's Finance Act, 2005 for the financial year commencing April 1, 2005.

It covered the employer's expenses on entertainment, travel, employee welfare, and accommodation
Hence, the correct option is (C).

27. Under the Banking Regulation Act, 1949, 21(A), the rate of interest charged by banking companies will not be subject to scrutiny by courts. Notwithstanding anything contained in the Usurious Loans Act, 1918 (10 of 1918) or any other law relating to indebtedness in force in any state, a transaction between a banking company and its debtor shall not be re-opened by any court on the ground that the rate of interest charged by the banking company in respect of such transaction is excessive.
Hence, the correct option is (C).

28. The provisions of this act are applicable only for NPA loans with outstanding above Rs.1 lakh. NPA loan accounts where the amount is less than 20% of the principal and interest are not eligible to be dealt with under this act.
Hence, the correct option is (D).

29. Unit banking is a limited way of banking where banks operate only from a single branch (or a few branches in the same area) taking care of the local community.

It is a system of banking that originated in US. In comparison to branch banking, the size of unit banks is very small.

Hence, the correct option is (C).

30. All banks which are included in the Second Schedule to the Reserve Bank of India Act, 1934 are Scheduled Banks.

These bank groups are:

1. State Bank of India and its Associates,
2. Nationalised Banks,
3. Private Sector Banks,
4. Foreign Banks, and
5. Regional Rural Banks.

Lawful purpose:- Section 3 states that a company may be formed for any lawful purpose. Thus, no company shall be formed for carrying on any unlawful objects. In case the Company proposed to be formed is a private company, the memorandum must be subscribed to by two or more persons.

Certain institutions including DFIs are notified by Government of India as Public Financial Institutions (PFI) under Section 4A of the Companies Act, 1956. The PFIs enjoy certain advantages under the Companies Act, 1956, Recovery of Debts due to Banks and FIs Act, 1993, Income Tax Act etc.

A foreign company is any company or body corporate incorporated outside India which, has a place of business in India whether by itself or through an agent, physically or through electronic mode; and. conducts any business activity in India in any other manner.

Hence, the correct option is (D).

31. Lok Adalats have been given statutory status under the Legal Services Authorities Act, 1987. Under the said Act, the award (decision) made by the Lok Adalat is deemed to be a decree of a civil court and is final and binding on all parties and no appeal against such an award lies before any court of law.

Hence, the correct option is (C).

32. An amalgamation is a combination of two or more companies into a new entity. Amalgamation is distinct from a merger because neither company involved survives as a legal entity. Instead, a completely new entity is formed to house the combined assets and liabilities of both companies.

Hence, the correct option is (C).

33. The full form of the SARFAESI Act is Securitisation and Reconstruction of Financial Assets and Enforcement of Security Interest Act, 2002. Banks utilize this act as an effective tool for bad loans (NPA) recovery. It is possible where non-performing assets are backed by securities charged to the bank by way of hypothecation or mortgage or assignment.

Hence, the correct option is (D).

34. In November 1994, RBI constituted the Board for Financial Supervision (BFS) under RBI (BFS) Regulations, 1994 to give undivided attention to the prudential supervision and regulation of banks, financial institutions, and non-bank financial institutions in an integrated manner.
Hence, the correct option is (B).

35. Action under provisions of the SARFAESI Act cannot be initiated by (RRB) Regional Rural Banks.

The Securitisation and Reconstruction of Financial Assets and Enforcement of Securities Interest Act, 2002 (also known as the SARFAESI Act) is an Indian law. It allows banks and other financial institutions to auction residential or commercial properties (of Defaulter) to recover loans.

Hence, the correct option is (C).

36. Publication only in a newspaper that is published every day is not true with regards to the publication of accounts and the balance sheet of a bank.

The balance sheet and profit and loss account prepared in terms of section 29 of the Act together with the Auditor's report shall be published within a period of six months from the end of the period to which they relate in a newspaper which is in circulation

at the place where the banking company has its principal office. Hence, the correct option is (C).

37. RBI's original share capital was divided into shares of 100 each fully paid, which were initially owned entirely by private shareholders. Following India's independence on 15 August 1947, the RBI was nationalized on 1 January 1949. Afterward, the majority of share capital in RBI was held by the Central Government.
Hence, the correct option is (B).

38. FEMA was passed in the winter session of Parliament in 1999, replacing the Foreign Exchange Regulation Act (FERA). It extends to the whole of India. Also, activities such as payments made to any person outside India or receipts from them are also involved.

Hence, the correct answer is (D).

39. The Information Technology Act 2000 is the prime legislation dealing with cyber offenses and electronic commerce in India which is based on the United Nations Model Law on Electronic Commerce adopted by the United Nations Commission on International Trade Law (UNCITRAL).

Hence the correct option is (B).

40. The bank is not liable to any endorsee or holder of a cheque, except when the bank is wound up, the holder of a cheque (issued by a customer of the bank having sufficient funds), becomes a creditor who is entitled to make a claim.
Hence, the correct option is (D).

41. Section 42 in Reserve Bank of India Act, 1934 regarding cash reserves of scheduled banks to be kept with RBI.

The Cash Reserve Ratio in India is decided by RBI's Monetary Policy Committee in the periodic Monetary and Credit Policy. The Reserve Bank of India takes stock of the CRR in every monetary policy review, which, at present, is conducted every six weeks. CRR is one of the major weapons in the RBI's arsenal that allows it to maintain a desired level of inflation, control the money supply, and also liquidity in the economy.

In view of the amendment carried out to RBI Act 1934, omitting sub-section (1B) of Section 42, the Reserve Bank does not pay any interest on the CRR balances maintained by SCBs with effect from the fortnight beginning March 31, 2007.

Every bank included in the Second Schedule shall maintain with the Bank an average daily balance the amount of which shall not be less than such percentage of the total of the demand and time liabilities in India of such bank as shown in the return referred to in sub-section.

Hence, the correct option is (A).

42. According to Section 26 in Banking Regulation Act, 1949 return of unclaimed deposits states that every banking company shall, within thirty days after the close of each calendar year, submit a return in the prescribed form and manner to the Reserve Bank as at the end of such calendar year of all accounts [in India] which have not been operated upon for ten years, provided that in the case of money deposited for a fixed period the said term of ten years shall be reckoned from the date of the expiry of such fixed period, provided further that every regional rural bank shall also furnish a copy of the said return to the

National Bank.
Hence, the correct option is (B).

43. Various forms/returns are given in the Banking Regulation (Co-operative Societies) Rules, 1966. All the mentioned returns, except quarterly return of NPA advances u/s 42 of RBI Act, are the various returns submitted to RBI.
Hence, the correct option is (B).

44. Regarding acceptance of deposits by banks-

(a) Banks can refuse to accept deposits from undesirable persons.

(b) For opening an account, an introductory reference is not mandatory.

(c) For the opening of an account, identification is essential.

(d) Banks can accept deposits of money only.

Accepting deposits is one of the two major activities of the Banks. Banks are also called custodians of public money. Basically, the money is accepted as a deposit for safekeeping. But since the Banks use this money to earn interest from people who need money, Banks share a part of this interest with the depositors.
Hence, the correct option is (D).

45. Aadhaar eSigns are recognized as an accepted method of secure electronic signatures as part of the Second Schedule of the Information Technology Act, 2010 (IT Act). The IT Act recognizes secure digital signatures having legal validity equivalent to that of physical signatures.

Hence, the correct option is (A).

46. For banking companies (private banks), it is prepared as per part I of Schedule VI of the Companies Act.

At the expiration of each calendar year or at the expiration of a period of twelve months ending with such date as the Central Government may, by notification in the Official Gazette, specify on this behalf, every banking company incorporated in India, in respect of all business transacted by it and every banking company incorporated outside India, in respect of all business transacted through its branches in India, shall prepare with reference to that year or period, as the case may be, a balance-sheet and profit and loss account as on the last working day of that year or the period, as the case may be in the form set out in the Third Schedule or as near thereto as circumstances admit.
Hence, the correct option is (B).

47. Foreign Exchange Management Act or FEMA states that 'authorized person' means an authorized dealer, money changer, or any other person authorized under section 10 (1) to deal in foreign exchange and foreign securities. These are authorized by RBI under section 10 of FEMA to deal in foreign exchange. An "Authorized Person" is also, not given a free hand to deal in Foreign Exchange. He has to furnish details and information, to Reserve Bank from time to time as may be required by it.

Hence, the correct option is (C).

48. Under the provisions of the RTI Act, any citizen of India may request information from a "public authority" (a body of Government or "instrumentality of State") which is required to

reply expeditiously or within thirty days.
Hence, the correct option is (B).

49. As per Section 68 of the Indian Contract Act, If a person, incapable of entering into a contract, or anyone whom he is legally bound to support, is supplied by another person with necessaries suited to his condition in life, the person who has furnished such supplies is entitled to be reimbursed from the property of such incapable person.

As per Section 68 of the Indian Contract Act, if necessities are supplied to minors, it is a valid agreement. Minor can also be a beneficiary.
Hence, the correct option is (C).

50. Section-209 of the Companies Act 1956 relates to the maintenance of proper books of accounts.

Section-209 is one of the most important sections in the Companies Act, 1956. This section deals with the requirements of maintenance of books of accounts and penalties for non-compliance. A detailed analysis of the provisions of Section 209 and its implication on other related sections is brought out in this article.

Hence, the correct option is (C).

51. Section 22 in Banking Regulation Act,1949 states that no company shall carry on banking business in India unless it holds a license issued on that behalf by the Reserve Bank, and any such license may be issued subject to such conditions as the Reserve Bank may think fit to impose.

Section 7 in Banking Regulation Act,1949 states that no company, other than a banking company, shall use as part of its name (or in connection with its business) any of the words "bank", "banker" or "banking" and no company shall carry on the business of banking in India unless it uses as part of its name at least one of such words. No firm, individual, or group of individuals shall, for the purpose of carrying on any business, use as part of its or his name any of the words "bank", "banking" or "banking company".
Hence, the correct option is (D).

52. The collection should be for the apparent tenor of the instrument in good faith and without negligence to any person in possession thereof under circumstances which do not afford a reasonable ground for believing that he is not entitled to receive payment of the amount therein mentioned.
Hence, the correct option is (C).

53. The Transfer of Property Act contains provisions relating to the transfer of 'actionable claims'. The transfer of an actionable claim, whether with or without consideration, shall be effected only by the execution of an instrument in writing and signed by the transferor or his duly authorized agent, shall be complete and effectual upon the execution of such instruments and thereupon, all the rights and remedies of the transferor, whether by way of damages or otherwise, shall vest in the transferee, whether such notice of the transfer as is hereinafter provided be given or not.
Hence, the correct option is (A).

54. Negotiable Instruments Act states that a cheque should have the following characteristics:

(1) It must be in writing

(2) It must contain an unconditional order to pay money only and not merely a request

(3) It must be signed by the drawer

(4) The parties must be certain

(5) The sum payable must also be certain

(6) It must comply with other formalities e.g. stamps, date, etc

Hence, the correct option is (D).

55. A floating charge is security, such as a mortgage or a lien, that has an underlying asset or group of assets that are subject to change in quantity and value. When businesses use floating charges, it does not affect their ability to use the underlying asset as normal. Only if the company fails to repay the loan or goes into liquidation does the floating charge become "crystallized" or frozen into a fixed charge and the lender becomes the first-in-line creditor to be able to draw against the underlying asset.

A floating charge is a particular type of security, available only to companies. It is an equitable charge on (usually) all the company's assets, both present, and future, on terms that the company may deal with the assets in the ordinary course of business. Very occasionally, the charge is over just a class of the company's assets, such as its stock.
Hence, the correct option is (C).

56. Conversion is often defined as other interference of a person's right to property without the owner's consent and without lawful justification. A conversion occurs when a person without authority or permission intentionally takes the personal property of another or deprives another of possession of the personal property.

Hence, the correct option is (D).

57. The Foreign Exchange Management Act, 1999 (FEMA) is an act of the Parliament of India "to consolidate and amend the law relating to foreign exchange with the objective of facilitating external trade and payments and for promoting the orderly development and maintenance of foreign exchange market in India.
Hence, the correct option is (C).

58. The beneficiary is the party who is to receive the benefit (payment) of the LC. The consignee of an LC and the beneficiary may not be the same. The credit is issued in the beneficiary's favor.
Hence, the correct option is (A).

59. A guarantee contract is to perform the obligation or to discharge the liability of a third party in case of its default.

A contract of guarantee always has three parties, they are:

1. the creditor
2. the principal debtor and
3. the surety

Whereas a contract of indemnity has two parties, the indemnifier and the indemnity holder. In a contract of indemnity, there is a single promise or contract, a promise to pay if there is a loss.

Option (D) is incorrect in the case of a contract of indemnity and guarantee.

Hence, the correct option is (D).

60. A financial guarantee is the type of bank guarantee which is issued by a bank and furnished by a bank's customer in lieu of earnest money or the security to be deposited with the beneficiary of the bank guarantee for the performance of a contract. These guarantees are given in lieu of purely monetary obligation (the obligation of the contractor to make earnest money deposit/guarantees to give to sale-tax department etc). Hence, the correct option is (B).

61. A mortgage by conditional sale is where the mortgagor sells the property to the mortgagee on the condition that in case of default of repayment of the mortgage money, the sale will become absolute, and on repayment of the money, the sale will become void and the mortgagee will transfer the property back to the mortgagor.

Hence, the correct option is (B).

62. A citizen has a right to obtain information in the form of diskettes, floppies, tapes, video cassettes, or in any other electronic mode or through print-out. The provided information is already stored in a computer or in any other device from which the information may be transferred to diskettes. Hence, the correct option is (D).

63. If a property's title has multiple mortgage liens and the loan secured by a first mortgage is paid off, the second mortgage lien will move up in priority and become the new first mortgage lien on the title. Documenting this new priority arrangement will require the release of the mortgage securing the paid-off loan. Thus, the priority will be according to the date. As mortgage in favor of Bank A was on January 14, 2007, and was the earliest, thus, will be dealt with first and subsequently Bank B (January 28, 2007) and Bank C (February 10, 2007). Hence, the correct option is (D).

64. Records should be maintained for all cash transactions where forged or counterfeit currency notes or bank notes have been used as genuine and where any forgery of a valuable security has taken place. Hence, the correct option is (D).

65. Credit Facility means the amount used by the Borrower under the Credit Facility Agreement, under the form of one or more lending products or products assimilated to lending products, as described in the Credit Facility Agreement, of the following type (without limitation)

(i) overdraft

(ii) credit line

(iii) object loan for financing current activity facility.

(iv) investment credit facility.

(v) credit facility for VAT financing related to investments.

(vi) Guarantee Facility.

(vii) Multiproduct Facility.

(viii) credit facility for delivery documents.

(ix) Endorsement Facility.

(x) Discounting Facility for Negotiable Instruments.

(xi) Discounting Facility for Letters of Credit.

(xii) forfaiting.
Hence, the correct option is (D).

66. Hypothecation is used for creating a charge against the security of movable assets, but here the possession of the security remains with the borrower itself. Thus, in case of default by the borrower, the lender (to whom the goods/security has been hypothecated) will have to first take possession of the security and then sell the same.

The best example of this type of arrangement is a car loan. In this case, the car/vehicle remains with the borrower but the same is hypothecated to the bank/financer. In case the borrower defaults, banks take possession of the vehicle after giving notice and then sell the same and credit the proceeds to the loan account. Hence, the correct option is (C).

67. Two conditions are necessary to enable a partner to sue his co-partners or the- firm. First, the firm should be registered and second, the name of the partner suing must figure in registration. The scope of the sub-section was examined by the Bombay High Court in S. H. Patel v. Husseinbhai Mohd, a case where the action was between two former partners to enforce an agreement restraining the outgoing partner from carrying on in some area of any business similar to that of the firm and the court had to examine whether such suit was maintainable the firm being unregistered. Hence, the correct option is (D).

68. The guidelines for the nature of records to be maintained by a bank under the Prevention of Money Laundering Act, 2002 are issued by RBI and SEBI from time to time.

Every banking company or financial institution or intermediary, as the case may be, shall maintain the records of the identity of its clients. Hence, the correct option is (C).

69. It is to provide for setting out the practical regime of right to information for citizens to secure access to information under the control of public authorities, in order to promote transparency and accountability in the working of every public authority, the constitution of a Central Information Commission and State Information Commissions and for matters connected therewith or incidental thereto. There is no prescribed form of application for seeking the information as the application can be made on plain paper. The information seeker is not required to give reasons for seeking information. Hence, the correct option is (B).

70. A floating charge is a security interest or lien over a group of non-constant assets, that change in quantity and value. A floating charge is used as a means to secure a loan for a company. The assets used in a floating charge are usually short-term current assets that the company consumes within one year.

Hence, the correct option is (C).

71. All companies having limited liability are required to use the term 'limited' or 'private limited'. But under Section 25, companies are allowed to dispense with the use of the term 'limited' or 'private limited' from their names after obtaining a license from the regional director. This helps the company to enjoy limited liability without disclosing to the public the nature of liability of its members.
Hence, the correct option is (D).

72. Companies Act 1956 has not been amended to bring it in tune with the Information Technology Act, 1999.

The Companies Act, 1956 empowers the Central Government to inspect the books of accounts of a company, to direct special audit, to order an investigation into the affairs of a company and to launch prosecution for violation of the Companies Act, 1956.
Hence, the correct option is (D).

73. The borrower may have to inevitably file an appeal before the Debt Recovery Tribunal (DRT) and Debts Recovery Appellate Tribunal (DRAT) under Section 17 of the SARFAESI Act, 2002.

The law under Section 17 of the SARFAESI Act gives a period of 45 days from the date of the receipt of the possession notice under Section 13(2) of the Acct the Borrower can file an appeal before the Debt Recovery Tribunal.

Hence, the correct option is (C).

74. In that case, the Supreme Court was dealing with the validity of the SARFAESI Act. The Court struck down Section 17(2) of the Act as ultra vires Article 14 of the Constitution of India. Thus, the complete statement is SARFAESI Act has been declared valid by Supreme Court but it struck down Section 17(2) of the Act, in the case of Mardia Chemicals vs Union of India and others, which provided for the deposit of 75% of the amount due to the bank before approaching DRT.
Hence, the correct option is (B).

75. The Act is applicable also to housing finance companies whose names are notified by the Central Government for such applicability. The provisions of the Act, relating to the enforcement of the security interest, applies to cases in which the security interests are created for due repayment of financial assistance.

Hence, the correct option is (C).

76. No suits to enforce a right arising from a contract shall be instituted in any Court by or on behalf of a firm against any third party unless the firm is registered and the persons suing are or have been shown in the Register of Firms as partners in the firm.

The effects of non-registration of a partnership firm are provided under Section 69^2 of the Act, whereby a partner of an unregistered firm cannot sue the firm or other partners enforce a right arising from a contract.

Hence, the correct option is (B).

77. If the directors of a company die in an accident, the company will still exist.
If the company has more than one director, the company can still run as usual. Practically speaking, the remaining directors will divide the deceased shareholder's responsibilities between them.
Hence, the correct option is (C).

78. Under the RTI Act, 2005, the information can be accessed under the control of a public authority. For this purpose, the public authority means any authority established

(a) by or under the Constitution

(b) by any other law made by Parliament

(c) by any other law made by State Legislature

(d) by notification issued or order made by the appropriate Government

Hence, the correct option is (D).

79. Under the provisions of the act, any citizen of India may request information from a public authority, be it a body of Government or instrumentality of the state, expeditiously or within 30 days. The focus of the paper is on the information which can be disclosed and which is exempted under the Right to Information Act 2005.
Hence, the correct option is (D).

80. Under the erstwhile Companies Act, 1956, a private company could start its business immediately upon receiving a certificate of incorporation. Private companies do not require to obtain a certificate of commencement of business from concerned Registrar of Companies under section 149 of Companies Act, 1956.

Under the Companies Act, 1956 a private company and a public limited company not having share capital are not required to comply with any other formalities and may commence its business activities immediately after obtaining the certificate of incorporation from the concerned Registrar of Companies.

Hence, the correct option is (B).

81. Negotiable Instruments Act, 1881 governs the transactions through cheques.

The entire processing of cheques and their payment are all governed under the covenants of the Negotiable Instruments Act, 1881, which necessitate that these instruments are in writing and have to be physically presented for payment in due course.

Hence, the correct option is (B).

82. Certificate of the corporation is like a Birth certificate of the company because the company came into existence from the date of the issue of a certificate of incorporation. It is legal proof of the fact that the company is incorporated. After incorporation, the company gets separated from its members.

Before the enactment of Companies Act, 2013 it was settled law that once the required documents have been delivered to the Registrar of Companies and the necessary fee paid, the Registrar, after satisfying himself, issues a certificate of incorporation which shall be a piece of conclusive evidence that all the requirements of the Companies Act have been complied with in respect of registration and matters precedent and incidental thereto.

"Private companies are not required to obtain a Certificate of Commencement". Thus, statement (d) is incorrect.

Hence, the correct option is (B).

83. A lease of immovable property for any other purpose shall be deemed to be a lease from month to month, terminable, on the part of either lessor or lessee, by fifteen days' notice.
Hence, the correct option is (D).

84. The statement "When a company creates a charge on its assets and fails to get the charge particulars filed and registered".

(a) any person interested in the charge can file and get it registered.

(b) if the charge is not filed and registered, the creditor becomes an unsecured creditor in the event of liquidation of the company.

(c) if the charge remains unregistered, the loan becomes due immediately.

(d) it is the responsibility of the company to file the charge within the given time period.

A 'charge' is the security a company gives for a loan. For example, a mortgage is a type of charge. The Companies Act, 2013 defines a Charge as an interest or lien created on the assets or property of a Company or any of its undertaking as security and includes a mortgage U/s 2(16). The Company may also issue Debentures to raise funds which may carry a right/ interest in the Assets/Properties of the company.

Hence, the correct option is (D).

85. For hypothecation as per the SARFAESI Act-

(a) It is a charge on movable assets.

(b) It is in favor of the secured creditor.

(c) It is without the delivery of possession.

"Hypothecation" means a charge in or upon any movable property, existing or future, created by a borrower in favor of a secured creditor without delivery of possession of the movable property to such creditor, as a security for financial assistance and includes floating charge and crystallization of such charge into fixed charge on movable property.
Hence, the correct option is (B).

86. Therefore, the SARFAESI Act as a whole applicable to whole India including the State of J&K. The verdict clearly provides that provisions of the SARFAESI Act, 2002 are within the legislative competence of Parliament and could be enforced in Jammu and Kashmir.

The act allows taking the matter to high courts only in some matters related to the implementation of the act in Jammu & Kashmir. However, high courts have been entertaining writ petitions under Article 226 (Power to issue writs) of the Constitution of India. It is possible where non-performing assets are backed by securities charged to the bank by way of hypothecation or mortgage or assignment.
Hence, the correct option is (B).

87. When the SARFAESI Act was challenged, the Supreme Court in Mardia Chemicals Ltd. vs Union of India, (2004) 4 SCC 311 had upheld the validity of the SARFAESI Act, except Section 17(2) of the SARFAESI Act which required depositing 75% of the amount claimed before entertaining an appeal under Section 17 of the SARFAESI Act.
Hence, the correct option is (B).

88. Prevention of Money Laundering Act, 2002 was enacted to fight against the criminal offence of legalizing the income/profits from an illegal source. The Prevention of Money Laundering Act, 2002 enables the Government or the public authority to confiscate the property earned from the illegally gained proceeds.

The Act was formulated for the following objectives: Prevent money-laundering. Provide for the confiscation of property derived from, or involved/used in, money-laundering. Provide for matters connected and incidental to the acts of money laundering.

Hence, the correct option is (D).

89. The regulations exclude a few persons from the application of the regulations. They are specific family trusts, ESOP trusts (conditions), employee welfare trusts, gratuity trusts, holding companies' within the meaning of Section 4 of the Companies Act, 1956, securitization trusts, securitization company, reconstruction company registered with RBI, any such pool of funds which is directly regulated by any other regulator in India.
Hence, the correct option is (B).

90. Under the act in consideration, to show the intention to take possession, the creditor is required to obtain possession of the security by giving a notice of 60 days.
Hence, the correct option is (D).

91. A lease is a legal document outlining the terms under which one party agrees to rent property from another party and the periodic payment made to the owner of a property for the use of the said property is rent. Thus, both are different.

Hence, the correct option is (C).

92. Banks should maintain for at least ten years from the date of cessation of transaction between the bank and the client, all necessary records of transactions, both domestic or international, which will permit reconstruction of individual transactions.

Hence, the correct option is (B).

93. In case there is a broad agreement, the account would be classified as a fraud, else based on the majority rule of agreement amongst banks with at least 60% share in the total lending, the account would be red-flagged by all the banks and subjected to a forensic audit commissioned or initiated by the consortium leader or the largest lender.
Hence, the correct option is (D).

94. The forms prescribed by the Central Government for registration are as under:

FORM I - For Creation and modification of charge.

FORM II - For particulars of satisfaction of charge.

FORM III - For securitization or reconstruction of financial assets.

FORM IV - For the satisfaction of securitization or reconstruction of financial assets.

Thus, all transactions need registration.
Hence, the correct option is (D).

95. If one is aggrieved by the decision, one may, within 30 days of the date of receipt of the award, appeal against the award before the appellate authority. The appellate authority may, if he/she is satisfied that the applicant had sufficient cause for not making an application for appeal within time, also allow a further period not exceeding 30 days.
Hence, the correct option is (D).

96. The partnership firm to be registered under the Indian Partnership Act, 1932 should be under the notice of the registrar of firms of the area in which the business of the firms is conducted.

As provided in Section 59, a partnership is said to be registered when a registrar is well pleased with the fidelity of application filed according to section 58 and an entry of the statement in the register known as Register of Firms is recorded.

Hence, the correct option is (A).

97. A property can be sold without the intervention of the court if it is located at only Chennai, Mumbai, and Kolkata or towns notified by the state government.

Following conditions should comply under Section 53A,

The contract should be for transfer of immovable property and from therein the term necessary to constitute transfer should be certainly ascertained.

The transferee should be ready and willing to perform his part of the contract.

Hence, the correct option is (D).

98. The maximum maturity period of funds/instruments in the money market is 364 days.

The money market is a market for short-term financial assets. The most important feature of a money market instrument is that it is liquid and can be turned over quickly at low cost and provides an avenue for equilibrating the short-term surplus funds of lenders and the requirements of borrowers.

Hence, the correct option is (D).

99. Under Section 17-A of the Recovery of Debts Due to Banks and Financial Institutions Act, 1993, the Chairperson of Appellate Tribunal may transfer any case from one tribunal to another depending on the merits of the case within the jurisdiction of the appellate tribunal, if an application seeking transfer is filed.
Hence, the correct option is (C).

100. Recovery of debt due to banks and Financial Institutions Act, 1993 Section 2(g) states that "debt" means any liability (inclusive of interest) which is claimed as due from any person by a bank or a financial institution or by a consortium of banks or financial institutions during the course of any business activity undertaken by the bank or the financial institution or the consortium under any law for the time being in force, in cash or otherwise, whether secured or unsecured, or assigned, or whether payable under a decree or order of any civil court or any arbitration award or

otherwise or under a mortgage and subsisting on, and legally recoverable on, the date of the application.

Hence, the correct option is (D).

101. The application shall be disposed of, as far as possible, within 180 days from the date of its receipt. A certificate will be issued to the Recovery Officer for recovery of the amount of debt specified in the certificate.
Hence, the correct option is (B).

102. Penalty for furnishing false particulars within the meaning In section 70, for the words "shall be punishable with imprisonment which may extend to three months, or with fine, or with both".
Hence, the correct option is (C).

103. 38 states that the High Court can order the winding up of a banking company on certain grounds stated therein and such grounds do not exclude the application of Ss. 391,392,433 and 533 of Companies Act, 1956. Such provisions of this section are also stated not to be prejudicial to the provisions under $.37(1)$ of the act. The Reserve Bank is required to apply for the winding up of the banking company if the central government directs it to do so after an inspection under section 35 of the Act.

Hence, the correct option is (B).

104. "Bankers' books" include ledgers, day-books, cash-books, account-books and all other records used in the ordinary business of the bank, whether these records are kept in written form or stored in microfilm, magnetic tape or in any other form of mechanical or electronic data retrieval mechanism, either onsite or at an offsite location including a back-up or disaster recovery site or both. Thus, all the statements are correct.
Hence, the correct option is (D).

105. RBI regulates and supervises the functions of NBFCs in accordance with the provisions of the RBI Act 1934. The registration of NBFC shall be carried out in accordance with the rules and regulations set out in Section 45-IA of the RBI Act 1934.

Hence, the correct option is (B).

106. Quasi-judicial bodies are such institutions which have the power of enforcement of law but are not courts. These bodies can inquire, investigate, summon & award legal penalties to any administrative agency. Generally, these bodies have limited judiciary power in specialized areas.

The National Consumer Disputes Redressal Commission (NCDRC), India is a quasi-judicial commission in India that was set up in 1988.
Hence, the correct option is (C).

107. Corporate governance is about promoting corporate fairness, transparency, and accountability. Corporate governance deals with how a corporation is governed.
Hence, the correct option is (D).

108. A preliminary decree was ordered to be drawn up. Thereafter, as the defendants had failed to pay the decretal amount, final decree proceedings were initiated.

Hence, the correct option is (B).

109. The Board of Directors of a company can exercise the following powers on behalf of the company only by means of resolutions passed at meetings of the Board:

- To make calls on shareholders in respect of money unpaid on their shares,

- To authorize buy-back of securities under section 68,

- To issue securities, including debentures, whether in or outside India,

- To borrow monies,

- To invest the funds of the company,

- To grant loans or give guarantee or provide security in respect of loans,

- To approve the financial statement and the Board's report,

- To diversify the business of the company,

- To approve amalgamation, merger, or reconstruction.

Hence, the correct option is (B).

110. When at the desire of the promisor, the promisee or any other person has done or abstained from doing something or does or abstains from doing something, such act or abstinence or promise is called a consideration for the promise. Thus, all are true.
Hence, the correct option is (D).

111. No partner would be liable on account of the independent or unauthorized actions of other partners, thus allowing individual partners to be shielded from joint liability created by another partner's wrongful business decisions or misconduct.
Hence, the correct option is (C).

112. Section 31 of the Negotiable Instruments Act, 1881 states that when a customer had sufficient balance in his account, the banker is bound to honor such a cheque and if he fails to do so, he shall compensate the drawer for any loss or damage caused by such default.
Hence, the correct option is (D).

113. Balance of trade (BOT) is the difference between the value of a country's imports and exports for a given period and is the largest component of a country's balance of payments (BOP).
Hence, the correct option is (A).

114. According to section 106 of TPA, 1882, if there is an absence of a written contract or a local usage to the contrary then in the case, a lease of immovable property for manufacturing and agriculture purpose will be valid till the time until it was terminated by either of the party, by 6 months notice and if there is a lease any other purpose except agriculture or manufacturing then it will be terminated by 15 days notice.
Hence, the correct option is (A).

115. Where, under a contract of sale, the property in the goods is transferred from the seller to the buyer, the contract is called a "sale", but where the transfer of the property in the goods is to take place at a future time, or subject to some condition thereafter to be fulfilled, the contract is called an "agreement to sell".
Hence, the correct option is (B).

116. Unless the Article (Section 152 of Companies Act, 2013) provides retirement of all the directors, at least $\frac{2}{3}$ directors of a public company shall be persons whose period of office is liable to determination by retirement of directors by rotation.
Hence, the correct option is (D).

117. In the absence of a contract or local law or usage to the contrary, a lease of immovable property for agricultural or manufacturing purposes shall be deemed to be a lease from year to year, terminable, on the part of either lessor or lessee, by six months' notice.
Hence, the correct option is (A).

118. Right to Information is an act to provide for setting out the practical regime of right to information for citizens to secure access to information under the control of public authorities, in order to promote transparency and accountability in the working of every public authority, the constitution of a Central Information Commission and State Information Commissions and for matters connected therewith or incidental thereto.

Hence, the correct option is (D).

119. Public authorities are the repository of information which the citizen have right to have under the Right to Information Act, 2005. As defined in the Act, a " Public authority " is any authority or body or institution of self government established or constituted by or under the Constitution; or by any other law made by the Parliament or a State Legislature; or by notification issued or order made by the Central Government or a State Government.

Hence, the correct option is (D).

120. In October 1993, another Committee headed by Rashid Jilani chairman of Punjab National Bank also suggested an alternative to the existing system of lending by way of cash credit for financing working capital requirements.
Hence, the correct option is (A).

Q.1 When is it necessary for a bank to form a consortium for lending a borrower though RBI has waived requirement for the same

A. when credit facilities are more than 15% of capital fund of the financing bank in case of single borrowers.

B. when credit facilities are more than 40% of the capital fund of the financing bank in case of a group.

C. when financing an infrastructure project.

D. Only (A) and (B)

Q.2 Members of FSDC includes

(i) Heads of financial sector Regulators (RBI, SEBI, PFRDA, IRDAI & FMC).

(ii) Finance Secretary and/or Secretary Department of Economic Affairs.

(iii) All four Deputy Governors of the RBI.

A. Only (i) and (ii)

B. Only (i) and (iii)

C. Only (ii) and (iii)

D. (i), (ii) and (iii)

Q.3 Under Section 37 of the Banking Regulation Act, a moratorium order can be issued by the High Court for a maximum total period of

A. one month.

B. six month.

C. one year.

D. None of these

Q.4 When a banking company is placed under moratorium under Section 45 of B.R.Act, the RBI must prepare a scheme

A. VRS for staff.

B. capital buy back.

C. reconstruction of the company or amalgamation with any other bank.

D. None of these

Q.5 Which of the following is correct about consortium financing by banks?

A. A minimum number of consortium members should be 2 and the maximum number should be 4

B. Every bank will have the same asset classification

C. Minimum share of a bank in the consortium should be 10%

D. The banks will have a pari passu charge on the securities charged to them

Q.6 Which of the following a notice must specify in case of foreclosed loans?

A. It should cover entire loan liability including installments not due

B. The notice must include details such as the borrower and lender's name and address, the property address, and the nature of the default

C. It must mention future interest payable till the date of repayment

D. All of the above

Q.7 The minimum period of a certificate of deposit is:

A. 7 days

B. 10 days

C. 15 days

D. 30 days

Q.8 Principal function of banks are

A. accepting deposits.

B. lending and investing.

C. non fund business and remittance services.

D. All of the above

Q.9 What is Reverse Repo?

(i) It is a method of borrowing against certain securities for a short period.

(ii) It is a process where lender levels against the securities with a commitment to take back the securities from the borrower against payment at a specified price.

(iii) It is helpful in contracting liquidity in the system.

A. Only (i) and (ii)

B. Only (i) and (iii)

C. Only (ii) and (iii)

D. (i), (ii) and (iii)

Q.10 To take care of temporary liquidity problems of central and state government, what kind of loan is given by RBI?

A. Treasury bills

B. Dated securities

C. Short duration bonds

D. Ways & means advances

Q.11 The advising banks responsibility is

A. to inform the issuing bank as to whom to issue the letter of credit.

B. to advise the buyer the dispatch of documents by the seller.

C. to inform the beneficiary/seller about the letter of credit.

D. None of the above

Q.12 The advising bank is also called the

A. Confirming Bank.

B. Notifying Bank.

C. Reimbursing Bank.

D. None of the above

Q.13 Authentication of an electronic record by a subscriber by means of an electronic method of procedure in accordance with provisions of Section 3 of Information Technology Act, is called

A. digital signature.

B. asymmetric cryptosystem.

C. electronic monitoring.

D. keypair.

Q.14 The banking ombudsman can be an arbitrator in disputes between

A. two banking companies.

B. two or more customers.

C. a bank and the government.

D. None of the above

Q.15 Directions can be issued to banking companies on loans and advances

A. in strict confidence.
B. in public interest.
C. in the interest of borrowers.
D. None of the above

Q.16 In case of fraud committed by the debtor on whose behalf the bank had given a guarantee, the bank
A. need not pay the beneficiary.
B. has to pay the beneficiary.
C. direct the beneficiary to sue to debtor.
D. None of the above

Q.17 The Letter of Credit is opened on the request of
A. issuing bank.
B. applicant.
C. beneficiary.
D. confirming bank.

Q.18 If a civil court has already given a decree then the recovery certificate can be issued by
A. any different court.
B. at the request of any of the parties.
C. DRT only.
D. None of the above

Q.19 Under the SARFAESI Act who has the power to condone delay in filling of the particulars?
A. An arbitrator
B. Registrar
C. Central registrar
D. Registrar of assurances

Q.20 The owner of a financial asset acquired by a securitisation company is called
A. purchaser.
B. seller.
C. originator.
D. vendor.

Q.21 From the following which function is of securitisation company?
A. Acquisition of loan transaction from the lender
B. Help the lender in recovery by sale of charged property
C. Take legal steps against the defaulter borrower on behalf of the lender
D. Acquisition of financial assets from the originator

Q.22 Working Capital Demand Loan was recommended by
A. Rashid Jilani.
B. N. Vaghul.
C. K. Kannan.
D. C. Rangarajan.

Q.23 How many types of 'R' return are required to be submitted at present.
A. 5
B. 6
C. 7
D. 2

Q.24 Name the different types of 'R' returns?
A. Nostro & Vostro
B. Nostro
C. Vostro
D. None of the above

Q.25 Four statements are given below. Some statements are not possible. Choose the statement which is possible?
A. Hypothecation can become a pledge
B. Pledge and third party pledge there is no difference
C. A mortgage is applicable to the Vehicle as a security

D. For the transfer of goods, the assignment is used

Q.26 A foreigner spouse of an Indian citizen is
(i) Non-Resident Indian (NRI).
(ii) Person of Indian Origin (PIO).
A. Only (i)
B. Only (ii)
C. Either (i) or (ii)
D. Neither (i) nor (ii)

Q.27 In documentary credit transactions
A. all parties deal with documents and not goods.
B. all parties deal in documents and goods as well.
C. buyer and seller deal in goods and banks in documents.
D. all parties deal in goods only.

Q.28 _______ suggests Human Resource Strategy in itself may not be effective.
A. Peter Drucker
B. Tony Grundy
C. John Zimmerman
D. Anonymous

Q.29 The buyer or importer who procures a letter of credit from his banker is called
A. opener of the credit.
B. beneficiary of the credit.
C. negotiator of the credit.
D. None of these

Q.30 Non-resident Indian is defined for banking purpose in
A. FEMA.
B. Income Tax Act 1961.
C. Wealth Tax Act 1957.
D. None of the above

Q.31 Import licenses are valid for shipment
A. 12 months from the date of issuance of a licence.
B. 1 week after the arrival of goods into the country.
C. upto last day of the month in which they expire.
D. 18 months from the date of arrival of goods.

Q.32 The face value of an Import License should take care of
A. cost of goods only.
B. cost, Insurance and Freight (i.e) CIF c. CIF plus interest.
C. CIF, Interest and agency commission if any.
D. customs manual.

Q.33 The rate applicable for an export bill tendered for negotiation is
A. bill buying rate.
B. bill selling rate.
C. composite rate.
D. TT buying rate.

Q.34 What type of charge is created when the security for the loan is the document of title to goods (such as Railway receipt)?
A. Hypothecation
B. Lien
C. Pledge
D. Assignment

Q.35 If a person seeking information is not provided information within the prescribed period (normally 30 days), he can make an appeal
A. within 30 days.
B. within 50 days.
C. within 6 months.
D. within one year.

Q.36 The maximum number of directors in a private company can be_____.

A. 3   **B.** 7   **C.** 15   **D.** 5

Q.37 At least _____ of the total number of directors of a public company are to be persons whose period of office is liable to determination by retirement by rotation.

A. 2   **B.** 7
C. two-third   **D.** None of the above

Q.38 Every public company or a private company which is a subsidiary of a public company, having a paid-up share capital of Rupees_____must have a managing or whole-time director or a manager.

A. five crore   **B.** five lakh
C. one crore   **D.** one lakh

Q.39 A system of a secure key pair consisting of a private key for creating a digital signature and a public key to verify the digital signature is called

A. digital signature.
B. asymmetric cryptosystem.
C. electronic monitoring.
D. e-commerce.

Q.40 Trusts of Hindus are governed by the

A. Parliament Act.
B. Indian Trust Act.
C. Wakf Act.
D. Religious and Charitable Endowments Act.

Q.41 Trusts of Muslims are governed by the

A. Parliament Act.
B. Indian Trust Act.
C. Wakf Act.
D. Religious and Charitable Endowments Act.

Q.42 The person given license to issue digital signature certificate u/s 24 of Information Technology Act is called

A. Certifying Authority.
B. DGC Authority.
C. Digital Signature Controller.
D. Controller of Certifying Authorities.

Q.43 The banking ombudsman may reject the complaint on the following grounds

A. complaint is without sufficient cause.
B. complaint is not pursued with reasonable diligence.
C. there is no loss or damage or inconvenience suffered by the complaint.
D. All of the above

Q.44 Which of the following the banking ombudsman does not cover?

A. Financial institutions
B. Non- banking financial companies
C. Non- scheduled banks
D. All of the above

Q.45 The banking ombudsman receives the maximum number of complaints in respect of

A. Foreign Bank.
B. Public Sector Bank.
C. Regional Rural Bank.
D. Co-operative Bank.

Q.46 Which of the following are the norms of awarding compensation by the banking ombudsman?

A. Banking ombudsman does not have unlimited powers to allow compensation
B. The maximum limit of compensation is Rs. 10 lakh
C. No compensation will be awarded in excess of that which is necessary
D. All of the above

Q.47 In case of non-compliance of the award by the bank the baking ombudsman will report to

A. Reserve Bank of India.
B. Supreme Court.
C. Finance Ministry.
D. Consumer Protection Forum.

Q.48 If a person commits an offence under the Prevention of Money Laundering Act 2002, shall be liable for fine

A. up to Rs.10 lakh.   **B.** up to Rs.5 lakh.
C. up to Rs.2 lakh.   **D.** up to Rs.1 lakh.

Q.49 The SARFAESI Act is applicable to secured creditors only to enforce the securities criteria

A. without the intervention of court or tribunal.
B. after taking permission of court or tribunal.
C. in case of assets on which charge is registered.
D. None of the above

Q.50 After using the securitisation measures a bank can proceed further

A. the civil court.
B. DRT.
C. both as the case may be.
D. None of the above

Q.51 In Mardia case what the Supreme Court declared as invalid?

A. Entire SARFAESI Act, 2002
B. Creation of security interest
C. Formation of Reconstruction Companies
D. Condition to pay 75% of the amount as pre-condition while preferring an appeal to the DRT

Q.52 Which of the following is an exception of the doctrine of indoor management, i.e. the person dealing with the company can suffer loss?

A. Where a person dealing with a company has actual knowledge of internal irregularity
B. Where the situation is such that a person dealing with a company could have obtained information about internal irregularity
C. Where an official of the company is acting unauthorisedly and the person dealing with the company has information

about this

D. All of the above

Q.53 Asset Reconstruction company has to get registration from

A. RBI.

B. its own bank.

C. Both (A) and (B)

D. None of the above

Q.54 The minimum number of members required in a private company is

A. 3 **B.** 7 **C.** 1 **D.** 2

Q.55 Most of the complaints are settled through

A. mutual agreement.

B. award.

C. bank itself.

D. before proceeding to agreed stage.

Q.56 What is the object of introducing the banking ombudsman scheme, 2006?

A. For effective monitoring of the NPA accounts in the banks

B. It is the RBI agency to regulate the disputes amongst the banks

C. To enable resolution of complaints relating to banking services

D. To facilitate the satisfaction or settlement of complaints relating to certain services rendered by banks

Q.57 RBI undertakes banking business for the State Government under the provision of

A. Sec 22 of RBI Act.

B. Sec 21 of RBI Act.

C. Sec 20 of RBI Act.

D. Agreement between RBI & Government u/s 21 A of RBI Act.

Q.58 A property mortgaged (Equitable mortgage) is in a village that is not a notified area. The bank branch which gave the loan is in a Notified area. If the bank wishes to file a suit, then,

A. the suit has to be filed in the district headquarters of the bank branch.

B. suit to be filed with the court in whose jurisdiction the property mortgaged is situated.

C. such loan not possible (Property in a different area and the lending bank in another area.

D. None of these

Q.59 A Co-operative bank can be which of the following:

(i) Primary Co-operative Bank.

(ii) District Central Co-operative Bank.

(iii) State Co-operative Bank.

A. only (i) and (ii) **B.** only (i) and (iii)

C. only (ii) and (iii) **D.** (i), (ii) and (iii)

Q.60 A Co-operative Bank can be which of the following?

A. Primary Co-operative Bank

B. District Central Co-operative Bank

C. State Co-operative Bank

D. All of the above

Q.61 A Banking company having operations in India could be constituted as a

A. body corporate under a Special Act.

B. registered under the Companies Act.

C. a foreign company under provisions of Companies Act.

D. All of the above

Q.62 There is an FDR of A and B but A dies before its maturity. B also dies one week after his death. FD amount is payable to

A. legal heirs of A.

B. legal heirs of B.

C. legal heirs of A and B.

D. legal heirs of the person who died later.

Q.63 Which of the following can become members of a company?

A. A partnership firm

B. An insolvent person

C. A person of unsound mind

D. A company

Q.64 If a cheque is crossed as account payee, this is the direction of ___ to ___

A. payee, paying bank.

B. payee, collecting bank.

C. drawer, paying bank.

D. drawer, collecting bank.

Q.65 Payments for the retirement of bills against imports into India must be received by

A. directly by the exporter.

B. directly by the importer.

C. authorized Dealer.

D. RBI.

Q.66 A person is presumed to have gone through the Articles of Association and Memorandum of Association available with the office of RoC although he might have actually not laid his hands on these documents. This is called the doctrine of

A. Ultra-vires.

B. Constructive notice.

C. Indoor management.

D. Outdoor management.

Q.67 Analysis of the balance sheet of a partnership firm shows that its total net worth is more than the total outside liabilities

A. it can be termed as a desirable situation.

B. it can be termed as an excellent and desirable situation.

C. it reflects the conservatism on the part of the management.

D. it reflects the risk appetite of the management.

Q.68 Acceptance of deposits is regulated by Central Govt. under Companies (Acceptance of Deposit) Rules 1975 in respect of

A. banks.

B. companies.

C. non-bank finance companies.

D. All of the above

Q.69 What is the maximum time for settlement of a claim before passing an award by the banking ombudsman ?
A. Within 15 days from the date of receipt of the complaint
B. Within 30 days from the date of receipt of the complaint
C. Within 2 months from the date of receipt complaint
D. Within 2 months from the date of receipt complaint

Q.70 What is the maximum limit of compensation the banking ombudsman may award?
A. Rs. 1 lakh
B. Rs. 5 lakh
C. Rs. 20 lakh
D. No such limit

Q.71 What is the time limit to accept the recommendations of banking ombudsman by a bank?
A. One week
B. Two week
C. Three week
D. Four week

Q.72 The banking ombudsman scheme was implemented in India on
A. 14/6/1995.
B. 1/17/1995.
C. 2/10/1995.
D. 15/12/1995.

Q.73 Which is the banks covered under the Banking Ombudsman Scheme, 2006?
A. Scheduled Commercial Banks
B. Regional Rural Banks
C. Scheduled Primary Cooperative Bank
D. All of the above

Q.74 The banking ombudsman scheme 1995 was amended in________.
A. 2000
B. 2001
C. 2002
D. 2004

Q.75 The usual form of a contract of agency is by way of a
A. power of attorney.
B. indemnity bond.
C. guarantee bond.
D. None of the above

Q.76 If a banking company is found to be not complying with the requirement of Prevention of Money Laundering Act 2002, the Director can impose a fine of
A. Rs.10000.
B. Rs.20000.
C. minimum Rs.10000 and maximum Rs.1 lakh.
D. minimum Rs.10000 and maximum Rs.5 lakh.

Q.77 There is an agreement between the parties for the specific performance of a contract. The limitation in this case is
A. 3 years, from the date fixed for performance.
B. 3 years, from the date of the contract.
C. 12 years, from the date fixed for performance.
D. 30 years, from the date fixed for performance.

Q.78 Which of the following is correct in the context of partnership firms?
A. If one partner cheats on a customer of the firm, other partners are not liable
B. For a partnership, it is compulsory to prepare a partnership deed
C. The partners can freely decide their mutual rights and liabilities

D. The nature of the business of the firm can be changed only with the consent of the majority of partners

Q.79 Which of the following is not an essential element of a contract of sale under the Sale of Goods Act?
A. There is a bilateral contract i.e. between seller and buyer
B. The consideration can be money or exchange of goods
C. The property is the movable property and not immovable property
D. The contract of sale can be oral or in writing

Q.80 Who has been authorized by RBI to deal in foreign exchange transactions?
A. Authorized Agency
B. Authorized People
C. Authorized Company
D. Authorized Dealer

Q.81 X purchased DD from Bank-B in favour of Y. DD has been misplaced in transit and bank has delayed the issue of duplicate DD due to completion of formalities
A. Y can file complaint in consumer court.
B. X and Y, together can file complaint in consumer court.
C. Y cannot file complaint as he has not purchased any service from the bank.
D. Y can file complaint with permission of X.

Q.82 Which of the following can make complaint under Consumer Protection Act?
A. The consumer himself
B. The voluntary consumer association
C. The Central or State Government
D. In case of death of the consumer, the complaint cannot be made

Q.83 If a return of loss is not filed on time _____
A. it can be filed any time to carry forward loss to set off in future years.
B. it cannot be filed subsequently.
C. subsequently but the carry forward loss will not be allowed to be set off in future years.
D. None of the above

Q.84 A customer is illiterate and finds it difficult to represent himself before the Ombudsman. He engages an advocate to handle his complaint________
A. a person can engage his representative including an advocate as per the scheme.
B. an advocate can be engaged with the permission of Ombudsman.
C. services of advocate are not permitted to be availed under the scheme to represent the complainant.
D. advocate can be engaged provided he does not claim any professional fee.

Q.85 Which particular provision was suggested by Supreme Court to be removed from the SARFAESI Act, in case of Mardia Chemicals vs Union of India and others?
A. Deposit of 75% of the amount of loan if the borrower wants to approach DRT against possession of the security
B. Deposit of 50% of the amount of loan if the borrower

wants to approach DRT against possession of the security

C. Deposit of 50% of amount of loan if the borrower wants to appeal to DRAT against DRT

D. Deposit of 75% of the amount of loan if the borrower wants to appeal to DRAT against DRT

Q.86 The agencies appointed under Consumer Protection Act are___

A. completely judicial in nature.

B. not judicial in nature.

C. quasi judicial in nature.

D. None of the above

Q.87 The penalty for not maintaining the required amount of SLR shall be paid within a period of ___ from the date on which a notice issued by the Reserve Bank demanding payment of the same is served.

A. 7 days   **B.** 10 days   **C.** 14 days   **D.** 15 days

Q.88 No banking company shall hold shares in any company, whether as pledgee, mortgagee or absolute owner, of an amount exceeding

A. 30% of the paidup share capital of that company.

B. 30% of its own paid-up share capital and reserves.

C. whichever is less between A and B.

D. None of the above

Q.89 Reserve Bank had removed Chairman/Director/Chief Executive Officer/other officer/employee of the banking company from office. Such person_____

A. can appeal to the Central Government within 30 days from the date of communication to him of the order.

B. can appeal to the Central Government within 60 days from the date of communication to him of the order.

C. can appeal to the Central Government within 90 days from the date of communication to him of the order.

D. can't appeal.

Q.90 In a Bill of exchange normally who is not the Drawee?

(i) The person ordering for payment

(ii) The person directed to pay

(iii) The beneficiary

A. Only (i) and (ii)   **B.** Only (i) and (iii)

C. Only (ii) and (iii)   **D.** (i), (ii) and (iii)

Q.91 Which entity regulates and supervises NBFCs?

A. SEBI   **B.** RBI

C. Ministry of Finance   **D.** NABARD

Q.92 Who is entrusted with the power to lay down instructions to the banks in India for audits?

A. RBI   **B.** Finance Ministry

C. State Government   **D.** None of the above

Q.93 When did the Banking Regulation Act come into effect?

A. 16th March 1949   **B.** 10th March 1949

C. 12th March 1950   **D.** 6th March 1950

Q.94 When did the Banking Regulation Act, 1949 become applicable to the state of Jammu & Kashmir?

A. 1949   **B.** 1979   **C.** 1956   **D.** 1966

Q.95 The Banking Regulation Act was initially passed by what name?

A. Banking Firms Act, 1949

B. Banking Companies Act, 1949

C. Banking Units Act, 1949

D. None of the above

Q.96 Who has been given the power under the Banking Regulation Act 1949 to grant license to banks?

A. Reserve Bank of India

B. State Government

C. Central Government

D. All of the above

Q.97 In which year the Banking Regulation Act 1949 was amended to make it applicable to cooperative banks?

A. 1962   **B.** 1964   **C.** 1969   **D.** 1965

Q.98 Which of the following entities are not covered under the Banking Regulation Act 1949?

A. Public Sector Banks

B. Co-operative Banks

C. Primary Agricultural Credit Society

D. All of the above

Q.99 Who regulates the District Central Cooperative Banks in India?

A. RBI

B. State Government

C. Central Government

D. SEBI

Q.100 Which section was added in the Banking regulation Act to include the Cooperative Banks under its purview?

A. Section 61   **B.** Section 56

C. Section 35   **D.** Section 28

Q.101 Which of the following is not a feature of document of title to goods undersection 2(4) of Sale of Goods Act?

A. A proof of possession of goods

B. Document of control of goods

C. Document that can be transferred by endorsement and delivery

D. The transferee gets defect free title even when the title of the transferor is defective

Q.102 Which of the following is not a document of title to goods?

A. Bill of lading   **B.** Airway bill

C. Railway receipt   **D.** Warehouse receipt

Q.103 The transfer of an interest in the immovable property by a person, to secure payment of the loan obtained, is called

A. mortgage.   **B.** assignment.

C. pledge.   **D.** hypothecation.

Q.104 Which of the following are the requirements of a securitized company?

A. It should be an independent company

B. It should be registered with RBI

C. It will be a public financial institution

D. All of the above

Q.105 For regulation and development of the insurance sector of the country the Government has formed

A. SEBI.

B. Reserve Bank of India.

C. Insurance Regulatory and Development Authority.

D. General Insurance Corporation.

Q.106 Which of the following is true in the context of a life insurance policy?

A. The policy is issued by the life insurance corporation or general insurance corporation

B. The contract of insurance is a contract of utmost reliability

C. The assignee of life policy cannot sue in his own name

D. The insured should have insurable interest in the policy

Q.107 What is the punishment under Consumer Protection Act for complaints of frivolous nature?

A. Only fine up to Rs.10000

B. Only imprisonment up to 3 years

C. Fine of Rs.2000 to Rs.10000 or imprisonment of 1 month to 3 years

D. Fine of up to Rs.10000 and/or imprisonment up to 3 years

Q.108 A Macro-Financial Monitoring Group (MFMG) is chaired by-

A. Finance Minister.

B. Governor, RBI.

C. Chief Economic Adviser.

D. DG, RBI (in-charge of financial stability).

Q.109 The monetary and credit policy statement of RBI is not called?

(i) Annual Policy Statement,

(ii) Credit policy of RBI,

(iii) Economic Policy

A. Only (i) and (ii)

B. Only (i) and (iii)

C. Only (ii) and (iii)

D. (i), (ii) and (iii)

Q.110 Terms Bull market and Bear market is associated with which branch of commercial activity ?

A. Foreign Trade

B. Banking

C. Share Market

D. Manufacturing

Q.111 The priority of charge under the Central Registry provisions, under SARFAESI Act, shall be on the basis of________

A. the charge created over the security first shall have the priority.

B. first in time registered to get priority over the person doing registration at a later time.

C. priority shall be determined by the authority heading the central registry.

D. priority shall be with reference to the purpose of the loan given against the security.

Q.112 The period of limitation for a loan under an agreement that it shall be payable on demand is and begins from____

A. 3 years, when there was loan default.

B. 3 years, from date of loan/document.

C. 2 years, from due date.

D. 3 years, from due date of the loan.

Q.113 If an existing company incorporated for secularization wants to undertake securitization activities after application of SARFAESI Act____

A. it has to incorporate a separate company.

B. it is deemed to have acquired the rights to undertake securitization activities under SARFAESI Act.

C. it is required to obtain registration with RBI within 6 months from commencement of the Act.

D. the existing companies do not require any registration with RBI.

Q.114 Before taking possession of a security under SARFAESI Act, the bank is required to issue notice to the borrower under provisions of____

A. Section 10 (3) of SARFAESI Act.

B. Section 13 (2) of SARFAESI Act.

C. Section 14 (1) of SARFAESI Act.

D. Section 17 (2) of SARFAESI Act.

Q.115 The ornaments kept by the bank in safe custody have been damaged, the loss

A. shall be of the bank.

B. shall be not of the bank, if bank had taken adequate care.

C. shall be of the bank, even if the bank had taken adequate care.

D. the bailor.

Q.116 A person dealing with a company cannot take the plea that he had no notice of contents of Articles of Association and Memorandum of Association due to

A. doctrine of ultra-vires.

B. doctrine of constructive notice.

C. doctrine of indoor management.

D. doctrine of outdoor management.

Q.117 Bank-B had sanctioned a loan to XYZ but it found to be inadequate to start the business, by the borrower____

A. complaint under Consumer Protection Act is possible.

B. complaint under Consumer Protection Act is possible only if the borrower suffers loss and able to prove.

C. complaint under Consumer Protection Act is not tenable.

D. complaint under Consumer Protection Act is tenable.

Q.118 Which of the following does match with regard to jurisdiction of the consumer courts?

A. Distt. Forum - covering the Distt.

B. State Commission - Covering the State

C. Apex Commission - Covering the entire country

D. None of the above

Q.119 An order was passed by a civil court after enactment of RDDB Act (DRT Act) 1993 but before the establishment of DRT having jurisdiction for that particular area____

A. order passed by civil court was not in its jurisdiction.

B. order passed by civil court was in jurisdiction of DRT.

C. order passed by civil court was in its jurisdiction.

D.   None of the above

Q.120 If a partnership is for a fixed period and it is continued even after the fixed period____

A.   it becomes illegal relationship.
B.   it is converted into a partnership at will.
C.   it becomes partnership for unlimited period.
D.   it becomes a particular partnership.

// Smart Answer Sheet //

Correct — Indicates percentage of students who answered questions correctly.

Skipped — Indicates percentage of students who skipped questions.

Q.	Ans.	Correct / Skipped
1	D	47.51 % / 21.59 %
2	A	14.29 % / 37.54 %
3	B	38.21 % / 34.22 %
4	C	46.18 % / 38.54 %
5	D	27.24 % / 38.54 %
6	D	43.85 % / 36.55 %
7	A	23.92 % / 37.87 %
8	D	47.84 % / 37.21 %
9	B	17.61 % / 38.54 %
10	D	37.21 % / 36.54 %
11	C	32.23 % / 35.54 %
12	B	29.24 % / 37.21 %
13	A	45.18 % / 33.89 %
14	A	25.25 % / 37.54 %
15	B	33.55 % / 35.89 %
16	B	39.2 % / 34.89 %

Q.	Ans.	Correct / Skipped
17	B	43.19 % / 37.87 %
18	D	5.65 % / 37.21 %
19	C	40.53 % / 12.96 %
20	C	37.21 % / 33.89 %
21	C	18.94 % / 32.56 %
22	A	28.9 % / 38.21 %
23	D	29.57 % / 21.93 %
24	A	46.51 % / 38.54 %
25	A	21.26 % / 38.21 %
26	B	17.61 % / 37.21 %
27	A	20.6 % / 30.56 %
28	B	12.96 % / 40.86 %
29	A	31.23 % / 32.89 %
30	A	41.2 % / 36.21 %
31	C	16.61 % / 37.21 %
32	C	11.63 % / 34.88 %

Q.	Ans.	Correct / Skipped
33	A	19.27 % / 23.59 %
34	C	20.27 % / 37.21 %
35	A	41.2 % / 35.54 %
36	C	40.86 % / 35.22 %
37	C	49.5 % / 38.21 %
38	A	28.57 % / 36.55 %
39	B	31.56 % / 38.21 %
40	B	32.56 % / 37.21 %
41	C	47.51 % / 33.55 %
42	A	21.26 % / 37.54 %
43	D	56.81 % / 34.22 %
44	D	25.58 % / 37.88 %
45	B	54.82 % / 33.22 %
46	C	14.29 % / 37.54 %
47	A	46.84 % / 35.55 %
48	B	22.92 % / 37.88 %

Q.	Ans.	Correct / Skipped
49	A	29.9 % / 38.21 %
50	B	34.22 % / 36.54 %
51	D	52.49 % / 34.55 %
52	D	39.53 % / 35.89 %
53	A	39.87 % / 37.87 %
54	D	43.85 % / 36.22 %
55	A	44.52 % / 35.55 %
56	D	31.56 % / 37.88 %
57	D	30.56 % / 38.88 %
58	B	39.87 % / 36.54 %
59	D	52.49 % / 35.88 %
60	D	57.14 % / 33.89 %
61	B	13.29 % / 38.21 %
62	C	48.17 % / 36.88 %
63	D	29.24 % / 35.54 %
64	D	21.26 % / 37.54 %

Q.	Ans.	Correct / Skipped
65	C	36.21 % / 36.55 %
66	B	27.24 % / 36.88 %
67	B	18.27 % / 38.54 %
68	B	8.31 % / 37.87 %
69	B	40.86 % / 37.88 %
70	C	35.55 % / 37.54 %
71	D	32.89 % / 24.59 %
72	A	25.25 % / 35.22 %
73	D	51.16 % / 37.88 %
74	C	26.91 % / 36.88 %
75	A	30.56 % / 37.88 %
76	C	31.89 % / 36.55 %
77	A	15.95 % / 39.2 %
78	C	14.29 % / 36.54 %
79	B	18.94 % / 25.91 %
80	D	40.86 % / 35.22 %

Q.	Ans.	Correct / Skipped
81	C	44.52 % / 33.55 %
82	D	10.63 % / 36.21 %
83	C	39.53 % / 39.54 %
84	C	25.58 % / 36.55 %
85	A	29.57 % / 37.87 %
86	C	41.53 % / 36.88 %
87	C	18.6 % / 38.21 %
88	C	36.88 % / 37.54 %

Q.	Ans.	Correct / Skipped
89	A	35.22 % / 38.87 %
90	B	20.27 % / 37.87 %
91	B	49.5 % / 37.88 %
92	A	50.83 % / 37.87 %
93	A	41.53 % / 33.89 %
94	C	26.58 % / 38.87 %
95	B	46.84 % / 35.88 %
96	A	52.16 % / 36.21 %

Q.	Ans.	Correct / Skipped
97	D	24.58 % / 38.88 %
98	C	47.84 % / 36.88 %
99	A	22.92 % / 35.88 %
100	B	32.56 % / 35.88 %
101	D	32.23 % / 39.53 %
102	B	29.24 % / 37.87 %
103	A	52.16 % / 37.54 %
104	D	42.52 % / 36.22 %

Q.	Ans.	Correct / Skipped
105	C	54.49 % / 37.87 %
106	D	17.61 % / 38.54 %
107	A	13.29 % / 33.89 %
108	C	18.6 % / 38.54 %
109	C	15.28 % / 34.22 %
110	C	53.49 % / 37.21 %
111	B	18.6 % / 28.91 %
112	B	21.93 % / 38.87 %

Q.	Ans.	Correct / Skipped
113	C	29.9 % / 31.56 %
114	B	30.23 % / 39.54 %
115	B	28.57 % / 35.88 %
116	B	23.59 % / 38.2 %
117	C	24.25 % / 29.57 %
118	C	29.57 % / 37.21 %
119	C	25.25 % / 29.9 %
120	B	35.88 % / 34.22 %

Performance Analysis	
Avg. Score (%)	31.0%
Toppers Score (%)	92.0%
Your Score	

//Hints and Solutions//

1. For meeting escalations in capital expenditure to be incurred under the rehabilitation programme, banks/financial institutions may provide, where considered necessary, appropriate additional financial assistance up to 15 per cent of the estimated cost of rehabilitation by way of contingency loan assistance. Interest on this contingency assistance may be charged at the concessional rate allowed for working capital assistance.

Banks should undertake proper scrutiny of the relevant loan applications and satisfy themselves, among other things, about the genuineness of the purpose, the quantum of the financial assistance required, the creditworthiness of the borrower, his repayment capacity, etc. and also observe the usual safeguards, such as, obtaining periodical stock statements, carrying out periodical inspections, determining drawing power strictly on the basis of the stock held, maintaining a margin of not less than 40 to 50 per cent, etc. They should also ensure that materials used up in the construction work are not included in the stock statements for the purpose of determining the drawing power.

Hence, the correct option is (C).

2.

- Governor Reserve Bank of India (RBI).
- Finance Secretary and/ or Secretary, Department of Economic Affairs (DEA).
- Secretary, Department of Financial Services (DFS).
- Secretary, Ministry of Corporate Affairs.
- Secretary, Ministry of Electronics and Information Technology.

Hence, the correct option is (A).

3. Under section 37 of the Banking Regulation Act 1949, provides that when a banking company is temporarily unable to meet its obligations, it may apply to the High court praying for an order staying the commencement on the continuance of all actions and proceeding against it for a period not exceeding 6 months, such suspension of business.
Hence, the correct option is (B).

4. In terms of section 45 of the Banking Regulation Act, 1949 (10 of 1949), during the period of moratorium, the Reserve Bank of India may, if so considered necessary in the public interest or in the interest of the depositors or to secure the management of the banking company, frame a scheme of reconstruction or amalgamation.

Hence, the correct option is (C).

5. A consortium bank is a subsidiary bank, which numerous other banks create. These banks might create a consortium bank to fund a large-scale project that is too large for one bank to complete itself, such as providing affordable homeownership for low- and moderate-income home buyers or to execute a large deal, such as selling loans in the loan syndication market.

Hence, the correct option is (D).

6. Once the lender has decided to initiate foreclosure, it must adhere to the state laws. Most states require the lender to supply the borrowers with a notice at this point. Typically, it is referred to as a notice of default. This document can be served by a sheriff, marshall or someone else appointed by the court.

Hence, the correct option is (D).

7. The minimum period of a certificate of deposit is 7 days.

The maturity period of Certificates of Deposit (CDs) issued by banks should not be less than 7 days and not more than one year, from the date of issue. A certificate of deposit (CD) is a product offered by banks and credit unions that provides an interest rate premium in exchange for the customer agreeing to leave a lump-sum deposit untouched for a predetermined period of time.

Hence, the correct option is (A).

8. Banks borrow from individuals, businesses, financial institutions, and governments with surplus funds (savings).Through the process of taking deposits, making loans, and responding to interest rate signals, the banking system helps channel funds from savers to borrowers in an efficient manner.

Hence, the correct option is (D).

9. Reverse repo rate is the rate at which the central bank of a country (Reserve Bank of India in case of India) borrows money from commercial banks within the country. It is a monetary policy instrument which can be used to control the money supply in the country.

Hence, the correct option is (B).

10. Ways & Means advances to take care of temporary liquidity problems of central and state government. The RBI as the banker to the State Governments provides Ways and Means Advances (WMA) to the States banking with it to help them to tide over temporary mismatches in the cash flow of their receipts and payments. Such advances are repayable in each case not later than three months from the date of making that advance.

Hence, the correct option is (D).

11. An 'advising bank (also known as a notifying bank) advises a beneficiary (exporter) that a letter of credit (L/C) opened by an issuing bank for an applicant (importer) is available. An advising bank's responsibility is to authenticate the letter of credit issued by the issuer to avoid fraud.

Hence, the correct option is (C).

12. An 'advising bank (also known as a notifying bank) advises a beneficiary (exporter) that a letter of credit (L/C) opened by an issuing bank for an applicant (importer) is available. The advising bank is usually located in the beneficiary's country.

Hence, the correct option is (B).

13. According to the Information Technology Act, 2000, digital signatures mean authentication of any electronic record by a subscriber by means of an electronic method or procedure in accordance with the provisions of section 3.

Hence, the correct option is (A).

14. The Reserve Bank of India (RBI) introduce the Banking Ombudsman Scheme (2002). The scheme has been revised to enable the Banking Ombudsman to function as an arbitrator on references to him of disputes either between banks and their customers or between two banks. The new Banking Ombudsman Scheme (2002) will cover all the regional rural banks in addition to all commercial banks and scheduled primary co-operative banks.

Hence, the correct option is (A).

15. The Reserve Bank of India has considered it necessary in the public interest and being satisfied that, for the purpose of enabling the Bank to regulate the financial system to the advantage of the country and to prevent the affairs of any Mortgage Guarantee Company from being conducted in a manner detrimental to the interest of investors or in any manner prejudicial to the interest of such MGCs and in the exercise of the powers conferred under section 45(A) of Reserve Bank of India Act, 1934 (Act 2 of 1934),
Hence, the correct option is (B).

16. Bank guarantee is often called "first demand" or "on-demand" guarantee because they are to be paid against the beneficiary first written demand for payment and no further documentation or proof of default is required.

Hence, the correct option is (B).

17. Letter of Credit is an assurance given by buyer's bank as opening bank to seller as beneficiary against sale of goods as per the terms and conditions mentioned in Letter of Credit. You (buyer) entered in to a contract with your overseas supplier to import machinery for production at your factory.
Hence, the correct option is (B).

18. Where a decree or order is passed by any Court before the commencement of the RDDB&FI (Amendment) Act, 2000 and has not yet been executed, then the decree-holder may apply to the Tribunal to pass an order for recovery of the amount and on receipt of that application under Section 31 A(1), the Tribunal may issue a certificate for recovery to a Recovery Officer.
Hence, the correct option is (D).

19. The scheme of the Act manifestly provides that the legislature has provided for application of the Limitation Act to original proceedings before the Tribunal under Section 19 only. The Appellate Tribunal has been conferred the power to condone delay beyond 45 days under Section 20(3) of the Act.

The particulars of every transaction of securitisation, asset reconstruction or creation of security interest shall be filed, with the Central Registrar in the manner and on payment of such fee as may be prescribed.
Hence, the correct option is (C).

20. Originator means the owner of a financial asset which is acquired by a securitisation company or reconstruction company for the purpose of securitisation or asset reconstruction.
Hence, the correct option is (C).

21. Functions of securitisation company.

a.)act as an agent for any bank or financial institution for the purpose of recovering their dues from the borrower on payment of such fees or charges as may be mutually agreed upon between the parties.

b.)act as a manager referred to in clause (c) of sub-section (4) of section 13 on such fee as may be mutually agreed upon between the parties.
c.)act as receiver if appointed by any court or tribunal.
Hence, the correct option is (C).

22. Working Capital Demand Loan (WCDL) is provided to meet working capital requirements. It shall be within the assessed working capital limits. It can be available as a sub-limit of funded working capital limit.

Hence, the correct option is (A).

23. There are two types of R-Returns. R-Return (NOSTRO) and R-Return (VOSTRO). A separate R-Return (NOSTRO) and a separate R-Return (VOSTRO) for each currency are required to be submitted irrespective of the number of accounts operated upon in that currency.

Hence, the correct option is (D).

24. Foreign exchange from India and affects the position of foreign currency assets or liabilities, is required to be reported to RBI.

There are two types of R-Returns are:

The terms Nostro and Vostro are used, mainly by banks, when one bank keeps money at another bank (in a correspondent account often called a Nostro or Vostro account). Both banks need to keep records of how much money is being kept by one bank on behalf of the other. In order to distinguish between the two sets of records of the same balance and set of transactions, banks refer to the accounts as Nostro and Vostro.

- A Nostro is our account of our money, held by the other bank.
- A Vostro is our account of other bank money, held by us.

Hence, the correct option is (A).

25. Other examples of this hypothecation are loans against stock and debtors. In such cases, if the bank feels that borrower is trying to cheat, then it can convert hypothecation to pledge i.e. it takes over possession of the goods and keeps the same under lock and key of the bank.

Hence, the correct option is (A).

26. A Person of Indian Origin (PIO) means a foreign citizen (except a national of Pakistan, Afghanistan, Bangladesh, China, Iran, Bhutan, Sri Lanka and/or Nepal)

- at any time held an Indian passport, or
- either of their parents/grandparents/great-grandparents was born and permanently resident in India as defined in Government of India Act, 1935 and other territories that became part of India thereafter provided neither was at any time a citizen of any of the aforesaid countries.
- is a spouse of a citizen of India or a PIO.

Hence, the correct option is (B).

27. Documentary credits (also known as letters of credit) are arrangements by banks for settling international commercial transactions. Provide a form of security for the parties involved. Ensure payment provided that the terms and conditions of the credit have been fulfilled.
Hence, the correct option is (A).

28. Tony Grundy suggests Human Resource Strategy in itself may not be effective. HR Strategy (Human Resource Strategy) is a designation for a long-term plan created to achieve objectives in the field of human resource and human capital management and development in the organization. Human Resource strategy is one of the outputs of strategic management in the field of human resources management.
Hence, the correct option is (B).

29. The applicant is the party who opens the Letter of Credit. Normally, the buyer of goods is the Applicant who opens a letter of credit. Letter of credit is opened as per his instruction and necessary payment is arranged to open Letter of credit with his bank.

Hence, the correct option is (A).

30. NRI for the purpose of bank accounts is as defined under FEMA. NRIs / PIOs / OCBs are permitted to open bank accounts in India out of funds remitted from abroad, foreign exchange brought in from abroad or out of funds legitimately due to them in India, with an authorised dealer.

Hence, the correct option is (A).

31. The validity of import licence from the date of issue of a licence shall be as follows:

i) Advance Licence as per chapter-7 and replenishment licence for Gem & Jewellery as per chapter- 8 of the Policy	18 months
ii)EPCG licence	24 months
iii) Others including CCP, DFRC and DEPB, unless otherwise specified	12 months
iv) Advance licence for Turnkey project	18 months or Co-terminus with the contracted duration of execution of the project whichever is later.
v) Advance Licence for Annual Requirement	12 months

Where the date of expiry of the licence falls before the last day of the month, the licence shall be deemed to be valid until the last day of the month.
Hence, the correct option is (C).

32. The value will always be CIF for imports and FOB in respect of exports. For imports if any local agency commission involved, the same also is added on CIF value of goods.
Hence, the correct option is (C).

33. Bills are export import proceeds. Bills buying rate is nothing but inward remittances, bill selling rate nothing but outward remittances. Foreign currency converted into domestic currency through bills buying rate; domestic currency converted into foreign currency through bill selling rate.
Hence, the correct option is (A).

34. A pledge is a bailment that conveys possessory title to property owned by a debtor to a creditor to secure repayment for some debt or obligation and to the mutual benefit of both parties. The term is also used to denote the property which constitutes the security. The pledge is a type of security interest.
Hence, the correct option is (C).

35. If an applicant is not supplied information within the prescribed time of thirty days or 48 hours, as the case may be, or is not satisfied with the information furnished to him, he may prefer an appeal to the first appellate authority who is an officer senior in rank to the Public Information Officer.
Hence, the correct option is (A).

36. The 1956 Act prescribed minimum 2 directors for a private and 3 for a public company respectively to constitute a Board. This criterion has been retained by the new Act, but the maximum limit of directors on the Board has now been raised from 12 to 15.
Hence, the correct option is (C).

37. Unless the article provides for the retirement of all the directors at every annual general meeting. Not less than 2/3rd (two-third) of the total number of directors of a public company shall be a person whose period of office is liable to determination by retirement of directors by rotation.
Hence, the correct option is (C).

38. As per section 203, every listed company or any public company having paid-up share capital of more than 10 crores or a company not falling under above two but having paid-up share capital of more than five crores is required to appoint a managing director/manager/whole-time director, company secretary, and chief executive officer.
Hence, the correct option is (A).

39. As per section 2(1) "asymmetric cryptosystem" means a system of a secure key pair consisting of a private key for creating a digital signature and a public key to verify the digital signature. The keys are simply large numbers that have been paired together but are not identical or asymmetric.

Hence, the correct option is (B).

40. Trusts in India are governed under the provisions of the Indian Trusts Act, 1882 (the "1882 Act"). In terms of the 1882 Act, a 'Trust' is an obligation annexed to the ownership of property, and arising out of a confidence reposed in and accepted by the owner, or declared and accepted by him for the benefit of another, of another and the owner.
Hence, the correct option is (B).

41. The 'Waqf Act, 1954' describes Waqf as, "the constant dedication by a soul confessing the Islam, of any 'movable' or 'immovable' property for any purpose approved by 'Muslim Law' as religious, pious or humane in the name of Allah.
Hence, the correct option is (C).

42. In cryptography, a Certificate Authority or Certification Authority (CA) is an entity that issues digital certificates. A digital certificate certifies the ownership of a public key by the named

subject of the certificate.
Hence, the correct option is (A).

43. The Banking Ombudsman may reject a complaint at any stage if it appears to him that a complaint made to him is: not on the grounds of complaint referred to above or the complaint is without any sufficient cause or the complaint that it is not pursued by the complainant with reasonable diligence.
Hence, the correct option is (D).

44. The banking ombudsman is anauthority originally established under the Banking Ombudsman Scheme, 1995 by theReserve Bank of India in exercise of the powers vested in it under Section 35A of theBanking Regulation Act. The scheme aimed at resolution and settlement of complaintsof the banking public against the commercial banks (excluding RRBs) and the scheduledprimary co-operative banks without resorting to courts. It was modified by the BankingOmbudsman Scheme, 2002 and later by the Banking Ombudsman Scheme, 2006 toenlarge the extent and scope of the authority and functions of banking ombudsman for'redressal of grievances against deficiency in banking services, concerning loans andadvances and other specified matters'. All commercial banks, regional rural banks andscheduled primary co-operative banks are required to comply with the modified scheme.
Hence, the correct option is (D).

45. The highest number of complaints were received against State Bank of India (46,994) followed by HDFC Bank at 12,044 and ICICI Bank at 10,465. The Ombudsman disposed of 96.5% of all complaints compared to 92% in the previous year indicating relatively speedy justice delivery.

Hence, the correct option is (B).

46. The amount, if any, to be paid by the bank to the complainant by way of compensation for any loss suffered by the complainant is limited to the amount arising directly out of the act or omission of the bank or ₹ 20 lakh (₹ Two Million), whichever is lower.

Hence, the correct option is (C).

47. The Banking Ombudsman shall report to the Reserve Bank the non-compliance by any bank of an Award which became binding on it and on receipt of such report the Review Authority shall pass necessary order. Jun 14, 2002.

Hence, the correct option is (A).

48. Whoever commits the offence of money-laundering shall be punishable with rigorous imprisonment for a term which shall not be less than three years but which may extend to seven years and shall also be liable to fine which may extend to five lakh rupees. The provisions of this section shall have effect as if for the words "which may extend to seven years", the words "which may extend to ten years" had been substituted.

Hence, the correct option is (B).

49. SARFAESI Act, 2002 is applicable only in the cases of secured loans where banks are in a position to enforce underlying securities such as mortgage, hypothecation, pledge etc. In all such cases, order from the court is not required unless the

security is fraudulent or invalid.
Hence, the correct option is (A).

50. After using the securitisation measures a bank can proceed further DRT. The Debts Recovery Tribunal (DRT) enforces provisions of the Recovery of Debts Due to Banks and Financial Institutions (RDDBFI) Act, 1993 and also Securitization and Reconstruction of Financial Assets and Enforcement of Security Interests (SARFAESI) Act, 2002.
Hence, the correct option is (B).

51. In Mardia Chemicals vs Union of India (2004) 21 ILD 521 SC, a three-member benchof the Supreme Court has declared this Act as constitutionally valid, except a part of theSection 17(2). Section 17(2) had laid down that when the lender intends to take the action of taking possession of the security asset, the borrower can file an appeal to theDRT only after depositing seventy-five per cent of the amount claimed by the lender.The Supreme Court has declared this condition of the deposit of 75% ofthe claim amount as unreasonable, oppressive, arbitrary and violative of Article 14 ofthe Constitution.
Hence, the correct option is (D).

52. Section 2 (20) of Companies Act, 2013 "Company" means a company incorporated under Companies Act. The company has a different and distinct personality from its members. It also has no strictly technical or legal meaning. A body corporate or corporation includes a company incorporated outside India but does not include a co-operative society registered under the law relating to co-operative societies, and any body corporate which the Central Government may, by notification, specify for this purpose. "Company" word derived from two words: "com"- group and "panies"- bread. Therefore, it means a group that eats their bread together.

Hence, the correct option is (D).

53. A company formed for the purpose of asset reconstruction and registered under the Companies Act, 1956 is called Reconstruction Company.

Acquisition of any right or interest, of any bank or financial institution, in any financialassistance, by any securitization company or reconstruction company, for the purpose of the realization of such financial assistance, is called asset reconstruction. In simple words,it is the takeover of loans or advances from the bank or financial institution for thepurpose of recovery.

On acquisition of a financial asset, the securitization or reconstruction company becomes the owner of the financial asset and steps into the shoes of the lender bank or financialinstitution. This acquisition can also be said to be, a sale of an asset without recourse tothe bank or financial institution. RBI is the regulatory authority for all securitization orreconstruction companies.
Hence, the correct option is (A).

54. The minimum number of members needed to form a private company is at least 2 members. The minimum number of members needed to form a Public Company is at least 7 members. The Maximum number of members in a Private Company is restricted to 200. The Public Company have no restriction on a maximum number of members.
Hence, the correct option is (D).

55. The Reserve Bank of India has released the annual report of the banking ombudsman for 2017-18 (running from July 1st, 2017 to June 30th, 2018). The report shows a marked rise in mutual settlement of 'maintainable' complaints compared to the previous two years and a corresponding decline in complaint rejections. Maintainable complaints are those that fall within the specified grounds for a complaint under the Ombudsman Scheme, 2006 and where due process is followed.

Out of the total number of maintainable complaints, 65.82% of banking complaints were disposed of by mutual settlement, up from 42.43% in 2016-17 and 35.93% in 2015-16. The rejection rate of 'maintainable' complaints fell correspondingly over the same period from 63.65% in 2015-16 to 33.82% in 2017-18. However continuing the trend of the previous year, the Ombudsman rejected nearly half the complaints it received as non-maintainable. The Ombudsman passed awards in a mere 0.159% of cases.
Hence, the correct option is (A).

56. The Banking Ombudsman Scheme, 2006 The Scheme is introduced with the object of enabling resolution of complaints relating to certain services rendered by banks and to facilitate the satisfaction or settlement of such complaints.
Hence, the correct option is (D).

57. The bank is the banker to the Central Government under Section 20 of the Act, andaccordingly, it is obligatory to undertake banking business for the Central Government.In the case of State Governments, their banking business is undertaken by the bank basedon agreements as provided in Section 21 A. Bank provides ways and means of advancesto the Central and State Governments. These are temporary advances to meet immediateneeds when there is an interval between expenditure and flow of revenue.
Hence, the correct option is (D).

58. A property mortgaged (Equitable mortgage) is in a village that is not a notified area. The bank branch which gave the loan is in a Notified area. If the bank wishes to file a suit, then the suit to be filed with the court in whose jurisdiction the property mortgaged is situated.

Hence, the correct option is (B).

59. Primary Co-operative Banks which are otherwise known as Urban Co-operative Banks are registered as Co-operative Societies under the Co-operative Societies Acts of the concerned States or the Multi-State Co-operative Societies Act function in urban areas and their business is similar to that of Commercial Banks.

A District Co-operative Central Bank (DCCB) is a co-operative bank operating at the district level in various parts of India. It was established to provide banking to the rural hinterland for the agricultural sector with the branches primarily established in rural and semi-urban areas.

The word 'State ' in the name of a state co-operative bank does not mean it is fully owned by State or State Government besides State Government other co-operative banks and district co-operative banks are also shareholders. In India 'State ' means the area of operation of the bank.

Hence, the correct option is (D).

60. Cooperative banking is retail and commercial banking organized on a cooperative basis. Cooperative banking institutions take deposits and lend money in most parts of the world.

It includes retail banking carried out by credit unions, mutual savings banks, building societies, and cooperatives, as well as commercial banking services provided by mutual organizations (such as cooperative federations) to cooperative businesses.

Hence, the correct option is (D).

61. Banking companies operating in India are constituted in the form of constituted under a special statute company registered under the Companies Act, 1956 or a foreign company society registered under the Societies Registration Act).

Hence, the correct option is (B).

62. Single holding with "Nomination" option If depositor dies before maturity, then the maturity proceeds will be payable to a nominee (as a custodian or trust). At a later stage, the amount will be fixed based on the WILL or Succession Certificate.

Hence, the correct option is (C).

63. Shareholders are also known as the members of a company. Under the Companies Act, 2013, any person can become a member and a person could mean an individual, body corporate or an association. The company law does not prescribe any disqualification, which would debar a person from becoming a shareholder of a company.
Hence, the correct option is (D).

64. A crossed cheque is a cheque that is payable only through a collecting banker and not directly at the counter of the bank. When two parallel transverse lines, with or without any words, are drawn generally, on the left-hand top corner of the cheque. An open cheque is a cheque where there is no crossing. Therefore, to encash the cheque no account is needed. One can encash it through the account of others. But if the cheque is crossed, then it can be encashed only through the account of the payee.

Hence, the correct option is (D).

65. Payments for the retirement of bills drawn under letters of credit as well as bills received from abroad for collection against imports into India must be received by authorized dealers, irrespective of the amount, by debit to the account of the importer.

Hence, the correct option is (C).

66. Constructive notice is the legal fiction that signifies that a person or entity should have known, as a reasonable person would have, of a legal action taken or to be taken, even if they have no actual knowledge of it. The doctrine is generally construed with regards to legal notices published, either by posting them at a designated place in a courthouse or publishing them in a newspaper designated for legal notices.

Hence, the correct option is (B).

67. TOL/TNW is a measure of a company's financial leverage calculated by dividing the total liabilities of the company by the total net worth of the business. Total outside liability is the sum of all the liabilities of the business and total net worth is the sum of share capital and surplus reserves of the company. This ratio gives an accurate picture of the businesses reliance on debt. A low TOL/TNW ratio signifies good levels of promoter's stake in the business, whereas a high TOL/TNW ratio shows low levels of promoter's stake in the business, which is considered risky. In the rating exercise, businesses with a TOL/TNW of less than 1 score the maximum amount of points while a TOL/TNW ratio of more than 3 is awarded no points. For most businesses, it would be good to have an average TOL/TNW ratio in the range of 1-2. In the given question TNW s more than TOL so ratio will be less than 1, it can be termed as an excellent and desirable situation. Hence, the correct option is (B).

68. Section 58A of the Companies Act, 1956 has put restrictions on acceptance of deposits by any company subject to rules being prescribed. Accordingly, Companies (Acceptance of Deposits) Rules, 1975 were prescribed which lay down various regulations and procedures for acceptance of deposits by companies.

Hence, the correct option is (B).

69. If a complaint is not settled by an agreement within a period of one month, the Banking Ombudsman proceeds further to pass an Award. Before passing an award, the Banking Ombudsman provides reasonable opportunity to the complainant and the bank, to present their case.
Hence, the correct option is (B).

70. Earlier, the banking ombudsman could only pass an award (a direction or an order) of up to Rs 10 lakh. This has now been increased to Rs 20 lakh. Additionally, the banking ombudsman can now grant a maximum compensation of Rs 1 lakh for loss of time and money, harassment and mental anguish suffered by the complainant.
Hence, the correct option is (C).

71. The Banking Ombudsman endeavors to promote, through conciliation or mediation, a settlement of the complaint by agreement between the complainant and the bank named in the complaint.

If the terms of settlement (offered by the bank) are acceptable to one in full and final settlement of one's complaint, the Banking Ombudsman will pass an order as per the terms of settlement which becomes binding on the bank and the complainant.

If a complaint is not settled by an agreement within a period of one month, the Banking Ombudsman proceeds further to pass an Award. Before passing an award, the Banking Ombudsman provides a reasonable opportunity to the complainant and the bank, to present their case.

Hence, the correct option is (D).

72. The Banking Ombudsman Scheme is an expeditious and inexpensive forum for bank customers for resolution of complaints relating to certain services rendered by banks. The Banking Ombudsman Scheme is introduced under Section 35 A of the Banking Regulation Act, 1949 by RBI with effect from June14,1995.

Hence, the correct option is (A).

73. Scheduled Commercial Banks- The scheduled commercial banks are those banks which are included in the second schedule of RBI Act 1934 and which carry out the normal business of banking such as accepting deposits, giving out loans and other banking services.

Regional Rural Banks- Regional Rural Banks are Indian Scheduled Commercial Banks operating at the regional level in the different states of India. They have been created with a view of serving primarily the rural areas of India with basic banking and financial services.

Primary Cooperative Banks- popularly known as Urban Cooperative Banks (UCBs) are registered as cooperative societies under the provisions of, either the State Cooperative Societies Act of the State concerned or the Multi-State Cooperative Societies Act, 2002.

Hence, the correct option is (D).

74. The Banking Ombudsman Scheme was first introduced in India in 1995 and was revised in 2002. The current scheme became operative from 1 January 2006 and replaced and superseded the banking Ombudsman Scheme 2002. Presently the Banking Ombudsman Scheme 2006 (As amended up to July 1, 2017) is in operation.

Hence, the correct option is (C).

75. A power of attorney (POA) is a legal document giving one person, the agent, or attorney-in-fact the power to act for another person, the principal.

The agent can have broad legal authority or limited authority to make decisions about the principal's property, finances, or medical care.

The power of attorney is often used when a principal becomes ill or disabled, or when they can't be present to sign necessary legal documents for financial transactions.

Hence, the correct option is (A).

76. Prevention of Money Laundering Act, 2002 is an Act of the Parliament of India enacted by the NDA government to prevent money-laundering and to provide for confiscation of property derived from money-laundering. PMLA and the Rules notified there under came into force with effect from July 1, 2005. The Act and Rules notified there under imposing obligation on banking companies, financial institutions and intermediaries to verify the identity of clients, maintain records and furnish information in a prescribed form to Financial Intelligence Unit - India (FIU-IND).

Hence, the correct option is (C).

77. The prescribed period of limitation for a suit of specific performance is 3 years from the date fixed for performance or if no such date is fixed, when the plaintiff has noticed that performance is refused.

Hence, the correct option is (C).

78. Partners can determine their mutual rights and duties by a contract called partnership deed, which determines aspects of general administration, such as which partner will do what work,

what will be their share in profits, etc. It may be varied by express or implied consent of all the partners.

Such a deed can be expressly made or implied by a course of dealing. For example, if one partner checks accounts of the firm daily and others do not object, his conduct will be presumed to be a right of all partners in the absence of a written partnership deed between them. So they can themselves determine the rights of partners.

Hence, the correct option is (C).

79. Sale and agreement to sell.

(1) A contract of sale of goods is a contract whereby the seller transfers or agrees to transfer the property in goods to the buyer for a price. There may be a contract of sale between one part-owner and another.

(2) A contract of sale may be absolute or conditional.

(3) Where under a contract of sale the property in the goods is transferred from the seller to the buyer, the contract is called a sale, but where the transfer of the property in the goods is to take place at a future time or subject to some condition thereafter to be fulfilled, the contract is called an agreement to sell.

(4) An agreement to, sell becomes a sale when the time elapses or the conditions are fulfilled subject to which the property in the goods is to be transferred.
Hence, the correct option is (B).

80. An Authorised Dealer (AD) authorized by RBI to deal in foreign exchange transactions. An Authorised Dealer is any person specifically authorized by the Reserve Bank under Section 10(1) of FEMA, 1999, to deal in foreign exchange or foreign securities and normally includes banks. Dealing with authorized forex dealers ensures that your transactions are being executed in a legal and just way.

Hence, the correct option is (D).

81. While a cheque takes a specified time of a day or two to get cleared, the same cannot be said for the demand draft. There are no codified rules as to how long the banks have to take in clearing the DD, which is why the time taken by each bank varies. Ideally, it takes two business days for a demand draft to be cleared. So, Y cannot file a complaint as he has not purchased any service from the bank.
Hence, the correct option is (C).

82. Under the Consumer Protection Act "complainant" can be made by -

(i) A consumer.

(ii) Any voluntary consumer association registered under any law for the time being in force.

(iii) The Central Government or any State Government.

(iv) The Central Authority.

(v) One or more consumers, where there are numerous consumers having the same interest.

(vi) In case of death of a consumer, his legal heir or legal representative.

(vii) In case of a consumer is a minor, his parent or legal guardian.

Hence, the correct option is (D).

83. A return declaring loss should be filed before the due date and any delay in filing of such return declaring loss will result in denial of the benefit of carrying forward of such loss and set off in future years. Every person whose total income in a previous year exceeds the maximum amount which is not liable to tax is required to file his return by the due date prescribed in section 139. A company or partnership firm has to file its return of income. A corporate assessee is required to file its return of income in the prescribed Form No 1. Corporate assesses are required to file the return of income in computer media (e-filing). The due date for filing of this return is presently October 31 of the Assessment year. A return of income can be revised to correct any mistake in the computation of income in the original return by filing another return within one year from the end of the assessment year or before completion of the assessment whichever is earlier.

Hence, the correct option is (C).

84. A customer is illiterate and finds it difficult to represent himself before the Ombudsman. He engages an advocate to handle his complaint services of advocate are not permitted to be availed under the scheme to represent the complainant.

Any person who has a grievance against a bank relating to the banking services for reasons, may himself or through his authorized representative other than an advocate make a complaint to the banking ombudsman within whose jurisdiction the branch or office of the bank complained against is located. Complaints arising out of the operation of credit cards shall be filed before the banking ombudsman within whose jurisdiction the billing address of the complainant is located.

Hence, the correct option is (C).

85. After the Supreme Court decision in the Mardia case and its fall out on the very intention of the legislation giving importance for recovery and prevent long legal battles that borrowers create without any payment, the Government of India has issued a notification amending the Section 17(2) of the SARFAESI Act. The amendment now stipulates the payment of 50% amount instead of seventy-five per cent as originally enacted. An aggrieved person has now a right to refer the matter to DRT and then to the Appellate Tribunal by depositing 50% of the claimed amount.

Hence, the correct option is (A).

86. The Act was enacted with the objective, 'for better protection of the interests of consumers". Different authorities were established for the settlement of consumers' disputes. The Act is social welfare benefit oriented legislation for the consumer providing self contained quasi-judicial machinery to provide speedy and simple redress to consumer disputes. The quasi-judicial machinery is established at the district, state and central levels. They observe the principles of natural justice and are empowered to give relief of specific nature and, if required, award compensation to the consumers. The Act also provides penalties for non-compliance of the orders given by these authorities. The agencies appointed under Consumer Protection Act are quasi-judicial in nature.

Hence, the correct option is (C).

87. The penalty for not maintaining the required amount of SLR shall be paid within a period of 14 days from the date on which a notice issued by the Reserve Bank demanding payment of the same is served.

If a banking company fails to maintain the required amount of SLR, it shall be liable to pay to RBI in respect of that default, the penal interest for that day at the rate of three per cent per annum above the Bank Rate on the shortfall and if the default continues on the next succeeding working day, the penal interest

Hence the correct option is (C).

88. Sub-section (2) of Section 19 of the B.R. Act, provides that no banking company shall hold shares in any company, whether as pledgee, mortgagee or absolute owner, of any amount exceeding 30 per cent of the paid-up share capital of that company or 30 per cent of its own paid-up share capital and reserves, whichever is less. It may be noted that there are no statutory restrictions, unlike in the case of subsidiaries, on the activities of companies in which banks can hold equity within the ceiling laid down under Section 19(2) of the B.R. Act. In other words, these companies could be both financial services companies as well as companies not engaged in financial services.

Hence the correct option is (C).

89. Reserve Bank had removed Chairman/Director/Chief Executive Officer/other officer/employee of the banking company from office. Such person can appeal to the Central Government within 30 days from the date of communication to him of the order.

Reserve Bank is satisfied that in the public interest or for preventing the affairs of a banking company being conducted in a manner detrimental to the interests of the depositors or for securing the proper management of any banking company it is necessary so to do, the Reserve Bank may, for reasons to be recorded in writing, by order, remove from office, with effect from such date as may be specified in the order, 2[any chairman, director,] chief executive officer (by whatever name called) or other officer or employee of the banking company.

Hence the correct option is (A).

90. The drawer after writing the bill of exchange has to sign it as a maker of the bill of exchange. Drawee is the person upon whom the bill of exchange is drawn. Drawee is the purchaser or debtor of the goods upon whom the bill of exchange is drawn. The payee is the person to whom the payment is to be made.

Hence, the correct option is (B).

91. The Department of Non-Banking Supervision (DNBS) is entrusted with the responsibility of regulation and supervision of Non-Banking Financial Companies (NBFCs) under the regulatory provisions contained under the Reserve Bank of India Act, 1934.

The Reserve Bank has been given the powers under the RBI Act 1934 to register, lay down policy, issue directions, inspect,

regulate, supervise and exercise surveillance over NBFCs that meet the 50-50 criteria of principal business.

Hence the correct option is (B).

92. The banking regulation Act empowers RBI to regulate the operations of banks lay down instructions for audits, control moratorium, mergers and liquidation issue directives in the interests of the public good.

Hence the correct option is (A).

93. The Banking Regulation Act, 1949 is a legislation in India that regulates all banking firms in India. Passed as the Banking Companies Act 1949, it came into force from **16 March 1949** and changed to Banking Regulation Act 1949 from 1 March 1966. It is applicable in Jammu and Kashmir from 1956.

Hence the correct option is (A).

94. Initially, this act was passed as Banking Companies Act, 1949 and it was applicable to the whole of India except Jammu & Kashmir. It became applicable to Jammu and Kashmir from 1956.

The banking regulation act of 1949 extends to the entire nation. Other acts are used as secondary to this act e.g. negotiable instrument act, Companies Act 1956. Passed as the Banking Companies Act 1949, it came into force16 March 1949 and changed to Banking Regulations Act 1949 it was made applicable to Jammu & Kashmir in the year 1956. The Banking Regulation Act is not pertinent to primary agricultural credit societies, non-agricultural primary credit societies and cooperative land mortgage banks.

Hence the correct option is (C).

95. Initially, the Banking Regulation Act was passed as the Banking Companies Act, 1949. It was changed to the Banking Regulation Act, 1949 from March 1, 1966. The Banking Regulation Act, 1949 is a legislation in India that regulates all banking firms in India.

Hence, the correct option is (B).

96. The Banking Regulation Act, 1949 is a legislation in India that regulates all banking firms in India. The Act gives the Reserve Bank of India (RBI) the power to license banks, have regulation over shareholding and voting rights of shareholders supervise the appointment of the boards and management regulate the operations of banks lay down instructions for audits control moratorium, mergers and liquidation issue directives in the interests of public good and on banking policy, and impose penalties.

Hence the correct option is (A).

97. Initially, the law was applicable only to banking companies. But, 1965 it was amended to make it applicable to cooperative banks and to introduce other changes. In terms of sub-section (2) of Section 22 of the Banking Regulation Act, 1949, the primary (urban) cooperative banks existing in the country as on March 1, 1966, were required to apply to the Reserve Bank of India.

Hence the correct option is (D).

98. Banking in India is mainly governed by the Banking Regulation Act, 1949 and the Reserve Bank of India Act, 1934. The

Reserve Bank of India and the Government of India exercise control over banks from the opening of banks to their winding up by virtue of the powers conferred under these statutes. All the regulatory provisions are not uniformly applicable to all banks. The applicability of the provisions of these Acts to a bank depends on its constitution; that is, whether it is a statutory corporation, a banking company or a co-operative society. In this unit, we look at the definition of banking, the constitution of different types of banks and applicability of regulatory laws, the general framework of the regulatory laws and the role of regulators namely, the Reserve Bank of India and the government. So, Banking Regulation Act applicable to banks and not to Primary Agricultural Credit Society.

Hence the correct option is (C).

99. Reserve Bank of India (RBI) regulates and supervises the banking functions of State Cooperative Banks (StCBs)/District Central Cooperative Banks (DCCBs)/Urban Cooperative Banks (UCBs) under the various provisions of the Banking Regulation Act, 1949.

Hence the correct option is (A).

100. In 1965, the Act was amended to include cooperative banks under its purview by adding Section 56. Cooperative banks, which operate only in one state, are formed and run by the state government. But, RBI controls the licensing and regulates the business operations.

With the introduction of Section 56 in the Banking Regulation Act, 1949 with effect from 1965, co-operative banks have come under the regulatory purview of the Reserve Bank. While the formation and management of co-operative societies operating in one state only (including those conducting banking business) are under the control of the State Government, licensing and regulation of banking business rest with the Reserve Bank. Thus, there is dual control of State Governments and the Reserve Bank over these banks.

Hence, the correct option is (B).

101. From the Section 2(4) of the act, we can say that this "includes the bill of lading, dock-warrant, warehouse keeper's certificate, railway receipt, multimodal transport document, warrant or order for the delivery of goods and any other document used in the ordinary course of business as proof of the possession or control of goods or authorizing or purporting to authorize, either by endorsement or by delivery, the possessor of the document to transfer or receive goods thereby represented."

Hence, the correct option is (D).

102. An air waybill or air consignment note is a receipt issued by an international airline for goods and an evidence of the contract of carriage, it is a document of title to the goods. Hence, the air waybill is non-negotiable.

Hence, the correct option is (B).

103. The 'Transfer of Property Act 1882' says "A mortgage is the transfer of an interest in specific immovable property for the purpose of securing the payment of money advanced or to be advanced by way of loan, an existing or future debt, or the

performance of an engagement which may give rise to a pecuniary liability".

Hence, the correct option is (A).

104. Securitization is the procedure where an issuer designs a marketable financial instrument by merging or pooling various financial assets into one group. The issuer then sells this group of repackaged assets to investors. Securitization offers opportunities for investors and frees up capital for originators, both of which promote liquidity in the marketplace.

However, securitization most often occurs with loans and other assets that generate receivables such as different types of consumer or commercial debt. It can involve the pooling of contractual debts such as auto loans and credit card debt obligations.

Hence, the correct option is (D).

105. Insurance Regulatory and Development Authority of India (IRDAI), is a statutory body formed under an Act of Parliament, i.e., Insurance Regulatory and Development Authority Act, 1999 (IRDAI Act 1999) for overall supervision and development of the Insurance sector in India.

Hence, the correct option is (C).

106. A beneficiary can be a person or a business. In any case, a beneficiary must have an insurable interest in the person who is being insured. With regards to life insurance, someone having an insurable interest in you means that they would experience financial loss and hardship should you die.

Hence, the correct option is (D).

107. The punishment under the Consumer Protection Act for complaints of frivolous nature only fine up to Rs.10000. The imposition of a penalty for frivolous consumer claims. There needs to be a guard against such frivolous complaints and therefore imposed a 25,000 rs fine on the complainant for a frivolous complaint.

Hence, the correct option is (A).

108. Macro-Financial Monitoring Group (MFMG) is chaired by Chief Economic Adviser and has representation from all the Departments of the Ministry of Finance. Representatives of financial sector regulators i.e. RBI, SEBI, IRDAI, PFRDA are special invitees for the MFMG meetings.

Hence, the correct option is (C).

109. (i) Credit policy of RBI - This method used by RBI is known as the monetary policy. Credit policy forms a sub part of the monetary policy. It is used to decide the quantum and the rate of interest at which credit is given by the banks. However, the objective of a contractionary policy is to raise interest rates to rein in inflation.

(ii) Economic Policy - An economic policy is a course of action that is intended to influence or control the behavior of the economy. Economic policies are typically implemented and administered by the government.

Hence, the correct option is (C).

110. Bull market and the Bear market is associated with which branch of commercial Share Market. A bull market is a market that is on the rise and where the economy is sound while a bear market exists in an economy that is receding, where most stocks are declining in value.

Hence the correct option is (C).

111. The priority of charge under the Central Registry provisions, under SARFAESI Act, shall be on the basis of first in time registered to get priority over the person doing registration at a later time.

According to the proposed change in the Sarfaesi Act, whoever registers their charge on an asset first with the designated central registry will get priority over others in recovering the dues by attaching the assets.

Hence, the correct option is (B).

112. Article 21 provides that for money lent under an agreement that it shall be payable on demand, the period of limitation (3 years) begins to run when the loan is made. A term loan is a monetary loan that is repaid in regular payments over a set period of time. Term loans usually last between one and ten years but may last as long as 30 years in some cases. A term loan usually involves an unfixed interest rate that will add additional balance to be repaid.

Hence, the correct option is (B).

113. If an existing company incorporated for secularization wants to undertake securitization activities after application of SARFAESI Act it is required to obtain registration with RBI within 6 months from commencement of the Act. The financial sector has been one of the key handlers in India's efforts to achieve success in rapidly developing its economy. Since our existing legal framework relating to commercial transactions has not kept pace with the changing commercial practices and financial sector reforms. This ensures the slow pace of recovery of defaulting loans and escalating levels of nonperforming assets of banks and financial institutions.

Hence, the correct option is (C).

114. Before taking possession of security under the SARFAESI Act, the bank is required to issue a notice to the borrower under provisions of Section 13 (2) of the SARFAESI Act.

Section 13(2) of the Sarfaesi act provides where any borrower, who is under a liability to a secured creditor under a security agreement, makes any default in repayment of secured debt or any instalment thereof, and his account in respect of such debt is classified by the secured creditor as a non-performing asset.

Hence, the correct option is (B).

115. As per safe deposit memorandum of hiring locker, the bank will not be responsible for any loss or damage of the contents kept in the safe deposit vault as a result of any act of war or civil disorder or theft or burglary and the contents will be kept by the hirer at his or her sole risk and responsibility. While the bank will exercise all such normal precautions, it does not accept any liability or responsibility for any loss or damage whatsoever sustained to items deposited with it.

Hence, the correct option is (B).

116. A person dealing with a company cannot take the plea that he had no notice of contents of Articles of Association and Memorandum of Association due to the doctrine of constructive notice.

The following are the practical effects of the doctrine of constructive notice:

(a) He who deals with the company is deemed to have notice of the public documents whether he has actually seen them or not.

(b) Another effect is that a person dealing with the company is not only deemed to have noticed but is also presumed to have read those documents and to have understood not only the company's powers but also of its officers.

(c) The doctrine of constructive notice is of a negative nature in the sense that it stops a person from contending (arguing) that he had no notice of the contents of the documents.

Hence, the correct option is (B).

117. Bank-B had sanctioned a loan to XYZ but it found to be inadequate to start the business, by the borrower complaint under Consumer Protection Act is not tenable.

An Act to provide for the protection of the interests of consumers and for the said purpose, to establish authorities for timely and effective administration and settlement of consumers' disputes and for matters connected therewith or incidental thereto.

Hence the correct option is (C).

118. National Consumer Disputes Redressal Commission (NCDRC). A national-level court works for the whole country and deals compensation claimed exceeds rupees one crore. The National Commission is the body of Consumer Courts it is also the highest appellate court in the hierarchy.

Hence, the correct option is (C).

119. An order was passed by a civil court after enactment of RDDB Act (DRT Act) 1993 but before the establishment of DRT having jurisdiction for that particular area order passed by the civil court was in its jurisdiction.

The Committee on the Financial System has considered the setting up of the Special Tribunals with special powers for adjudication of such matters and speedy recovery as critical to the successful implementation of the financial sector reforms.

Hence the correct option is (C).

120. If a partnership is for a fixed period and it is continued even after the fixed period it is converted into a partnership at will.

It extends to the whole of India except the State of Jammu and Kashmir.

It shall come into force on the 1st day of October 1932, except section 69 which shall come into force on the 1st day of October 1933.

Hence the correct option is (B).

Q.1 Which of the following groups is not included in the term 'goods', as per the Sale of Goods Act?

A. Shares and stocks

B. Grass and shares

C. Actionable claims and stock

D. Stocks and grass

Q.2 A suit is deemed to have been instituted (filed) in a court.

A. When the court fee has been paid.

B. When the plaint is presented to the proper officer in the court.

C. When the plaint has been acknowledged by the court.

D. Any of the above

Q.3 Which of the following are essential functions of banks as indicated in Section 5(b) of the Banking Regulation Act?
(i) Accept deposits and lend or invest such deposits
(ii) Accept deposit and undertake non-fund based business
(iii) Accept deposits and undertake remittance business
(iv) Lend, invest, and issue letters of credit

A. (i) and (iv) only

B. (i) and (iii) only

C. (iii) only

D. (i) only

Q.4 Private Sector Banks are regulated by
(i) Companies Act 1956
(ii) Banking Regulation Act 1949
(iii) RBI Act 1934
(iv) Banking Companies (Acquisition & Transfer of Undertakings) Act 1970

A. (i), (ii) and (iii) only

B. (ii), (iii) and (iv) only

C. (i), (iii) and (iv) only

D. (i) to (iv) all

Q.5 Other than the business specified u/s 6 (1) of the Banking Regulation Act, a bank can undertake any other business which can be prescribed/decided by
(i) Central Government
(ii) RBI
(iii) Board of the Bank
(iv) Ministry of Corporate Affairs

A. (i) and (ii) only

B. (ii) and (iii) only

C. (iv) only

D. (i) only

Q.6 Time required for obtaining a copy of the order or award shall be excluded while computing the limitation period for:

A. Filing review application

B. Filing revision

C. Filing an application to set aside the award

D. All of the above

Q.7 Which of the following are regulated by the Banking Regulation Act 1949?
(i) Public Sector Banks
(ii) State Bank Group Banks

(iii) RRBs
(iv) Coop Land Mortgage Banks

A. (i) to (iv) all

B. (i) to (iii) only

C. (i), (ii) and (iv) only

D. (i), (iii) and (iv) only

Q.8 Who can suspend the operation of the banking company and on whose recommendations?

A. RBI, on the recommendations of Central Government

B. RBI, on its own

C. Central Govt, on its own

D. Central Govt, on recommendations of RBI

Q.9 As per the Sale of Goods Act, ____ goods mean the goods identified and agreed upon, at the time a contract of sale is made.

A. Future

B. Specific

C. Movable

D. Immovable

Q.10 In the context of Cooperative Banks, which of the following statements are correct?
(i) Coop bank operating in one State obtains registration under State Coop Societies Act.
(ii) For coop banks operating in more than one State, Central Govt. appoints Registrar.
(iii) Coop banks are under the purview of BR Act u/s 56.
(iv) Where coop bank is registered under DICGC Act, RBI can order its winding up.

A. (i) to (iv) all

B. (i) to (iii) only

C. (i), (iii) and (iv) only

D. (ii) and (iv) only

Q.11 Before declaring a dividend, a banking company has to reduce its profits
(i) Preliminary or share selling expenses
(ii) Organization expenses
(iii) Brokerage and loss incurred
(iv) Bad debts for which adequate provision has been made

A. Only (i) to (iii)

B. Only (ii) to (iv)

C. Only (i) and (iv)

D. Only (ii) and (iii)

Q.12 As per the Sale of Goods Act, ____ goods are those which are to be manufactured by the seller after making a contract of sale.

A. Future

B. Specific

C. Movable

D. Immovable

Q.13 Which of the following statements are not correct in connection with shareholding in an Indian bank under the provision of BR Act?

A. There is no ceiling on a person's holding of shares.

B. No shareholder can exercise voting rights in excess of

a10% of total voting rights.

C. The provision of a 10% ceiling restricts the transfer and registration of such transfer.

D. The provisions of the companies Act also govern the transfer of shares of banking companies.

Q.14 In the case of non-resident persons, which of the following incomes is/are taxable?

A. Earned in India only

B. Earned while outside India only

C. Earned outside India, when in India only

D. All of the above

Q.15 RBI can appoint Chairman of a bank
(i) If the office is lying vacant and not filled immediately
(ii) If in the opinion of RBI, such vacant position is to be against the interest of the banking company
(iii) And such appointment shall be for a maximum period of 5 years
(iv) And there is provision for re-appointment after the initial period

A. (i) to (iv) all correct

B. (i), (ii) and (iv) are correct

C. (i), (ii) and (iii) are correct

D. (ii), (iii) and (iv) are correct

Q.16 In the context of the capital of a bank,
(i) The authorized capital means the maximum limit of share capital which the bank is authorized to have under its memorandum.
(ii) The amount of share capital that is subscribed and received is called paid-up capital.
(iii) The amount of share capital which is issued and paid-up is called subscribed capital.

A. (i) to (iii) all correct

B. (i) and (ii) only are correct

C. (i) and (iii) only are correct

D. (ii) and (iii) only are correct

Q.17 Banks are required to deposit the number of TDS (sale of the movable asset), in the govt. account:

A. Within one month from date of deduction

B. Within 7 days from date of deduction

C. Within 7 days from close of the month, during which deduction is made

D. Within one month from close of the month, during which deduction is made

Q.18 Under the Sale of Goods Act, if the sale is by sample, which of the following implied conditions is not correct?

A. Bulk shall correspond with the sample in the quality.

B. Buyer shall have an opportunity to compare the bulk with the sample.

C. Goods shall be free from any defect, rendering them un-merchantable, which would not be apparent on a reasonable examination of the sample.

D. None of the above

Q.19 While issuing a banking license for a foreign bank, RBI, in addition to usual consideration, takes into account
(i) Whether the business will be carried by the company in the public interest
(ii) Whether the law of the country where the bank originated discriminates against Indian banks
(iii) Whether the company complies with provisions of the BR Act, as applicable to foreign companies

A. (i) (ii) and (iii)   **B.** (i) and (ii) only

C. (ii) and (iii) only   **D.** (i) and (iii) only

Q.20 Which of the following statements is not correct?

A. Coop Bank operating in more than one state is registered under the Multi-State Coop Societies Act.

B. The government can exempt a bank from provisions of the Banking Regulation Act, on its own.

C. The company matters relating to a banking company are regulated by an authority under the Companies Act.

D. Banks undertake to trade in shares subject to regulation by SEBI.

Q.21 RBI cannot give directions to banks for loans and advances in respect of which of the following?

A. Purpose of which the loan can be allowed

B. Margin to be maintained for secured advances

C. Maximum amount of loan that may be sanctioned to one company, firm or association of persons

D. None of the above

Q.22 If a security is in possession of a bank, it can be sold by the bank:

A. By filing a suit under SARFAESI Act

B. By giving 60-day notice under provisions of SARFAESI Act

C. By giving reasonable time notice under provisions of Indian Contract Act

D. Under reasons of SARFAESI Act or Indian Contract Act, at the discretion of the bank

Q.23 Which of the following regarding the return of GST is/are correct?

A. GSTR-1 is to be filed by all normal taxpayers who are registered under GST. It is to be filed monthly, except in the case of small taxpayers with turnover up to Rs.1.5 crore in the previous financial year, who can file the same on a quarterly basis.

B. GSTR-2A is the return containing details of all inward supplies of goods and services i.e. purchases made from registered suppliers during a tax period.

C. GSTR-3 is to be filed by all normal taxpayers registered under GST, however, the filing of the same has been suspended ever since the inception of GST.

D. All of the above

Q.24 Banks are required to transfer a part of their profits to a Reserve Fund:
(i) U/S 17-1 of BR Act
(ii) And the amount is to be 20% of such profits
(iii) After payment of dividend
(iv) And commercial banks operating in India should transfer not less than 25 per cent of the 'net profit'

A. (i), (ii), (iii) and (iv)

B. (i), (ii) and (iii) only

C. (i), (ii) and (iv) only

D. (ii), (iii) and (iv) only

Q.25 A banking company can amalgamate with another banking company of its own, called _____ amalgamation. Central Govt. can also order amalgamation of two banking companies u/s 396 of ___, in consultation with ___.

A. Voluntary, RBI Act, SEBI

B. Voluntary, Companies Act, RBI

C. Voluntary, RBI Act, RBI

D. Voluntary, Companies Act, SEBI

Q.26 As per the Sale of Goods Act, the _____ of the seller is terminated when the buyer gets possession of the goods.

A. Warranty

B. Condition

C. Lien

D. Agreement

Q.27 A Lok Adalat has jurisdiction:

A. To decide a case as per its own judgment

B. To determine and arrive at a compromise or settlement

C. To decide a case as per its own judgment based on evidence produced before it

D. All of the above

Q.28 A public corporation is set up:

A. By Special Act of Parliament

B. By special order of the Government

C. Under the Indian Companies Act, 1956

D. None of the above

Q.29 Central Govt. can make rules for the preservation of records/books u/s _____ of BR Act. RBI can make rules u/s _____ of BR Act and banks can return the paid instruments to customers u/s _______ of BR Act.

A. 45Z, 35, 45Y

B. 45Y, 35A, 45Z

C. 21A, 35A, 51Z

D. 21A, 35A, 45Z

Q.30 Which of the following pairs does not match?

A. A corresponding new bank established under Banking Companies (Acquisition and Transfer of Undertakings) Act 1970 - State Bank

B. A principal coop bank in a district - Central Coop Bank

C. A coop society, the primary objective of which is to finance its members – coop credit society

D. The Bank which promotes an RRB - sponsor bank

Q.31 Under the provision of the SBI Act, 1955, SBI is managed by

(i) A board consisting of Chairman, Vice Chairman, maximum two Mg. Directors etc.

(ii) Chairman and Mg. Director is appointed for a period not exceeding 5 years

(iii) Local Boards are set up where the bank has Local HO

(iv) Local Boards consists of Chairman and other elected and nominated members

A. (i) to (iv) are correct

B. (i) to (iii) only are correct

C. (ii), (iii) and (iv) are correct

D. (i), (iii) and (iv) are correct

Q.32 A bank has made payment across the counter, of a cheque issued as a crossed cheque and the holder claims damages from the bank. Under such circumstances, the bank is liable:

A. To the drawer of the cheque

B. To the true owner of the cheque, i.e. holder

C. To the drawer and also the payee

D. All of the above

Q.33 Under provisions of the SARFAESI Act, the security receipt evidence:

A. Undivided right or interest of the purchaser, in the security

B. Independent right or interest of the purchaser, in the security

C. An exclusive right or interest of the purchaser, in the security

D. The exclusive right or interest of the seller, in the security

Q.34 A bank makes payment of two cheques on which, later it is found that the signatures of the drawer are forged. The first account is that of a company and the 2nd account is a joint account in which signatures of one of the account holders are real.

A. The bank is liable for the first cheque and for half the amount in the 2nd case.

B. The bank is liable for both the cheques.

C. The bank is liable for the 1st cheque and not liable for the 2nd cheque.

D. The bank is not liable for any of the cheques if payment is in due course.

Q.35 Under FEMA, the term authorized person means:

A. Authorized dealers, money changers and all banks

B. Authorized dealers and all banks

C. Authorized dealers and money changers

D. All of the above

Q.36 Right to information available to Indian citizens under RTI Act 2005 does not include which of the following rights?

A. Inspection of documents of records

B. Taking notes of documents

C. Taking certified samples of the material

D. None of the above

Q.37 The Board of Directors of a company cannot pass a valid resolution unless it is passed in a meeting in respect of which of the following?

A. Issues of debentures

B. Investment of funds of the company

C. Borrowing or lending of money

D. None of the above

Q.38 Under RTI Act 2005, information can be obtained by:

A. Any person in India including artificial persons

B. Companies, firms, corporations etc

C. Indian citizens

D. All of the above

Q.39 Banks can issue notice for enforcement of security interest under the SARFAESI Act when:

A. There is a default by borrower and security is in possession of the bank

B. The account is NPA and security is in possession of the bank

C. The account is a suit filed and security is in possession of the bank

D. The account is a suit filed and security is in possession of the borrower

Q.40 In a limited liability partnership, the rights and obligations of the partners are as per:

A. Certificate of Incorporation

B. Schedule II to the LLP Act

C. Agreement between Partners Act

D. Agreement between partners and if there is no such agreement, then as per Schedule I to the LLP Act

Q.41 Which of the following characteristics of a company is not true?

A. Liability of the shareholders is to the extent of a nominal value of the shares held by them

B. A company is a group of shareholders and is not different from them

C. A company is created through a legal process called incorporation which is completed by the issue of a Certificate of Incorporation by RoC

D. A company, being a legal person, has all the rights and obligation to sue or to be sued

Q.42 A trust is governed by:

(i) Trust Act 1882, if it is a private trust

(ii) Public Trust Act, if it is a public trust

(iii) Waqf Act if it is a Muslim trust

A. (i) to (iii) are correct

B. (ii) and (iii) are correct

C. (i) and (iii) are correct

D. None of these

Q.43 If the information does not relate to his organization, the Central Assistant public information officer has to forward the request for information to the concerned public authority within:

A. 5 days   **B.** 1 week   **C.** 21 days   **D.** 30 days

Q.44 In the pledge, the possession of goods is with the creditor (pawnee) which can be

(i) Actual – where the goods are actually in possession of the creditor

(ii) Symbolic – where the pawnor hands over the control of the goods to the pawnee without actual delivery

(iii) Trust receipt – where the goods are released to the pawnor without payment, by the pawnee on the basis of an undertaking

A. Only (i) and (iii) are correct

B. Only (ii) and (iii) are correct

C. Only (i) is correct

D. All (i) to (iii) are correct

Q.45 If a banking company fails to ensure compliance with obligations under the prevention of Money Laundering Act 2002, the director can impose a fine of:

A. Min Rs. 1,000 and max Rs. 1 lakh

B. Min Rs. 5,000 and max Rs. 2 lakh

C. Min Rs. 50,000 and max Rs. 5 lakh

D. Min Rs. 10,000 and max Rs. 1 lakh

Q.46 If a person commits offense under Prevention of Money Laundering Act, 2002, he shall be liable for fine:

A. Up to Rs. 10 lakh   **B.** Up to Rs. 5 lakh

C. Up to Rs. 2 lakh   **D.** Up to Rs. 1 lakh

Q.47 Which of the following is the most appropriate difference between a deferred payment guarantee and a term loan?

A. A term loan is sanctioned for purchase of fixed assets and DPG for purchase of current assets.

B. TL is a fund based loan and DPG is a semi-fund based loan.

C. In TL, funds outlay is immediate but in DPG, it is contingent.

D. In TL, an appraisal is more detailed than the appraisal of the DPG proposal.

Q.48 The mortgage in which the mortgager transfers the possession to the mortgagee is called ______. In such mortgage, (there is)/(there is no), personal liability of the mortgage.

A. English mortgage, there is

B. Mortgage by conditional sale, there is no

C. Simple mortgage, there is no

D. Usufructuary mortgage, there is no

Q.49 Which of the following statements is correct?

A. A certificate of incorporation is required by a public company only and not by a private company.

B. Certificate of commencement of business is conclusive proof of the existence of a company.

C. A certificate of incorporation is conclusive proof of the existence of a company.

D. A certificate of commencement of business is required by a private company only.

Q.50 Under FEMA 1999, there is the provision of appeal. The first such appeal can be made to:

A. Director (Appeals)   **B.** Appellate Tribunal

C. High Court   **D.** Supreme Court

Q.51 A public company may be a company limited by:

A. Shares   **B.** Guarantee

C. Shareholders   **D.** Both (A) and (B)

Q.52 A mortgage when created through an instrument in writing (called mortgage deed) is required to be registered with ____ within ____ months if the value of mortgage money is Rs.____.

A. Registrar of Firms, 4 months, 100 or more

B. Registrar of Assurances, 4 months, 100 or more

C. Registrar of Companies, 34 months, 100 or more

D. Registrar of Assurances, 3 months, 100 or more

Q.53 The primary function of an office is ______.

A. Making, using and preserving records

B. Remuneration personnel

C. Carrying out the management policies

D. Safeguarding of authority means

Q.54 The offences that are compoundable under any law, cannot be brought within the purview of which of the following?

A. Lok Adalat
B. DRT
C. Civil Court
D. High Court

Q.55 Which of the following parties in a bill of exchange do not match?

A. Maker - the debtor who is to make the payment
B. Drawer - who makes the bill of exchange and orders the drawee to make
C. Payee - the person who is to obtain payment as per order of the drawer
D. Drawee - the debtor, liable on the bill to pay

Q.56 Which of these features of limited liability partnership is not correct as per LLP Act 2008?

A. LLP is a separate legal entity
B. LLP is separate from its partners
C. LLP is taxed as a partnership
D. None of the above

Q.57 A guarantee which is issued by a bank, guaranteeing the timely payment of instalment to the supplier, by the applicant (borrower), for the machinery purchased on a long term credit from the supplier, is called:

A. Standby guarantee
B. Performance guarantee
C. Deferred payment guarantee
D. Statutory guarantee

Q.58 A person residing in India:

A. Can own foreign currency or immovable property if it was held when he was resident outside India
B. Can transfer foreign currency or immovable property if it was held when he was resident outside India
C. Can invest in foreign currency or immovable property if it was held when he was resident outside India
D. All of the above

Q.59 Which of the following statements is not correct in the context of the sale of goods?

A. A contract of sale can be absolute.
B. A contract of sale can be conditional.
C. In an absolute contract, there are no conditions to be fulfilled by the seller or buyer.
D. In a conditional contract, the goods are transferred later but the sale takes place beforehand.

Q.60 In case of mortgage, (a) the limitation period against the mortgager for personal liability is _____ years (b) against the mortgaged property, it is _____ years and (c) for foreclosure, it is _____ years.

A. 12, 12, 30
B. 3, 12, 30
C. 12, 12, 12
D. 3, 12, 12

Q.61 Which of the following documents is of title to goods?
(i) Bill of lading
(ii) Warehouse receipt
(iii) Delivery order
(iv) Airway bill

A. (i) to (iv) all
B. (i) to (iii) only
C. (i), (iii) and (iv) only
D. (ii), (iii) and (iv) only

Q.62 In case of creation of equitable mortgage, the property which is to be equitably mortgaged must be located in:

A. Notified towns only
B. Chennai, Mumbai or Kolkata only
C. Any place
D. Either A or B

Q.63 (i) A mortgage deed is a document in which the mortgagor transfers an interest in real estate to a mortgagee.
(ii) Debentures provide voting rights to the holders of the debentures in general meetings.
(iii) The assignee of the life policy can not sue in his own name.
(iv) Borrowers can pledge the documents of title to goods.

A. (i) to (iv) are correct
B. (i), (ii) and (iii) are correct
C. (i), (iii) and (iv) are correct
D. (ii), (iii) and (iv) are correct

Q.64 Which of the following is not a capital account transaction?

A. An Indian company purchased office space outside India
B. Indian Govt. made repayment of installment of a loan taken from US Government
C. An individual purchased shares on a stock exchange in London
D. Export of goods made on a deferred payment basis

Q.65 Financial Stability Report is published on ___ basis?

A. Yearly
B. Monthly
C. Quarterly
D. Half-yearly

Q.66 A lease for agricultural or manufacturing purpose can be terminated by the lesor or lessee by giving_________notice to one another.

A. 1 Month
B. 2 Month
C. 6 Month
D. 12 Month

Q.67 Compared to a public company, a private limited company is at a disadvantage because:
(i) It cannot invite the public to subscribe to its shares (ii) It has to observe restrictions on the transfer of its shares because the number of members is limited (iii) It has limited growth due to fewer shareholders(iv) It cannot obtain a loan from a bank

A. (i) to (iv) are correct
B. (i), (ii) and (iii) are correct
C. (i), (iii) and (Diiv) are correct
D. (ii), (iii) and (iv) are correct

Q.68 Which of the following has the authority under the SARFAESI Act to prescribe income recognition, accounting standards, and provisioning norms for Securitisation or Reconstruction Companies?

A. RBI

B. RRBs

C. SEBI

D. Company Law Board

Q.69 What is the function of the public key out of the pair of keys used in an electronic signature?

A. To create an electronic signature

B. To verify an electronic signature

C. To create and verify an electronic signature

D. All of the above

Q.70 When the sake of security is made by the creditor under the SARFAESI Act, the sale proceeds are to be utilized
(i) First towards costs incidental to preservation and protection of security
(ii) For dues of the secured creditor
(iii) Surplus to the person entitled thereto in accordance with the rights and interests

A. (i) to (iii) all correct

B. Only (i) and (ii) correct

C. Only (ii) and (iii) correct

D. Only (i) and (iii) correct

Q.71 Which among the following is an umbrella organisation for operating retail payments and settlement systems in India?

A. RBI

B. NPCL

C. Indian Banks' Association

D. None of the above

Q.72 After receipt of notice of possession from the bank, if the borrower transfers, other than in the normal course of business, any of his assets without the consent of the bank, what is the punishment under the SARFAESI Act?

A. There is punishment in the form of fine only.

B. There is punishment in the form of imprisonment for up to 2 years.

C. The punishment can be in the form of the fine and imprisonment up to 1 year or both.

D. There is no provision of any punishment.

Q.73 Which among the following is not a product of NPCI?

A. UPI **B.** NFS **C.** IMPS **D.** RTGS

Q.74 The provisions of the SARFAESI Act are applicable in which of the following transactions?

A. A lien or pledge on any goods as per Indian Contract Act

B. Security interest created on agricultural land

C. Loan amount above Rs. 1 lakh

D. Balance amount less than 20% of the principal amount and interest

Q.75 As per Rules under Prevention of Money Laundering Act 2002, the banks are not required to obtain which the following documents while opening an account of a company?

A. Certificate of Incorporation

B. Memorandum of Association and Articles of Association

C. Board resolution and official valid document in respect of the person operating the account

D. None of the above

Q.76 Under provisions of Right to Information Act, where the information is supplied by a 3rd party and is treated as confidential by that 3rd party and this information is sought by any person, the Public Information Officer shall give notice within ___ from date of receipt of such request to such 3rd party about his intention to disclose the information.

A. 5 days

B. 1 week

C. 10 days

D. No such notice is required

Q.77 The Tribunal is a quasi-judicial body and the selected candidates are appointed on tenure basis, i.e. for a period of ______ from the date they enter upon the office of the Tribunal or till they attain the age of________, whichever is earlier.

A. 5 years, 62 years **B.** 6 years, 62 years

C. 3 years, 62 years **D.** 5 years, 70 years

Q.78 A complaint that is made to Ombudsman should not relate to an issue
(A) Already settled by the Ombudsman
(B) Pending with a court
(C) Already decided by a court
(D) Where limitation period has expired

A. (A), (B) and (C) only

B. (B), (C) and (D) only

C. (A), (C) and (D) only

D. (A), (B), (C) and (D) all

Q.79 When the suit is filed by the bank with DRT, DRT summons the defendant requiring him to show cause within ______ days from ____ as to why the relief prayed for by the bank, should not be granted.

A. 30, date of summons

B. 45, receipt of summons

C. 30, service of summons

D. 45, date of summons

Q.80 In which of the following mortgages is the property is transferred by the mortgage absolutely with a condition for retransfer by the mortgagee?

A. Simple mortgage

B. English mortgage

C. Equitable mortgage

D. Usufructuary mortgage

Q.81 When the borrower wants to file an appeal against the order of DRT, which of the following is not correct?

A. He can do so within 45 days of receipt of order by him.

B. He can do so by depositing 75% of the amount of order.

C. He can do so by filing an appeal with High Court or DRAT.

D. He can do so without depositing any amount when permitted by DRAT.

Q.82 Which among the following cannot be considered as consumer under the provisions of Consumer Protection Act?

A. Purchase of goods which have been fully paid

B. Purchase of goods which have been partly paid

C. Purchase of goods for commercial purpose

D. User of goods purchased by another person

Q.83 When a bank is to send a certified copy of bank records to a court, the bank is to give a certificate that should contain all of the following, except that:

A. The entry is a true copy

B. The entry is contained in bank books

C. The entry was made in the ordinary course of business

D. Such record is not in the custody of the bank

Q.84 Bank B has received a notice from Recovery Officer of DRT attaching the balance lying in the current account of XYZ Pvt. Ltd.

A. The bank will ignore the notice as such authority is not vested with the Recovery Officer of DRT.

B. The bank will inform the Recovery Officer that his order cannot be complied with as he has no such authority.

C. The bank will follow the order as Recovery Officer can issue such order similar to the one given u/s 226 of Income Tax Act.

D. The bank will follow the order because the recovery of due amount of some other bank is involved.

Q.85 The lease for agricultural and manufacturing purposes is deemed to be a lease from year to year and it can be terminated by giving _____ notice.

A. 2 month **B.** 3 month

C. 6 month **D.** 12 month

Q.86 Which of these functions of public and private keys is correct?

A. Private key verifies the digital signatures and public-key creates the digital signature.

B. Public key verifies the digital signatures and private key creates the digital signature.

C. The private key and public key are used to verify the digital signatures.

D. The private key and public key are used to create digital signatures.

Q.87 An agreement that cannot be enforceable by law is called:

A. Quasi-agreement **B.** Void agreement

C. Voidable agreement **D.** Immoral agreement

Q.88 Distt. forum is headed by a person who is or has been qualified to be a _____ Judge. The other _____ members of not less than _____.

A. Distt, 3, 35 years

B. Distt, 3, 27 years

C. Distt, 2, 35 years

D. High Court, 3, 35 years

Q.89 In the execution of mortgage decree, the decree-holder can bring the mortgaged properties to sale:

A. Without first seeking an order of attachment of court

B. After seeking an order of attachment of court

C. After obtaining an order from the court

D. None of the above

Q.90 A contract is valid only when there is a valid consideration, but in the case of a contract of guarantee, no consideration passes between the bank and the guarantee. The contract is still valid because:

A. Guarantor has signed the contract with his free will

B. A guarantor is a major person and contracts with a major person is valid

C. Anything done for the benefit of the borrower is sufficient consideration for the guarantor

D. Guarantor's liability is secondary (as the borrower is primarily liable) and hence, no consideration is required

Q.91 Which of the following statement is correct in the context of a bank guarantee:

A. The liability of the bank is secondary and that of the borrower primary.

B. The liability of the bank is primary and that of the borrower secondary.

C. The liability of the bank and that of the borrower is primary.

D. The liability of the bank as well as that of the borrower secondary.

Q.92 Which of the following is true?

A. Bailor is the person who receives the goods as security for the loan.

B. When documents are delivered by a customer for safe custody to the bank and the bank takes due care, but there is a loss to documents, the bank is liable to the customer.

C. If the bailor has knowledge about the defect in the goods due to which bailee suffers a loss, the bailor is liable.

D. Bailee can use the goods as he likes and is not liable for damages for such use.

Q.93 As a part of corporate governance, the concept of 'fit and proper' relates to which of the following aspects?

A. Appointment of directors of banks

B. Management of banks

C. While deciding Board of directors

D. Staff of banks

Q.94 Under the Sale of Goods Act, the term 'caveat emptor' means:

A. An instruction to the buyer to buy only if he likes

B. A condition binding the buyer and seller to agree to certain conditions of the sale

C. A warning for the sale buyer to be cautious while buying

D. A right of the seller, whether to sell the goods or not

Q.95 A partnership is a contract with all of the following features, except that the:

A. The contract can be oral contract also

B. The contract is to carry any type of business, lawful or otherwise

C. Business is to be carried to make profits and share profits

D. The mutual relationship between partners is of agency

Q.96 X, the natural guardian of M, the minor, wants to mortgage the property in the name of M to secure a loan for the benefit of the minor.

A. The property in the name of M cannot be mortgaged.

B. The property in the name of M can be mortgaged if the loan is for benefit of the minor.

C. The property in the name of M can be mortgaged if the loan is for benefit of the minor with permission of the court only.

D. The property in the name of M can be mortgaged if the loan is for benefit of the minor with permission of the registrar of assurances.

Q.97 A contract without _______ is void.

A. Cash
B. Consideration
C. Indemnity
D. Guarantee

Q.98 The provisions in respect of enhancing the borrowing powers of the Board of a public limited company or subsidiary of a public limited company, by the shareholders, are given in section ____ of the Companies Act 2013.

A. 125
B. 163
C. 180
D. 194

Q.99 As per SEBI guidelines, the minimum percentage of independent directors out of total should be _____ of a ______.

A. 25%, public company
B. 50%, public company
C. 50%, listed company
D. 25%, listed company

Q.100 A guarantee which extends to a series of transactions is known as a ________ guarantee.

A. Continuing
B. Invalid
C. Irrevocable
D. General

Q.101 Tax assessed by AO shall be paid within _______ days.

A. 30
B. 45
C. 60
D. None of these

Q.102 _______ means voluntary transfer of possession from one person to another.

A. Delivery
B. Lien
C. Indemnity
D. Suit

Q.103 If the stipulation agreed to between the parties is essential to the main purpose of the contract, then such a stipulation is known as a/an _________.

A. Condition
B. Warranty
C. Implied condition
D. Guarantee

Q.104 If the sale of goods is by ________, there is an implied condition that the goods shall correspond with the description.

A. Description
B. Sample
C. Oral agreement
D. Written contract

Q.105 Provision for deduction of tax at source are as per Section_____ of Income Tax Act, 1961.

A. 192
B. 193
C. 194
D. None of the above

Q.106 The usual form of contract of agency is by way of a/an ___________.

A. Power of attorney
B. Indemnity bond
C. Guarantee bond
D. None of these

Q.107 In a government company, the government holds at least _________ per cent of the paid-up capital.

A. 12
B. 15
C. 50
D. 51

Q.108 When the _______ is in possession of goods, a lien can be exercised.

A. Seller
B. Buyer
C. Agent of the buyer
D. Carrier

Q.109 The maximum number of directors in a public company can be ________.

A. 3
B. 7
C. 12
D. 15

Q.110 The minimum number of members required in a public company is ________.

A. 3
B. 7
C. 12
D. 2

Q.111 Schedule III Part II of the Companies Act, 2013 deals with which one of the following?

A. Format of Balance Sheet
B. Format of Profit and Loss Account
C. Format of Trading Account
D. Format of Cash Flow

Q.112 The Sale of Goods Act was enacted on:

A. 18th July 1930
B. 15th March 1930
C. 15th July 1930
D. None of the above

Q.113 Additional directors are appointed by the _______.

A. Board of Directors
B. Promoters
C. Underwriters
D. Shareholders

Q.114 There are _____ parties in a contract of indemnity.

A. 2
B. 3
C. 4
D. 5

Q.115 Which among the following is a necessary condition for declaring it a company as a Govt. company under the provisions of Companies Act 1956?

A. It should be fully owned by the Central Government
B. It should be fully owned by the Central and State Government
C. At least 50% of the paid-up capital should be owned by the Government
D. At least 51% of the paid-up capital should be owned by the Government

Q.116 Casual vacancies in the board of directors are filled in by the ________.

A. Board of Directors
B. Promoters
C. Underwriters
D. Shareholders

Q.117 A private company should have a minimum paid-up capital or Rupees ________.

A. Five Crore
B. Five Lakh
C. One Crore
D. One Lakh

Q.118 Every public limited company must have a managing director or whole-time director, where paid-up share capital is:

A. Above Rs. 2 crore
B. Rs. 2 crore and above
C. Rs. 5 crore and above
D. Rs. 10 crore and above

Q.119 There is regular trade between two parties through letter of credit but they want that it may not be required to open a letter of credit again and again. What type of LC is suitable for them?

A. Irrevocable LC

B. Revolving LC

C. Red clause LC

D. Confirmed LC

Q.120 Which of the following documents is called charter of the company?

A. Certificate of Commencement of Business

B. Certificate of Incorporation

C. Articles of Association

D. Memorandum of Association

// Smart Answer Sheet //

Correct Indicates percentage of students who answered questions correctly.

Skipped Indicates percentage of students who skipped questions.

Q.	Ans.	Correct / Skipped
1	C	44.3 % / 21.49 %
2	B	13.6 % / 33.77 %
3	D	32.46 % / 32.45 %
4	A	25.88 % / 35.08 %
5	D	10.96 % / 36.85 %
6	D	36.4 % / 36.85 %
7	B	39.91 % / 36.41 %
8	D	26.75 % / 36.85 %
9	B	39.04 % / 36.84 %
10	A	28.07 % / 37.28 %
11	A	24.12 % / 35.09 %
12	A	43.42 % / 35.97 %
13	C	17.98 % / 28.51 %
14	A	32.46 % / 35.08 %
15	B	11.84 % / 33.77 %
16	B	17.11 % / 32.45 %

Q.	Ans.	Correct / Skipped
17	D	10.09 % / 36.4 %
18	D	16.23 % / 38.59 %
19	A	44.3 % / 13.16 %
20	B	44.3 % / 23.24 %
21	D	28.95 % / 27.19 %
22	C	11.4 % / 34.21 %
23	D	43.86 % / 21.93 %
24	C	17.98 % / 30.7 %
25	B	41.67 % / 36.84 %
26	C	29.39 % / 37.72 %
27	B	24.56 % / 27.19 %
28	B	32.02 % / 35.52 %
29	B	25.88 % / 30.7 %
30	A	39.04 % / 34.21 %
31	A	31.14 % / 35.09 %
32	B	26.32 % / 31.57 %

Q.	Ans.	Correct / Skipped
33	A	15.79 % / 23.25 %
34	B	36.4 % / 31.58 %
35	C	27.63 % / 34.65 %
36	D	34.21 % / 32.9 %
37	D	13.16 % / 35.52 %
38	C	23.25 % / 36.84 %
39	B	30.7 % / 37.28 %
40	D	43.42 % / 36.84 %
41	B	30.26 % / 29.83 %
42	A	43.42 % / 34.21 %
43	A	22.81 % / 33.77 %
44	A	10.09 % / 35.52 %
45	D	46.05 % / 29.39 %
46	B	25.44 % / 34.21 %
47	C	33.33 % / 35.53 %
48	D	17.54 % / 36.41 %

Q.	Ans.	Correct / Skipped
49	C	21.93 % / 37.72 %
50	A	26.32 % / 36.84 %
51	D	43.42 % / 32.46 %
52	B	14.04 % / 28.94 %
53	A	40.35 % / 35.09 %
54	A	34.21 % / 36.4 %
55	A	30.26 % / 34.21 %
56	D	13.6 % / 35.08 %
57	C	45.61 % / 35.97 %
58	D	50.0 % / 36.4 %
59	D	26.32 % / 34.21 %
60	B	39.91 % / 30.7 %
61	B	34.65 % / 35.96 %
62	C	21.93 % / 36.84 %
63	C	22.81 % / 35.52 %
64	D	21.93 % / 35.96 %

Q.	Ans.	Correct / Skipped
65	D	14.47 % / 35.97 %
66	C	33.77 % / 36.84 %
67	B	35.96 % / 38.16 %
68	A	38.16 % / 36.4 %
69	B	29.39 % / 36.84 %
70	A	37.72 % / 39.03 %
71	B	38.6 % / 25.0 %
72	C	48.68 % / 27.64 %
73	D	28.07 % / 35.53 %
74	C	29.82 % / 36.85 %
75	D	32.46 % / 36.4 %
76	A	17.98 % / 36.41 %
77	A	30.26 % / 36.41 %
78	D	45.61 % / 37.28 %
79	C	14.47 % / 25.44 %
80	B	35.53 % / 30.26 %

Q.	Ans.	Correct	Skipped
81	C	17.98 %	27.2 %
82	C	28.51 %	34.21 %
83	D	36.84 %	36.41 %
84	C	39.47 %	36.41 %
85	C	36.4 %	36.85 %
86	B	38.16 %	36.84 %
87	B	35.53 %	36.84 %
88	C	24.12 %	36.84 %

Q.	Ans.	Correct	Skipped
89	A	16.67 %	37.72 %
90	C	17.11 %	37.28 %
91	B	25.88 %	37.28 %
92	C	25.0 %	36.4 %
93	A	39.91 %	28.51 %
94	C	25.0 %	36.4 %
95	B	23.68 %	35.97 %
96	C	25.0 %	35.96 %

Q.	Ans.	Correct	Skipped
97	B	48.68 %	36.85 %
98	C	16.23 %	39.03 %
99	C	15.79 %	35.09 %
100	A	54.39 %	33.77 %
101	A	39.04 %	35.96 %
102	A	47.81 %	36.84 %
103	A	21.93 %	36.84 %
104	A	33.33 %	36.41 %

Q.	Ans.	Correct	Skipped
105	C	30.7 %	36.41 %
106	A	38.16 %	37.72 %
107	D	51.75 %	32.9 %
108	A	33.77 %	35.53 %
109	D	45.18 %	28.94 %
110	B	35.96 %	34.22 %
111	B	33.77 %	26.32 %
112	B	25.88 %	34.21 %

Q.	Ans.	Correct	Skipped
113	A	53.51 %	28.07 %
114	A	50.0 %	34.65 %
115	D	48.68 %	35.53 %
116	A	40.35 %	35.97 %
117	D	28.51 %	26.75 %
118	C	40.79 %	34.21 %
119	B	47.37 %	26.31 %
120	D	32.89 %	29.39 %

Performance Analysis

Avg. Score (%)	26.0%
Toppers Score (%)	85.0%
Your Score	

//Hints and Solutions//

1. As per the Sale of Goods Act, "goods" means every kind of movable property other than actionable claims and stock.

"Every kind of movable property other than actionable claims and money; and includes stock and shares, growing crops, grass, and things attached to or forming part of the land which are agreed to be severed before sale or under the contract of sale will be considered goods". As you can see, shares and stocks are also defined as goods by the Act. The term actionable claims mean those claims which are eligible to be enforced or initiated by a suit or legal action. This means that those claims where an action such as recovery by auction, suit, refunds, etc. could be initiated to recover or realize the claim.

Hence, the correct option is (C).

2. Under the Limitation Act, 1963, a suit is instituted in an ordinary case, when the plaint is presented to the proper officer, or in an ordinary case when the plaint is presented to the proper officer.

(1) Every suit shall be instituted by presenting a plaint in duplicate to the Court or such officer as it appoints on this behalf.

(2) Every plant shall comply with the rules contained in Order VI and VII, so far as they are applicable.

(3) The plaint shall not be deemed to be duly instituted unless it complies with the requirements specified in sub-rules.

Hence, the correct option is (B).

3. As indicated in Section 5(b) of the Banking Regulation Act "banking" means the accepting, for the purpose of lending or investment, of deposits of money from the public, repayable on demand or otherwise, and withdrawal by cheque, draft, order or otherwise.
Hence, the correct option is (D).

4. Private Sector Banks are regulated by the Companies Act 1956, Banking Regulation Act 1949 and RBI Act 1934. All banks other than public sector banks are called Private Banks. These banks are registered under the Indian Companies Act, 1956. They are of two types-Indian Banks and Foreign Banks. Banks registered in India are called Indian Banks and those with their registered office outside India are called Foreign Banks. Private Sector Bank means banks licensed to operate in India under the Banking Regulation Act, 1949, other than Urban Co-operative Banks, Foreign Banks and banks licensed under specific Statutes.

Under the Banking Regulation Act, 1949, the RBI has been entrusted with the full responsibility of supervising and regulating private sector banks in India. Under Section 22 of the Banking Regulation Act, private banks are required to obtain a license from the RBI to carry on banking business in India.

The Preamble to the Reserve Bank of India Act, 1934 spells out the objectives of the Reserve Bank as: "to regulate the issue of banknotes and the keeping of reserves with a view to securing monetary stability in India and generally to operate the currency and credit system of the country to its advantage."

Hence, the correct option is (A)

5. In addition to the business of banking, a banking company may engage in any other forms of business which the Central Government may by notification in the Official Gazette, specify as a form of business in which it is lawful for a banking company to engage u/s 6(1).

Hence, the correct option is (D).

6. In computing the period of limitation for an appeal or an review application for leave to appeal or for revision or for review of a judgment, the day on which the judgment complained of was pronounced and the time requisite for obtaining a copy of the decree, sentence or order appealed from or sought to be revised or reviewed shall be excluded. In computing the period of limitation for an application to set aside an award, the time requisite for obtaining a copy of the award shall be excluded.
Hence, the correct option is (D).

7. In computing the period of limitation for an appeal or an application for leave to appeal or for revision or for review of a judgment, the day on which the judgment complained of was pronounced and the time requisite for obtaining a copy of the decree, sentence or order appealed from or sought to be revised or reviewed shall be excluded.

The Reserve Bank of India (RBI) regulates and supervises Public Sector And Private Sector Banks. Under the provisions of the Banking Regulation Act, 1949.

On 1 July 1955, the Imperial Bank of India became the State Bank of India. In 2008, the Government of India acquired the Reserve Bank of India's stake in SBI so as to remove any conflict of interest because the RBI is the country's banking regulatory authority.

Reserve Bank, as the regulator of Regional Rural Banks (RRBs), has been actively engaged from the very beginning in the review, examination and evaluation of customer service in RRBs by means of various guidelines issued from time to time to the RRBs.

Hence, the correct option is (B).

8. Under The Banking Regulation Act, 1949, Section 45 states Power of Reserve Bank to apply to Central Government for suspension of business by a banking company and to prepare a scheme of reconstitution of amalgamation.
Hence, the correct option is (D).

9. Under the Sale of Goods Act, specific goods mean goods identified and agreed upon at the time a contract of sale is made.

In sec 2(6) of the Act, future goods have been defined as the goods that will either be manufactured or produced or acquired by the seller at the time the contract of sale is made. The contract for the sale of future goods will never have the actual sale in it, it will always be an agreement to sell.

Hence, the correct option is (B).

10. (i) Coop bank operating in one State obtains registration under State Coop Societies Act.

(ii) For coop banks operating in more than one State, Central Govt. appoints Registrar. "

(iii) Coop banks are under the purview of BR Act u/s 56

(iv) Where coop bank is registered under DICGC Act, RBI can order its winding up.

Co-operative society other than a co-operative bank shall use as part of its name or in connection with its business any of the words "bank", "banker" or "banking", and no co-operative society shall carry on the business of banking in India unless it uses as part of its name at least of such words.

"Central Registrar" means the Central Registrar of Co-operative Societies appointed under sub-section (1) of section 4 and includes any officer empowered to exercise the powers of the Central Registrar under sub-section (2) of that section.

Hence, the correct option is (A).

11. No banking company shall pay any dividend on its shares until all its capitalised expenses (including preliminary expenses, organization expenses, share-selling commission, brokerage, amounts of losses incurred, and any other item of expenditure not represented by tangible assets) have been completely written off.
Hence, the correct option is (A).

12. Under Section 2 in the Sale of Goods Act, 1930, future goods mean goods to be manufactured or acquired by the seller after the making of the contract of sale.

In sec 2(6) of the Act, future goods have been defined as the goods that will either be manufactured or produced or acquired by the seller at the time the contract of sale is made. The contract for the sale of future goods will never have the actual sale in it, it will always be an agreement to sell.

Hence, the correct option is (A).

13. The provision of a 10% ceiling restricts the transfer and registration of such transfer.

Prior to the amendment, Section 7 enabled transfer of foreign contribution funds to other persons, both registered and not registered under the FCRA. Rule 24 of the Foreign Contribution (Regulation) Rules, 2011 (FCRR, 2011) permitted transfer of foreign contribution to persons not registered under the Act provided it does not exceed 10% of the total value of funds received. Pursuant to the amendment, Section 7 of FCRA bars the transfer of foreign contribution to any person, either registered or not registered under the Act.
Hence, the correct option is (C).

14. A person who is a non-resident, where the royalty is payable in respect of any right, property or information used or services utilized for the purposes of a business or profession carried on by such person in India or for the purposes of making or earning any income from any source in India.

Income that is deemed arose, received, or earned in India by a non-resident will be taxable.

Hence, the correct option is (A).

15. Power of Reserve Bank to appoint the chairman of the Board of Directors appointed on a whole-time basis or a managing director of a banking company: Where the office of a banking company is vacant, the Reserve Bank may if it is of opinion that the continuation of such vacancy is likely to adversely affect the interests of the banking company, appoint a person eligible under sub-section (4) of section 10B to be so appointed, to be the chairman of the Board of directors appointed on a whole-time basis.
Hence, the correct option is (B).

16. "Authorised capital" or "nominal capital" means such capital as is authorized by the memorandum of a company to be the maximum amount of share capital of the company.
"Paid-up share capital" or "share capital paid-up" means such aggregate amount of money credited as paid-up as is equivalent to the amount received as paid-up in respect of shares issued and also includes any amount credited as paid-up in respect of shares of the company, but does not include any other amount received in respect of such shares, by whatever name called.
Hence, the correct option is (B).

17. The income tax department has extended the time limit for depositing TDS on sale of the property. Such TDS can now be deposited within 30 days from the end of the month in which it was deducted. So, if you have deducted TDS on the property on 10th August 2016, you can deposit it by 30th September.
Hence, the correct option is (D).

18. A contract of sale or lease is a contract for sale or lease by sample if there is a term in the contract, express or implied, to that effect. In a contract for sale or lease by sample, (a) there is an implied condition that the bulk must correspond with the sample in quality, (b) there is an implied condition that the buyer or lessee must have a reasonable opportunity of comparing the bulk with the sample, and (c) there is an implied condition that the goods must be free from any defect rendering them unmerchantable that would not be apparent on a reasonable examination of the sample.
Thus, all are true.
Hence, the correct option is (D).

19. Procedurally, foreign banks are required to apply to RBI for opening their branches in India. Foreign banks' application for opening their maiden branch is considered under the provisions of Sec 22 of the BR Act, 1949. Before granting any license under this section, the general character of the proposed management of the proposed bank will be in the public interest or the interest of its depositors. RBI may require to be satisfied that the Government or the law of the country in which it is incorporated does not discriminate in any way against banks from India.

A foreign bank, which obtains an in-principle approval from the Reserve Bank for opening a WOS in India has to apply to the Registrar of Companies for registering the subsidiary as a company under the Companies Act, 1956 (Act 1 of 1956) and shall be required to comply with the provisions of that Act, to the extent they are applicable to banking companies as defined in Banking Regulation Act, 1949.

Hence, the correct option is (A).

20. The government can exempt a bank from provisions of the Banking Regulation Act, on its own.

A sub-broker acts on behalf of a trading member as an agent for assisting investors in dealing with securities. New Delhi: Sebi today said it has done away with the category of sub-brokers as market intermediaries, which require registration with the regulator.

An Act to consolidate and amend the law relating to co-operative societies, with objects not confined to one State and serving the interests of members in more than one State, to facilitate the voluntary formation and democratic functioning of co-perative s as people's institutions based on self-help and mutual aid and to enable them to promote their economic and social betterment and to provide functional autonomy and for matters connected therewith or incidental there to.

Hence, the correct option is (B).

21. Section 20(1) of the Banking Regulation Act, 1949 also lays down the restrictions on loans and advances to the directors and the firms in which they hold a substantial interest. Purchase of or discount of bills from directors and their concerns, which is in the nature of clean accommodation, is reckoned as 'loans and advances' for the purpose of Section 20 of the Banking Regulation Act, 1949. FAQs regarding the applicability of Section 20 of BR Act, 1949.

Banks are prohibited from entering into any commitment for granting any loans or advances to or on behalf of any of its directors, or any firm in which any of its directors is interested as partner, manager, employee or guarantor, or any company [not being a subsidiary of the banking company or a company registered under Section 8 of the Companies Act, 2013, or a Government company] of which, or the subsidiary or the holding company of which any of the directors of the bank is a director, managing agent, manager, employee or guarantor or in which he holds substantial interest, or any individual in respect of whom any of its directors is a partner or guarantor.

Hence, the correct option is (D).

22. The sale of the securities by the pawnee bank without giving reasonable notice to the pawner is bad and not binding on him. What Section 176 contemplates is not merely a notice but a reasonable notice, of the intended sale of the security by the creditor within a certain date so as to afford an opportunity to the debtor to pay up the amount within the time mentioned in the notice.
Hence, the correct option is (C).

23. GST return is a format where a taxpayer registered under the Goods and Services Tax (GST) law has to file for each registration separately. Also, the number of GST returns to be filed will be based on the type of taxpayer, such as regular taxpayer, composition dealer, e-commerce operator, TDS deductor, non-resident taxpayer, Input Service Distributor(ISD) etc. Usually, a regular taxpayer has to file two returns per month (GSTR-1, GSTR-3B) and an annual return (GSTR-9/9C) for each GST registration separately.

GSTR-1 is to be filed by all normal taxpayers who are registered under GST. It is to be filed monthly, except in the case of small taxpayers with turnover up to Rs.1.5 crore in the previous financial year, who can file the same on a quarterly basis.

GSTR-2A is the return containing details of all inward supplies of goods and services i.e. purchases made from registered suppliers during a tax period.

GSTR-3 is to be filed by all normal taxpayers registered under GST, however, the filing of the same has been suspended ever since the inception of GST.

Hence, the correct option is (D).

24. In terms of section 17 (1) and 11 (1)(b) (ii) of the Banking Regulation Act, 1949, banks are required to transfer, out of the balance of profit as disclosed in the profit and loss account, a sum equivalent to not less than 20 percent of such profit to Reserve Fund. This provision is a minimum requirement. Considering the imperative need for augmenting the reserves, it was advised to vide circular DBOD.No.BP.BC.24/21.04.018/ 2000-2001 dated September 23, 2000, that all scheduled commercial banks operating in India (including foreign banks) should transfer not less than 25 percent of the 'net profit' (before appropriations) to the Reserve Fund with effect from the year ending 31 March 2001.

Hence, the correct option is (C).

25. Voluntary Amalgamation: A banking company may be amalgamated with another banking company.

Amalgamation by Govt: After Consultation with RBI, Central Govt. is empowered to order amalgamation of two banking companies (u/s 396 of Companies Act).

Where the Central Government is satisfied that it is essential in the public interest that two or more companies should amalgamate, then, notwithstanding anything contained in sections 394 and 395 but subject to the provisions of this section, the Central Government may, by order notified in the Official Gazette, provide for the amalgamation of those companies into a single company with such constitution ; with such property, powers, rights, interests, authorities and privileges ; and with such liabilities, duties, and obligations; as may be specified in the order."

Hence, the correct option is (B).

26. The unpaid seller of goods loses his lien thereon —

(a) When he delivers the goods to a carrier or other bailee for the purpose of transmission to the buyer without reserving the right of disposal of the goods;

(b) When the buyer or his agent lawfully obtains possession of the goods; (c) by waiver thereof.

According to subsection (1) of Section 49 of the Sale of Goods Act, 1930, an unpaid seller loses his lien: If he delivers the goods to a carrier or other bailee for transmission to the buyer without reserving the right of disposal of the goods. When the buyer or his agent obtains possession of the goods lawfully.

Hence, the correct option is (C).

27. The power and jurisdiction of Lok Adalat are confined only to passing of award based on a compromise or settlement between the parties. It has no adjudicatory or judicial functions and its functions relate purely to conciliation.

Hence, the correct option is (B).

28. A public corporation is set up by special order of the Government.

In India, a public corporation is a business that's created by the legislature or an act of parliament, and its name is notified in the official gazette of the state or central government. There are many businesses that were created in India by the government in the form of a service organization.

Hence, the correct option is (B).

29. In exercise of the powers conferred by section 45Y of the banking regulation Act, 1949 (10 of 1949), the Central Government, after consultation with the Reserve Bank of India, hereby makes the following rules, namely: Every banking company shall preserve, in good order, its books, accounts and other documents, relating to a period of not less than five years immediately preceding the current calendar year.
Reserve Bank may, having regard to the factors specified in sub-section (1) of section 35A, by an order in writing, direct any banking company to preserve any of the books, accounts or other documents mentioned in those rules, for a period longer than the period specified for their preservation, in the said rules.
45Z states - Nomination for return of articles kept in safe custody with banking company where any person leaves any article in safe custody with a banking company such person may nominate, in the prescribed manner, one person to whom in the event of the death of the person leaving the articles in safe custody, such article may be returned by the banking company.
Hence, the correct option is (B).

30. The Department of Co-operative Bank Regulation (DCBR) regulates State Co-operative Banks (StCBs), District Central Co-operative Banks (DCCBs), and Urban Cooperative Banks (UCBs).

A sponsoring bank in relation to a Regional Rural Bank is a Bank by which such an RRB is sponsored. It is the duty of a sponsor bank to aid and assist the RRB sponsored by it.

"Corresponding new bank" means a corresponding new bank constituted under Sec 3 of the Banking Companies (Acquisition and Transfer of Undertakings) Act. Thus, it is under the Banking Regulation Act, 1949.

Hence, the correct option is (A).

31. Under provisions of SBI Act 1955, SBI is managed by - The Central Board and it should consist of the following, namely: (a) a chairman and a vice-chairman to be appointed by the Central Government in consultation with the Reserve Bank The chairman and the vice-chairman and each managing director shall hold office for such term, not exceeding five years, as the Central Government may fix when appointing them and shall be eligible for reappointment. A Local Board is constituted for the new local head office, any person who is, at the time of such constitution or holding office as a member of a Local Board for an existing local head office. Local Board consists of Chairman and other elected and nominated members.
Hence, the correct option is (A).

32. The bank is always liable to the person whomsoever the cheque is favorable too, not the bearer. Thus, in the given case, the bank is liable to the true owner of the cheque.

A crossed check is any check that is crossed with two parallel lines, either across the whole check or through the top left-hand corner of the check. This double-line notation signifies that the check may only be deposited directly into a bank account.

Hence, the correct option is (B).

33. The securitization involves two stages. In the first stage, it is the acquisition of financial assets and undivided interest therein. The second stage is the issue of security receipts in favor of investors for the purpose of raising money from investors.

Hence, the correct option is (A).

34. The National Commission held that the bank couldn't escape responsibility in comparing signatures. Thus, in both the given cases, the bank is liable for both the cheques.

Hence, the correct option is (B).

35. Sec 2 (c) of FEMA 1999 defines Authorised Persons means as Authorised Dealer, Money Changer, Offshore Banking Unit or any other person authorized u/s 10 (1) to deal in Foreign Exchange or Foreign Securities.

Hence, the correct option is (C).

36. RTI Act 2005 is to provide for setting out the practical regime of right to information for citizens to secure access to information under the control of public authorities, in order to promote transparency and accountability in the working of every public authority, the constitution of a Central Information Commission and State Information Commissions and for matters connected therewith or incidental thereto. All the mentioned are true with respect to the act.
Hence, the correct option is (D).

37. When it is not feasible to call a board meeting and approval of directors is required on an urgent basis. In such cases, resolution can be passed through circulation.

As per section 175 of the companies Act, 2013 read with Rule 5 of companies (Meeting of the board and its powers) Rules, 2016 and Secretarial Standards-1 issued by the Institute of company Secretaries of India, the company to pass a resolution by circulation without convening a board meeting or a committee meeting, as the case may be.

Hence, the correct option is (D).

38. Under the provisions of the RTI Act, any citizen of India may request information from a "public authority" (a body of Government or "instrumentality of State") which is required to reply expeditiously or within thirty days. The authorities under the RTI Act 2005 are called public authorities.

Right to Information Act 2005 mandates timely response to citizen requests for government information.

Hence, the correct option is (C).

39. Banks can issue a notice for enforcement of security interest under the SARFAESI Act when the account is NPA and security is in possession of the bank. The SARFAESI Act, 2002 gives powers of "seize and desist" to banks. Banks can give notice in writing to the defaulting borrower requiring it to discharge its liabilities within 60 days. If the borrower fails to comply with the notice, the Bank may take recourse to one or more of the following measures: Take possession of the security for the loan Sale or lease or assign the right over the security Manage the same or appoint any person to manage the same.

Hence, the correct option is (B).

40. The mutual rights and duties of the partners and the mutual rights and duties of the LLP and its partners shall be determined on the basis of the LLP agreement between the partners or between the limited liability partnership and its partners. If there is no agreement as to any matter, the mutual rights and duties of the partners and the mutual rights and duties of the LLP and its partners shall be determined by the provisions relating to that matter as set out in the First Schedule.
Hence, the correct option is (D).

41. A company has a distinct legal entity independent of its members. It can own property, make contracts, and file suits in its own name. Shareholders are not the joint owners of the company's property. A shareholder cannot be held liable for the acts of the company. Similarly, members of the company are not its agents.

Hence, the correct option is (B).

42. Trusts and charitable institutions registered under the Indian Trusts Act, 1882. Public Trust Act, if it is a public trust. Those engaged in purely religious and charitable work registered under the Religious Endowments Act, 1863; the Charitable and Religious Trusts Act, 1920; the Waqf Act, 1995 and similar other State Acts. As a legal transaction, the Waqif (settler) appoints himself or another trustworthy person as Mutawalli (manager) in an endowment deed (Waqfnamah) to administer the Waqf (charitable trust).
Hence, the correct option is (A).

43. The Central Public Information Officer or State Public Information Officer, as the case may be, shall, within five days from the receipt of the request, give written notice to such third party of the request.

Where a Central Public Information Officer or the State Public Information Officer, as the case may be, intends to disclose any information or record, or part thereof on a request made under this Act, which relates to or has been supplied by a third party and has been treated as confidential by that third party, the Central Public Information Officer or State Public Information Officer, as the case may be, shall, within five days from the receipt of the request, give a written notice to such third party of the request and of the fact that the Central Public Information Officer or State Public Information Officer, as the case may be, intends to disclose the information or record, or part thereof, and invite the third party to make a submission in writing or orally, regarding whether the information should be disclosed, and such submission of the third party shall be kept in view while taking a decision about disclosure of information: Provided that except in the case of trade or commercial secrets protected by law, disclosure may be allowed if the public interest in disclosure outweighs in importance any possible harm or injury to the interests of such third party.

Hence, the correct option is (A).

44. In the case of pledge, the possession of pledged goods will be passed on to the pawnee from the pawnor, and the

possession of moveables will be transferred to the pawnee and he will be in possession and the pawnor will not be able to enjoy the same as the possession has already been parted with the goods. So, pledge deals with the transfer of possession of the moveable property to the creditor as security to the loan advances.

Hence, the correct option is (A).

45. If the director, in the course of any inquiry, finds that a reporting entity or its designated director on the board or any of its employees has failed to comply with the obligations, then, without prejudice to any other action that may be taken under any other provisions of this Act, he may by an order, levy a fine on such reporting entity or its designated director on the Board or any of its employees, which shall not be less than 10,000 rupees but may extend to 1 lakh rupees for each failure.
Hence, the correct option is (D).

46. Persons found guilty of an offense of Money Laundering are punishable with imprisonment for a term which shall not be less than three years but may extend up to seven years and shall also be liable to a fine up to Rs. 5 lakh (Section 4 of the Act).

Hence, the correct option is (B).

47. A term loan is a loan from a bank for a specific amount that has a specified repayment schedule and a fixed or floating interest rate. Thus, it is fund based. However, DPG is a payment guarantee issued to your exporter for deferred or timely payment of the goods, and corresponding interest. ICBC undertakes to pay your exporter in the event you are unable to pay the principal and interest as scheduled in the contract. Thus, that depends on the situation, i.e. contingent.
Hence, the correct option is (C).

48. A usufructuary mortgage is where the mortgagor delivers possession of the mortgaged property to the mortgagee and authorizes him to retain such possession until payment of the mortgage-money and to receive the rents and profits accruing from the property. In such a mortgage, there is no personal liability of the mortgager.

Hence, the correct option is (D).

49. Section 35 of the Companies Act, 1956 deals with the conclusiveness of the certificate of incorporation. It provides that "A certificate of incorporation given by the Registrar in respect of any association shall be conclusive evidence that all the requirements of this Act have been complied with in respect of registration and matters precedent and incidental thereto, and that the association is a company authorized to be registered and duly registered under this Act."
Hence, the correct option is (C).

50. Any person aggrieved by an order made by the adjudicating authority may prefer an appeal to the special director (Appeals).

Procedure for filing appeal every appeal presented to the special director (Appeals) under section 17 of the act shall be in the form I signed by the applicant. The appeal shall be filed in triplicate and accompanied by three copies of the order appealed against.

Hence, the correct option is (A).

51. A public company may be a company limited by shares or a company limited by guarantee with or without share capital.

A company limited by shares can be described as an incorporated business structure and is regarded as a legal person or entity, which is held responsible for its own debts. It is the most popular company structure out there and is normally created by people who wish to earn profits from their business ventures.

Hence, the correct option is (D).

52. A mortgage when created through an instrument in writing (called mortgage deed) is required to be registered with Registrar of Assurances within 4 months if the value of mortgage money is Rs. 100 or more. Registration is compulsory for other non-testamentary instruments which purport or operate to create, declare, assign, limit or extinguish, whether in present or in future, any right, title or interest, whether vested or contingent, of the value of one hundred rupees, and upwards, to or in immovable property.
Hence, the correct option is (B).

53. The primary function of an office is making, using, and preserving records. Processing and arranging information It is the most significant function of an office. The information collected and recorded cannot be readily used for decision making and other purposes in the organization. Therefore it must be processed and arranged.
Hence, the correct option is (A).

54. The offences which are compoundable under any law cannot be brought within the purview of the Lok Adalat. This means that the Lok Adalat has no authority of its own to pass judgments.

Nature of Cases to be Referred to Lok Adalat Any dispute which has not been brought before any court and is likely to be filed before the court. Provided that any matter relating to an offence not compoundable under the law shall not be settled in Lok Adalat.

Hence, the correct option is (A).

55. According to the bill of exchange, the drawee is to make the payment. Thus, 1 does not state the truth.

The drawee is the party that pays the sum specified by the bill of exchange. The payee is the one who receives that sum. The drawer is the party that obliges the drawee to pay the payee. The drawer and the payee are the same entity unless the drawer transfers the bill of exchange to a third-party payee.

Hence, the correct option is (A).

56. Some of the key features of LLPs are: They are a separate legal entity from their members. They have the benefit of limited liability for their members. They are taxed as a partnership. Thus, all the mentioned are the features of limited liability partnership.

Hence, the correct option is (D).

57. A deferred payment guarantee is a guarantee for a payment that has been deferred or postponed. The necessity to issue a deferred payment guarantee arises in the case of the purchase of capital goods like machinery.
Hence, the correct option is (C).

58. All the given options are true for a person residing in India or NRI, who is residing in India but was not previously.

A person resident outside India, not being a Non-Resident Indian or an Overseas Citizen of India, who is a spouse of a Non-Resident Indian or an Overseas Citizen of India may acquire one immovable property (other than agricultural land/ formhouse/ plantation property), jointly with his/ her NRI/ OCI spouse subject to the conditions laid down in regulation 6 of FEMA 21.

Hence, the correct option is (D).

59. A conditional contract is an agreement that is enforceable only if another agreement is performed or if another specific condition is satisfied. A conditional contract is also termed as a hypothetical contract.

Hence, the correct option is (D).

60. In the case of a mortgage, (a) the limitation period against the mortgager for personal liability is 3 years (b) against the mortgaged property, it is 12 years, and (c) for foreclosure, it is 30 years.

The property was mortgaged on 27.5.1122 (ME) (11.1.1947) for a period of 12 years. The period expired on 11.1.1959. Contention based on the observation of the learned Single Judge in Kunjamma's case (supra) is that since the mortgage money is not deposited before 11.11.1989, the right to redeem mortgage money is extinguished by operation of Article ".

According to the above judgment, in view of Article 61 of the Limitation Act, right to redeem mortgage is lost after 30 years from the date on which the mortgage money has become due. The period of limitation for foreclosure by a mortgagee is also 30 years and the starting point of limitation is the same.

Hence, the correct option is (B).

61. Bill of a lading-a detailed list of a ship's cargo in the form of a receipt given by the master of the ship to the person consigning the goods. A warehouse receipt is a document that provides proof of ownership of commodities (e.g. bars of copper) that are stored in a warehouse, vault, or depository for safekeeping. A Delivery Order (abbreviated D/O) is a document from a Consignee, or an owner or his agent of freight Carrier which orders the release of the transportation of cargo to another party.

An airway bill (AWB) or air consignment note is a receipt issued by an international airline for goods and evidence of the contract of carriage, but it is not a document of title to the goods. Hence, the airway bill is non-negotiable.

Under Article 124 of the Jaipur Act for a suit against the mortgagee with possession to redeem or recover the property mortgaged, a period of limitation of 30 years was provided from the date when the right to redeem the property to recover, possession accrued.

Hence, the correct option is (B).

62. A mortgage in which the lender is secured by taking possession of all the original title documents of the property that serves as security for the mortgage gives the mortgagee the right to foreclose on the property, sell it, or appoint a receiver in case

of nonpayment and it can be at any place.
Hence, the correct option is (C).

63. A mortgage deed is a document in which the mortgagor transfers an interest in real estate to a mortgagee for the purpose of providing a mortgage loan. The mortgage deed is the evidence of the interest transferred to the mortgage holder. An assignee can sue in his own name if he had complied with the Act (Policies of Assurance Act, 1867) and had obtained on assignment either by endorsement on the policy or by separate instrument. The borrower may pledge the documents of title with the bank and, on the other hand, manage to obtain the delivery of goods on the basis of indemnity bond or some other device. Debentures are generally freely transferable by the debenture holder. Debenture holders have no rights to vote in the company's general meetings of shareholders.
Hence, the correct option is (C).

64. Export of goods made on a deferred payment basis is not a capital account transaction. As defined in Section 2(e) of the FEMA, "capital account transaction" means transactions which alter the assets or liabilities, including contingent liabilities outside India, of persons resident in India or assets or liabilities, in India, of persons resident outside India and includes transactions referred to in section 6(3) of the FEMA

Hence, the correct option is (D).

65. The Financial Stability Reports, published on a half-yearly basis by the Reserve Bank of India, after approval by FSDC Sub-Committee. It is published in January and July every year.

Hence, the correct option is (D).

66. According to section 106 of TPA, 1882, if there is an absence of a written contract or a local usage to the contrary then in the case, a lease of immovable property for manufacturing and agriculture purpose will be valid till the time until it was terminated by either of the party, by 6 months notice and if there is a lease any other purpose except agriculture or manufacturing then it will be terminated by 15 days notice.

Hence, the correct option is (D).

67. The following are the disadvantages of a private limited company: The shares in a private limited company cannot be sold or transferred to anyone else without the agreement of other shareholders. It has limited growth and a restricted number of shareholders. It is not allowed to invite the public to subscribe to its shares.

A Private Limited Company is a company that is privately held for small businesses. The liability of the members of a Private Limited Company is limited to the number of shares respectively held by them. Shares of Private Limited Company cannot be publicly traded.

Private Limited Company is the simplest and a very popular form of Business Registration in India. It can be registered with a minimum of two people. Limited liability protection to shareholders, ability to raise equity funds, separate legal entity status make it the most recommended type of business entity for millions of small and medium-sized businesses that are family-owned or professionally managed.

Hence, the correct option is (B).

68. Reserve Bank of India has the authority under the SARFAESI Act to prescribe income recognition, accounting standards, and provisioning norms for Securitisation or Reconstruction Companies. The provisions of the guidelines and directions shall apply to SC/RC registered with the RBI under Section 3 of the SARFAESI Act, 2002.
Hence, the correct option is (A).

69. Using a public key is to authenticate that a message originated with a holder of the paired private key, or to encrypt a message with a public key to ensure that only the holder of the paired private key can decrypt it.

By adding public-key encryption to digital signature schemes, we can create a cryptosystem that can provide the four essential elements of security namely – Privacy, Authentication, Integrity, and Non-repudiation.

Hence, the correct option is (B).

70. The secured creditor may relinquish his security interest to the liquidation estate and receive proceeds from the sale of assets by the liquidator as per section 53.

(i) First towards costs incidental to preservation and protection of the security,

(ii) For dues of the secured creditor,

(iii) Surplus to the person entitled thereto in accordance with the rights and interests.

Hence, the correct option is (A).

71. National Payments Corporation of India (NPCI), an umbrella organisation for operating retail payments and settlement systems in India, is an initiative of Reserve Bank of India (RBI) and Indian Banks' Association (IBA) under the provisions of the Payment and Settlement Systems Act, 2007, for creating a robust Payment.
Hence, the correct option is (B).

72. If any person contravenes or attempts to contravene or abets the contravention of the provisions of this Act or of any rules made thereunder, he shall be punishable with imprisonment for a term which may extend to one year, or with fine, or with both.
Hence, the correct option is (C).

73. The National Payments Corporation of India (NPCI), incorporated by the Reserve Bank of India, functions as a hub for all electronic retail payment systems in the country. These retail payment systems include a diverse range of products, delivery channels, service providers and technology solutions.

Real-Time Gross Settlement (RTGAS) abbreviated as RTGS systems are specialist funds transfer systems where the transfer of money or securities takes place from one bank to any other bank on a "real-time" and on a "gross" basis.

Hence, the correct option is (D).

74. The provisions of the SARFAESI Act are applicable only for NPA loans with outstanding above Rs. 1 lakh. NPA loan accounts where the amount is less than 20% of the principal and interest

are not eligible to be dealt with under this Act.
Hence, the correct option is (C).

75. As per Rules under Prevention of Money Laundering Act 2002, the banks are required to obtain the following documents:

(i) Certificate of incorporation and memorandum and articles of association,
(ii) Resolution of the board of directors to open an account and identification of those who have authority to operate the account,
(iii) Power of Attorney granted to its managers, officers or employees to transact business on its behalf,
(iv) Copy of PAN allotment letter,
(v) Copy of the telephone bill.
Thus, all the given documents are important. Hence, the correct option is (D).

76. Where a Central Public Information Officer or a State Public Information Officer, as the case may be, intends to disclose any information or record, or part thereof on a request made under this Act, which relates to or has been supplied by a third party and has been treated as confidential by that third party, the Central Public Information Officer or State Public Information Officer, as the case may be, shall, within five days from the receipt of the request, give written notice to such third party of the request and of the fact that the Central Public Information Officer or State Public Information Officer, as the case may be, intends to disclose the information or record.
Hence, the correct option is (A).

77. The Tribunal is a quasi-judicial body set up under the provisions of the Recovery of Debts Due to Banks and Financial Institutions Act, 1993. The selected candidates will be appointed on tenure basis for a period of five years from the date they enter upon the office of the Tribunal or till they attain the age of 62 years, whichever is earlier.
Hence, the correct option is (A).

78. One's complaint will not be considered if:

- One has not approached his bank for redressal of his grievance first.
- The subject matter of the complaint is pending for disposal / has already been dealt with at any other forum like the court of law, consumer court etc.
- Frivolous or vexatious
- The institution complained against is not covered under the scheme.
- The subject matter of the complaint is not within the ambit of the Banking Ombudsman.
- If the complaint is for the same subject matter that was settled through the office of the Banking Ombudsman in any previous proceedings.

Hence, the correct option is (D).

79. Under DRT Act 19(4), on receipt of the application under sub-section(1) or (2), the Tribunal has to issue summons to the defendant requiring him to show cause within 30 days of the service of summons as to why the relief prayed for should not be granted.
Hence, the correct option is (C).

80. English mortgage - The borrower promises to repay the borrowed money on a certain date. The borrower transfers the property to the lender. The lender will re-transfer the property when the money is repaid. The mortgaged property is absolutely transferred to the mortgagee.
Hence, the correct option is (B).

81. Under the Securitisation And Reconstruction of Financial Assets and Enforcement of Security Interests (SARFAESI) Act 2002, an appeal can be filed before the DRAT against orders passed by the DRT.

Under sub-section (3) of section 20, of the The Recovery of Debts Due to Banks and Financial Institutions Act, 1993, an Appeal has to be filed within 45 days from the date on which a copy of the order aggrieved has been passed or deemed to have been passed by the Tribunal is received.
Hence, the correct option is (C).

82. The act has the provision of the Establishment of the CCPA which will protect, promote and enforce the rights of consumers. The CCPA will regulate cases related to unfair trade practices, misleading advertisements, and violation of consumer rights.

A person must hire or purchase any good or service for consideration which has been paid in full or in part. So, it can be said that to become a 'consumer' under this Act. The purchased good should not be used for reselling or any other commercial purposes.

Hence, the correct option is (C).

83. Bank records should be accompanied by a certificate in accordance with section 2(8) and 2A of the Act. The certificate is to ensure the accuracy and reliability of the entry in banking records. The printout of entry or copy of such printout along with the certificate by the branch manager/principal accountant and the person in charge of the computer resource which generated that entry together makes a "certified copy". A certified copy of any entry of banker's book shall be admissible prima facie as Evidence.

Hence, the correct option is (D).

84. Section - 226, Income Tax Act, 1961-2014 (3) The 11[Assessing] Officer 12 [or Tax Recovery Officer] may, at any time or from time to time, by notice in writing require any person from whom money is due or may become due to the assessee or any person who holds or may subsequently hold money, for or on account of the assessee to pay to the Assessing Officer or Tax Recovery Officer either forthwith upon the money becoming due or being held or at or within the time specified in the notice (not being before the money becomes due or is held) so much of the money as is sufficient to pay the amount due by the assessee in respect of arrears or the whole of the money when it is equal to or less than that amount.Save as otherwise provided in this sub-section, every person to whom a notice is issued under this subsection shall be bound to comply with such notice, and, in particular, where any such notice is issued to a post office, banking company or an insurer, it shall not be necessary for any passbook, deposit receipt, policy or any other document to be produced for the purpose of any entry, endorsement or the like being made before payment is made, notwithstanding any rule, practice or requirement to the contrary.Hence, the correct option is (C).

85. Section 106 of the transfer of property act 1882 deals with the duration of leases and states that in the absence of a contract, or local law or usage to the contrary, a lease of immovable property for agricultural or manufacturing purposes shall be deemed to be a lease from year to year, terminable on the part of either lessor or lessee, by 6 month notice and a lease of immovable property for any other purpose shall be deemed to be a lease from month to month, terminable, on the part of either lessor or lessee by 15-day notice.
Hence, the correct option is (C).

86. A digital signature in its simplest description is a hash of the data that is subsequently encrypted with the signer's private key. Since that is something only the signer has, that is where the trust comes from. Everyone has access to the signer's public key. So, to validate a digital signature, the recipient:

(1) Calculates a hash of the same data,

(2) Decrypts the digital signature using the sender's public key, and

(3) compares the 2 hash values. If they match, the signature is considered valid. If they don't match, it either means that a different key was used to sign it, or that the data has been altered.

Thus, public key helps in verification. The private key is used to encrypt the hash. The encrypted hash along with other information, such as the hashing algorithm, is the digital signature. Thus, it helps in creating the electronic signature.
Hence, the correct option is (B).

87. A void contract is an agreement not enforceable by law. A void contract is a contract which ceases to be enforceable by law. A contract when originally entered into may be valid and binding on the parties. It may subsequently become void.
Hence, the correct option is (B).

88. According to sub-section (1) of Section 10 of the Consumer Protection Act –

(a) The President of the Forum should be a person who is, or has been, or is qualified to be a District Judge.

(b) Two other members, one of whom shall be a woman, who shall have the following qualifications, namely: (i) Be not less than 35 years of age, (ii) Possess a bachelor's degree from a recognized university, (iii) Be persons of ability, integrity and standing.
Hence, the correct option is (C).

89. Under enforcement of mortgages through court, while executing the mortgage decree, the decree-holder can bring the properties mortgaged to sale without first seeking an order of attachment from the court.
Hence, the correct option is (A).

90. Black laws dictionary defines the term guarantee as the assurance that a legal contract will be duly enforced. A contract of guarantee is governed by the Indian Contract Act,1872 and includes 3 parties in which one of the parties acts as the surety in case the defaulting party fails to fulfill his obligations. Contracts of guarantee are mostly required in cases when a party requires a loan, goods or employment. The guarantor in such contracts assures the creditor that the person in need may be trusted and in case of any default, he shall undertake the responsibility to pay. Thus we can say the contract of guarantee is invisible security given to the creditor.

Hence, the correct option is (C).

91. A bank guarantee is a type of guarantee from a lending institution. The bank guarantee means a lending institution ensures that the liabilities of a debtor will be met. In other words, if the debtor fails to settle a debt, the bank will cover it.

There are two types of liability: Primary and Secondary-

The primarily liable parties are makers of notes and drawees of drafts (your bank is the drawee for your check), and their liability is unconditional. The secondary parties are drawers and indorsers.

Hence, the correct option is (D).

92. Bailor will not be liable for the defects which are not within his knowledge. However, if the bailor is aware of the defect, then he is liable to the bailee. The bailor must disclose to the bailee any faults or defects in the goods.
Hence, the correct option is (C).

93. According to the Reserve Bank, 'fit and proper' is for the status of the directors nominated by the Government or elected by the shareholders to the Boards of the Public Sector Banks.

The "fit and proper" criteria (or "fit and proper test") make reference to requirements for evaluating managers, directors, and shareholders. Particularly, the ability to fulfill their duties ("fitness"), as well as their integrity and suitability ("propriety"), are examined.

Hence, the correct option is (A).

94. The phrase Caveat Emptor means "let the buyer beware." The doctrine of caveat emptor is enshrined in Section 16 of the Sale of Goods Act, 1930.

It is the principle that the buyer alone is responsible for checking the quality and suitability of goods before a purchase is made.

Hence, the correct option is (C).

95. Under the partnership contract, any business should be in accordance with the laws. The owners are all personally liable for any legal actions and debts the company may face unless otherwise provided by law or in the agreement.

Contracts based on validity can come in five different forms, including valid contracts, void contracts, voidable contracts, illegal contracts, and unenforceable contracts. A valid contract is one that is legally enforceable, while a void contract is unenforceable and imposes no obligations on the parties involved.

Hence, the correct option is (B).

96. According to the Hindu Minority and Guardianship Act, 1956, the natural guardian of a Hindu minor cannot mortgage or

charge any part of the property of the minor without the permission of the court.

The long list of natural guardians existing under old Hindu law has been reduced to three only, namely the father, the mother, and the husband. It has been provided that a de facto guardian has no power to deal with a Hindu minor's property.

Hence, the correct option is (C).

97. Agreement without consideration is void unless it is in writing and registered or is a promise to compensate for something is done or is a promise to pay a debt barred by limitation law.
Hence, the correct option is (C).

98. The borrowing powers of the board of a public limited company are defined under section 180 ("Restrictions on powers of Board") of the companies act 2013.

The companies act 2013, imposes some restrictions on the general powers of the board. Pursuant to section 180 of the companies act 2013, the act specifies the powers which the Board can exercise only through approval of shareholders by special resolution.

Hence, the correct option is (C).

99. The revised clause 49 stipulates that in companies that have executive chairmen, at least 50% of the board is required to have independent directors. For listed companies with non-executive chairmen, one-third of the board must comprise independent directors.

Hence, the correct option is (C).

100. A Guarantee which extends to a series of transactions is called a continuing guarantee. A continuing guarantee may at any time be revoked by the surety, as to future transactions, by notice to the creditor.

Continuing Guarantee: It is a guarantee for a series of transactions. According to Section 129, continuing guarantee extends to a series of transactions. The liability of surety, in this case, extends to a number of transactions and he becomes liable for the unpaid balance at the end of the guarantee.
Hence, the correct option is (A).

101. Tax assessed by the Assessing Officer(AO) shall be paid within 30 days.

Response received from the taxpayer within 30 days from the issuance date of intimation will be considered before making the final adjustment and in case no response received within such period, adjustments arrived initially will be incorporated.

Hence, the correct option is (A).

102. "Delivery" means voluntary transfer of possession from one person to another.

Delivery of goods in the sale of goods act is defined as a voluntary transfer of possession from one person to another. Thus, to effect a valid delivery, goods from one person to another must be transferred willingly and not by means of fraud, theft, or force, etc.

Hence, the correct option is (A).

103. A condition is a stipulation essential to the main purpose of the contract, the breach of which gives rise to a right to treat the contract as repudiated. A warranty is a stipulation collateral to the main purpose of the contract, the breach of which gives rise to a claim for damages but not to a right to reject the goods and treat the contract as repudiated.
Hence, the correct option is (A).

104. Where there is a contract for the sale of goods by description, there is an implied condition that the goods shall correspond with the description and if the sale is by sample as well as by description, it is not sufficient that the bulk of the goods corresponds with the sample if the goods do not also correspond with the description.
Hence, the correct option is (A).

105. Section 194A deals with deduction of TDS on interest other than interest on securities like Interest on Fixed Deposits, Interest on Loans and Advances other than banks. Payments made to non-residents are also covered under TDS mechanism. However, tax in such a case is to be deducted as per Section 195.

Hence, the correct option is (C).

106. Agency law refers to the relationship between a person, or "agent", that acts on behalf of another person, company, or government, usually called the "master" or "principal". This form of agency can be, and often is, enforced by written agreements made through a power of attorney.
Hence, the correct option is (A).

107. Government companies are companies where the central govt. or one or more state govt. or the central and the state govt. (jointly) hold at least 51 percent of the paid-up capital.

Section 2(45) of the Indian companies act, 2013, defines a government company as, "Any company in which not less than 51% of the paid-up share capital is held by the central government, or by any state government."

Hence, the correct option is (D).

108. The unpaid seller's lien is a possessory lien, i.e. the lien can be exercised as long as the seller remains in possession of the goods. He may exercise his right of lien not with standing that he is in possession of the goods as agent or bailee for the buyer.
Hence, the correct option is (A).

109. The 1956 act prescribed minimum 2 directors for a private and 3 for a public company to constitute a Board. This criterion has been retained by the new act, but the maximum limit of directors on the board has now been raised from 12 to 15.
Hence, the correct option is (D).

110. A public company is a company that has a minimum paid-up share capital of Rs. 5 lakh. Hence, as prescribed by the Companies Act the minimum number of members to form a public company is 7.

Hence, the correct option is (B).

111. The Schedules under the Companies Act, 2013:

- Schedule I: Memorandum and Articles (Section 4 and 5)
- Schedule II: Depreciation (Section 123)

- Schedule III: Balance Sheet and Statement of Profit & Loss (Section 129), Part I Balance Sheet, Part II Profit and Loss Account
- Schedule IV: Code for Independent Directors (Section 149(8))
- Schedule V: Appointment of managing director, whole-time director or manager (Section 196 and 197)
- Schedule VI: Infrastructure Projects (Section 55 and 186)

Hence, the correct option is (B).

112. The Sales of Goods Act was enacted on 15th March 1930 and was enforced in July 1930.

A contract of sale of goods is a contract whereby the seller transfers or agrees to transfer the property in goods to the buyer for a price. There may be a contract of sale between one part-owner and another.

Hence, the correct option is (B).

113. The articles of a company may confer on its board of directors the power to appoint any person, other than a person who fails to get appointed as a director in a general meeting, as an additional director at any time who shall hold office up to the date of the next annual general meeting or the last date on which the annual general meeting should have been held, whichever is earlier.
Hence, the correct option is (A).

114. Indemnity contract includes two parties namely, indemnifier and indemnity holder. The person who is promising to pay compensation is called indemnifier and the person whose loss is compensated is called indemnity holder.
Hence, the correct option is (A).

115. Government companies, under the provisions of companies Act 1956, are the companies where the Central Govt. or one or more State Govt. or the Central and the State Govt. (jointly) hold, at least 51 percent of the paid-up capital.

In any government company, the minimum share of capital held by the government is not less than 51% of the total paid-up capital. 51 % of the total paid-up capital is held by the central government or state government or jointly.

Hence, the correct option is (D).

116. In the case of a public company, if the office of any director appointed by the company in general meeting is vacated before his term of office expires in the normal course, the resulting casual vacancy may, in default of and subject to any regulations in the articles of the company, be filled by the Board of Directors at a meeting of the board.
Hence, the correct option is (A).

117. According to the companies act, 2013, every company has to give a declaration to the registrar of companies, stating its paid-up capital is not less than Rs. five lakh in the case of public companies (the listed ones, as well as those that have raised money from the market through debt); and not less than Rs. one lakh in the case of private companies. This declaration is necessary for obtaining a commencement certificate for business. Hence, the correct option is (D).

118. Every public company or a private company which is a subsidiary of a public company, having a paid-up share capital of Rs. 5 crores or more, must have a managing director or whole-time director or manager.
Hence, the correct option is (C).

119. A revolving LC is a special letter of credit type which is structured in a way so that it revolves either in value or in time covering multiple shipments over a long period of time under the single letter of credit. As, in the given case, they don't want to open an LC again and again, so revolving LC is suitable for them.
Hence, the correct option is (B).

120. An important step in the formation of a company is to prepare a document called a memorandum of association. It is the charter of the company and is a very important document as it contains the basic conditions on which the company is incorporated.
Hence, the correct option is (C).

Q.1 ______ goods are to be manufactured/produced/acquired by the seller after making of the contract of sale.

A. Future
B. Specific
C. Moveable
D. Immoveable

Q.2 Who among the following can be an Authorised Dealer of Category III?

(i) Commercial Banks

(ii) RRBs

(iii) Select Financial and other institutions

A. Only (i)
B. Only (iii)
C. Only (ii) and (iii)
D. (i), (ii) and (iii)

Q.3 A lease for agricultural or manufacturing purpose can be terminated by the lessor or lessee by giving ________ notice to one another.

A. 1 month
B. 3 months
C. 6 months
D. 12 months

Q.4 Pari passu is a charge which does not indicate

(i) a first charge over securities.

(ii) equal charge to charge holders.

(iii) proportionate share to shareholders.

A. Only (i) and (ii)
B. Only (i) and (iii)
C. Only (ii) and (iii)
D. (i), (ii) and (iii)

Q.5 Banker's lien is a/an______

A. hypothecation.
B. mortgage.
C. implied pledge.
D. pledge.

Q.6 A Memorandum recording mortgage by deposit of title deeds does not require____.

A. registration
B. stamping
C. both Registration and Stamping
D. None of these

Q.7 In the case of _____ goods, Banker's lien is not applicable.

A. owner's
B. stolen
C. finished
D. None of these

Q.8 The right to ______ two accounts is known as set-off.

A. open
B. banker's right
C. combine
D. None of these

Q.9 The right of set-off is ________

A. customer's right.
B. banker's right.
C. banker's obligation.
D. bank's description.

Q.10 Garnishee order is issued by________.

A. police officer
B. revenue authority
C. enforcement authority
D. court of law

Q.11 What is the time limit for disposing an appeal by Appellate Authority ?

A. Within 2 months
B. Within 3 months
C. Within a month
D. No such limit

Q.12 How many Debt Recovery Appellate Tribunals have been set up?

A. 2
B. 5
C. 7
D. 10

Q.13 Where an appeal against the order of Appellate Tribunal can be made?

A. No where
B. High Court
C. Supreme Court
D. Concerned District Court

Q.14 No banking company can hold any immovable property howsoever acquired, except such as is required for its own use, for any period exceeding _____ from the acquisition thereof.

A. 3 years
B. 5 years
C. 7 years
D. 9 years

Q.15 What are the provisions of Section 141 of Companies Act?

A. The authority of the Registrar of Companies to allow the company to file particulars of charge after 30 days

B. The authority of Registrar of Companies to allow the company to file particulars of charge after 60 days

C. The authority of the Company Law Board to allow the company to file particulars of charge after 60 days

D. The authority of the Registrar of Companies to allow the company to file particulars of charge at any time

Q.16 A collecting bank gets protection for collecting a demand draft subject to certain conditions, u/s of ________.

A. 131, NI Act
B. 31, NI Act
C. 31, RBI Act
D. 131A, NI Act

Q.17 The objective of enactment of Consumer Protection Act 1986 is __________

A. to help bank customer to file suit in a consumer court.
B. better protection of the interests of the consumers.
C. a quick remedy to the consumer through normal courts.
D. All of the above

Q.18 Bank-A wants to file a suit in a DRT. The suit can be filed within the local limits of which of the following DRT (which one is not correct)________.

A. where the defendant resides or carries on the business
B. where any of the defendants (where there are more than one) resides or carries on the business
C. where the cause of action has arisen
D. it is at the discretion of the bank

Q.19 Previous year means the year, immediately preceding the _____ year, of an assessee _______.

A. financial year, calendar year
B. calendar year, assessment year

C. financial year, assessment year

D. assessment year, financial year

Q.20 When RBI appoint a suitable person in place of the Chairman or Director or Chief Executive Officer or other officer or employee who has been removed from his office, shall hold office for a period not exceeding _________ or such further periods not exceeding _________ at a time as the Reserve Bank may specify?

A. 3 years, 3 years

B. 3 years, 5 years

C. 5 years, 3 years

D. 5 years, 5 years

Q.21 Which of the following types of loss cannot be recovered under a contract of indemnity?

A. Damages paid in a suit.

B. Cost paid in a suit.

C. Payment made in compromise that are not contrary to the indemnity.

D. None of the above

Q.22 In case of pledge, the possession and ownership of the goods remain with _________.

A. possession with bank and ownership with borrower

B. possession with the borrower and ownership with the bank

C. possession and ownership with borrower

D. possession and ownership with the bank

Q.23 Every Chairman of the Board of Directors and Managing Director of a banking company shall be in the whole-time employment and shall hold office for maximum period of not exceeding _________.

A. 3 years   **B.** 5 years   **C.** 7 years   **D.** 9 years

Q.24 A contract to perform the promise or discharge the liability of a third party, if the third party defaults, is called a contract of ____.

A. insurance

B. guarantee

C. indemnity

D. assurance

Q.25 Which of the following paves the way for listing and trading of the issuer company's securities, whose securities are already not listed on the stock exchange?

A. Initial Public Offering

B. Further Public Offering

C. Bonus Issue

D. Right Issue

Q.26 A minor can be _______ of a partnership firm.

A. partner of the firm

B. admitted to the benefits

C. Either (A) or (B)

D. Neither (A) nor (B)

Q.27 The banker should not _______ the account of his customer unless there is a justifiable reason for the closure.

A. close

B. open

C. transfer

D. None of these

Q.28 Which of the following types of amounts do not form part of the term debt under the RDDB Act (DRT Act) 1993?

A. Fraud committed by an employee

B. Any liability payable under a mortgage or money payable under a decree or civil court

C. Any liability for which there is no security

D. None of the above

Q.29 The preferential payments shall be made by the official liquidator or adequate provision for such payments shall be made by him within_______ from the date of the winding-up order of the Bank.

A. 1 week

B. 1 month

C. 3 months

D. 6 months

Q.30 In a contract of indemnity, there are parties__________.

A. one party, the indemnifier

B. two parties, the insurer and the insured

C. two parties, the indemnifier, and the indemnity holder

D. two parties, the guarantor and the beneficiary

Q.31 Under which of the following, a protection is not available to the paying bank?

A. Section 10 of NI Act

B. Section 85 of NI Act

C. Section 89 of NI Act

D. Section 131 of NI Act

Q.32 Which one of the following requires lenders to provide standardized information?

A. TILA   **B.** RESPA   **C.** NCUA   **D.** UCC

Q.33 The Reserve Bank of India performs the supervisory function under the guidance of the ______.

A. Department of Economic Affairs

B. Ministry of Finance

C. Board for Financial Supervision (BFS)

D. Integrated Financial Management System

Q.34 Adjudicating Authority has to Endeavour to dispose of the complaint within______from the date of receipt of the complaint.

A. one year

B. 182 days

C. six months

D. four weeks

Q.35 Which of the following reasons prompted for setting up of the Debt Recovery Tribunal?

A. Under delay in setting the claims by courts

B. Delay in extension of the decree

C. Non-availability of Assets with the borrower due to inordinate delay in courts

D. All the above

Q.36 When financial institutions and banks undertake activities related to banking like investment, issue of debit and credit card etc then it is known as ________________.

A. Internet Banking

B. Universal Banking

C. Virtual Banking

D. Wholesale Banking

Q.37 Which one of the following is the ratio of the loan principal to the appraised value?

A. Combined Loan To Value: (CLTV) ratio

B. Loan-to-Value Ratio

C. Mortgage Loan

D. Statutory Liquidity Ratio

Q.38 A promissory note can be________

(i) Demand PN.

(ii) Usance PN.

A. Only (i)   **B.** Only (ii)

C. Either (i) or (ii)   **D.** Neither (i) nor (ii)

Q.39 Attachment order is issued by

A. the drawer of a cheque.

B. income-tax authorities.

C. manager of the bank.

D. None of these

Q.40 Which country started the first plastic notes?

A. Afghanistan   **B.** Argentina

C. Australia   **D.** Austria

Q.41 Which is the first Indian bank to open a branch outside India?

A. Andhra Bank   **B.** Bank of Baroda

C. Bank of India   **D.** Canara Bank

Q.42 In case of non-compliance with the orders of the forum by the trader or a person against whom the complaint was made the forum c/commission may fix the following penalties?

A. Imprisonment of one month and up to 3 years

B. A fine of not less than Rs. 2,000 but to more than Rs. 10,000

C. (A) or (B)

D. None of these

Q.43 The banking ombudsman scheme does not cover

A. scheduled commercial banks.

B. regional rural banks.

C. Co-operative banks.

D. financial institutions.

Q.44 Lok Adalat is organized by

A. state authority or district authority.

B. supreme court legal services committee.

C. high court legal services committee.

D. Any of the above

Q.45 A person is presumed to have gone through the Articles of Association and Memorandum of Association available with the office of RoC although he might have actually not laid his hands on these documents. This is called doctrine of

A. ultra-vires.

B. constructive notice.

C. indoor management.

D. outdoor management.

Q.46 An order has been passed by Distt. Forum under Consumer Protection Act, for payment of compensation. Its recovery shall be made by

A. referring the order to the collector to recover as land revenue.

B. filing of execution in a civil court.

C. recovery officer of DRT.

D. recovery officer on the pattern of DRT.

Q.47 While filing an appeal before the appellate tribunal if any amount is required to be deposited?

A. No, the amount is required to be deposited till the appellate tribunal decides

B. Yes, Court fee on the appeal amount is required to be paid

C. Yes, 75 percent of the amount determined by the tribunal is required to be deposited at the timing of filing of the appeal

D. Yes, after the admission of the appeal 75 percent of the amount determined by the tribunal is required to be deposited

Q.48 While dealing with shares and securities banks have to follow the regulations framed by _________.

A. company law board

B. registrar of companies

C. SEBI

D. FEDAI

Q.49 According to section 3 of Evidence Act, the Document can be

A. any matter expressed or described upon any substance by means of letter, figure, or marks.

B. any other means.

C. intends to be used for purpose of recording that matter.

D. All the above

Q.50 The term corresponding new bank under Banking Companies (Acquisition & transfer of undertaking) Act 1970 stands for

A. New Private Banks.   **B.** Old Private Banks.

C. RRBs.   **D.** Nationalised Bank.

Q.51 Which was the first committee recommended for establishment of special Recovery tribunals for Books and Financial Institution?

A. Tiwari committee

B. Ojha Committee

C. Narasimham Committee

D. Rangarajan Committee

Q.52 The main outcome of the FSLC's work was a draft________

A. Indian Financial Standards.

B. Indian Financial Code.

C. Indian Economic Code.

D. Indian Economic Standards.

Q.53 When the board of a banking company is ordered to be reconstituted under Section 10A of the BR Act, directors will be removed______for the purpose of reconstitution.

A. by rotation

B. by lots

C. by majority decision

D. None of the above

Q.54 For the purpose of exposure norms, what is the meaning of 'Group'?

A. Majority of the directors should be common

B. The Managing Director should be same

C. Commonality of Management and effective control

D. All of these

Q.55 The company-related issues of the banking companies are regulated by which of the following?

A. Banking Regulation Act, 1949

B. Reserve Bank of India Act, 1934

C. Both (A) and (B)

D. None of these

Q.56 Banks are undertaking to trading in shares and securities and this activity is regulated by

A. authorities under Companies Act.

B. Reserve Bank of India.

C. Central Government.

D. Securities and Exchange Board of India.

Q.57 The maximum number of members in case of a private limited company is _______.

A. 10   **B.** 20   **C.** 30   **D.** 200

Q.58 Central govt. can give direction to RBI only after consulting

A. Governor RBI.

B. Central Board of RBI.

C. Finance Commission.

D. President of India.

Q.59 The Companies Act applies to the banking companies

A. Irrespective whether the provisions of the Banking Regulation Act.

B. Insofar as the provisions are consistent with the provisions of the Banking Regulation Act.

C. In relation to their registration and winding up.

D. All the above

Q.60 The Banking Regulation Act applies to Co-Operative Banks

A. as provided in the State Co-operative Act.

B. as provided in the Central Co-operative Act.

C. as provided in the modification of Section 56.

D. as applicable to other Commercial Banks.

Q.61 In public sector banks, the shareholding of the Central government is _______.

A. not less than 50%   **B.** 51% or more.

C. more than 50%   **D.** less than 50%

Q.62 The moral beliefs held by an individual is known as_______.

A. values   **B.** rights   **C.** duties   **D.** personal

Q.63 Ethics is derived from the Greek word_______.

A. ethos   **B.** etho   **C.** ethic   **D.** ethical

Q.64 A banking company requires____from___ to undertake banking business as per the provision of Section_____of Banking Regulation Act.

A. registration, RBI, 23

B. license, RBI, 22

C. registration, registrar of companies, 24

D. certificate of commencement of business, registrar of companies, 24

Q.65 Which is the first bank established in India?

A. Bank of Calcutta

B. Bank of Hindustan

C. General Bank of India

D. State Bank of India

Q.66 Who is the founder of Punjab National Bank?

A. Bal Gangadhar Tilak

B. Bhagat Singh

C. Bipin Chandra Pal

D. Dyal Singh Majithia

Q.67 The shareholder of a banking company can exercise maximum____of the total voting rights of all shareholders.

A. 2%   **B.** 5%

C. 10%   **D.** No such limit

Q.68 The interests and rights of customers are given top priority in ______.

A. the vendor model   **B.** the civic model

C. the austere model   **D.** the artistic model

Q.69 Drawee of a Cheque is_______.

(i) an A/c holder

(ii) always a banker

A. Only (i)   **B.** Only (ii)

C. Either (i) or (ii)   **D.** Neither (i) nor (ii)

Q.70 The oldest form of business organization is _______.

A. partnership

B. sole proprietorship

C. joint-stock company

D. co-operative undertaking

Q.71 Which is the first Indian bank started solely with Indian capital investment?

A. Canara Bank

B. Central Bank of India

C. Punjab National Bank

D. State Bank of India

Q.72 Partnership may come into existence _______.

A. by the operation of law

B. by an express agreement only

C. by an express or implied agreement only

D. by inheritance of property

Q.73 Registration of partnership is ______.

A. optional under Indian Partnership Act

B. compulsory under the Indian Partnership Act

C. compulsory under the Income Tax Act

D. compulsory under Indian Contract Act

Q.74 The most important advantage of a joint-stock company form of business organization is that _______.

A. the liability of its member is limited

B. members can conveniently transfer their shares

C. it offers infinite scope for expansion

D. it mobilizes a vast amount of financial resources

Q.75 Letter of Credit where in addition to advance payment, the beneficiary is entitled to payment of storage charges is called_______.

A. LC

B. Red clause credit

C. Yellow clause credit

D. Green clause credit

Q.76 In the co-operative organization, the voting rights of members are _______.

A. in proportion to the capital paid by each member

B. equal, irrespective of the amount of capital contribution

C. in proportion to the nominal value of capital held by each member

D. in proportion to the total finance supplied including the amount of loan by each member

Q.77 Section 5(b) of_______ gives the definition of the term 'Banking'.

A. Contract Act

B. Banking Companies (Acquisition and Transfer of Undertakings) Act

C. Banking Regulation Act

D. Transfer of Property Act

Q.78 Principle functions of the Bank are

A. dispatch of statements.

B. adjustment of interoffice transactions.

C. clearing.

D. acceptance of deposits for lending and investment.

Q.79 In case of safe custody of articles relation between Bank and Customer is Bank_____and Customer_____.

A. agent, principal

B. lessor, lessee

C. bailor, bailee

D. debtor, creditor

Q.80 The line is a/an_____of the creditor to retain possession.

A. obligation

B. right

C. interest

D. protection

Q.81 As per RBI, for borrowers availing working capital credit facilities of Rs.10 crore and above from the banking system, the loan component should normally be % and the cash credit component should be.

A. 80%, 20%

B. 20%, 80%

C. 75%, 25%

D. 60%, 40%

Q.82 Which one of the following is open for public inspection and copying?

A. FACTA

B. FCRA

C. FDCPA

D. FOIA

Q.83 The minimum number of members for registration of a co-operative society is _______.

A. two

B. seven

C. ten

D. twenty

Q.84 Co-operative and public companies are similar in respect of _______.

A. the liability of members

B. the minimum number of members required for registration

C. the maximum number of members

D. method of distribution of profit

Q.85 Which section of IT Act deals with the appointment of the controller of certifying authorities?

A. Section 17

B. Section 15

C. Section 10

D. Section 5

Q.86 At the time of a new partner goodwill _______.

A. Belongs to all partners, new and old

B. Belongs only to the new partners who

C. Belongs only to the old partner who have credited it

D. None of the above

Q.87 What is the punishment for identity theft in the IT Act?

A. Three-year imprisonment or 2 lakh rupees penalty or both

B. Two-year imprisonment or 1 lakh rupees penalty or both

C. Three-year imprisonment or 1 lakh rupees penalty or both

D. None of the above

Q.88 A mortgage is defined under_______.

A. contract act

B. sale of goods act

C. transfer of property act

D. None of the above

Q.89 In a contract of guarantee the person who gives the guarantee is called_______.

(i) surety

(ii) principal debtor

A. Only (i)

B. Only (ii)

C. Either (i) or (ii)

D. Both (i) and (ii)

Q.90 The limit for the maximum number of members in a public company is restricted to _______.

A. 2000

B. 5000

C. 10000

D. unlimited

Q.91 One of your customers lost the Fixed Deposit Receipt issued by the bank. To obtain a duplicate FD he needs to furnish_______.

A. A Promissory Note

B. A Guarantee

C. A Letter of Credit

D. An Indemnity Bond

Q.92 A private company should have at least _______.

A. 2 members

B. 7 members

C. 10 members

D. 50 members

Q.93 When did the National Bank of Agriculture and Rural Development established?

A. July 1982

B. July 1969

C. June 1951

D. June 1961

Q.94 When did the government acquire RBI's shareholding (72.5%) in NABARD?

A. May 2008   **B.** June 2008
C. August 2008   **D.** March 2009

Q.95 When did the National Housing Bank start its operations?

A. July 1982   **B.** July 1988
C. April 1980   **D.** March 1971

Q.96 Who works as RBI's agent at places where it has no office of its own?

A. State Bank of India
B. Ministry of Finance
C. Government of India
D. International Monetary Fund

Q.97 A partnership firm cannot raise funds through _______.

A. bank loan   **B.** partners loan
C. debentures   **D.** partners capital

Q.98 Which of the following sources is not used for medium-term financing?

A. Issue of equity shares
B. Issue of debentures
C. Term loans from banks
D. Sale of current asset

Q.99 Which of the following securities proves a burden on the finances of the company, when the company is not earning profits?

A. Equity shares
B. Preference shares
C. Redeemable preference shares
D. Debentures

Q.100 In the case of co-operative banks which are registered under the Deposit Insurance and Credit Guarantee Corporation Act, who has the power to order their winding up?

A. State Government
B. Central Government
C. Reserve Bank
D. Any of the above

Q.101 What is the full form of CBS?

A. Core Banking Solutions
B. Core Banking Software
C. Core Banking System
D. Core Banking Service

Q.102 Which of the following rural bank is named after a river?

A. Prathama Bank
B. Varada Grameen Bank
C. Thar Anchalik Grameen Bank
D. Aravali Kshetriya Grameen Bank

Q.103 What is Scheduled Bank in India?

A. It is included in the II Schedule of Banking Regulation Act.
B. It is included in the II Schedule of Constitution.
C. It is included in the II Schedule of Reserve Bank of India Act.

D. None of these

Q.104 What is the animal on the insignia of the RBI?

A. Lion   **B.** Tiger   **C.** Panther   **D.** Elephant

Q.105 Preference shares are those which carry preferential right in respect of _______.

A. dividends
B. repayment of capital
C. both dividend and repayment of capital
D. right to vote on all important motions in AGM

Q.106 The number of Banks nationalized since 1969 is _______.

A. 8   **B.** 12   **C.** 14   **D.** 20

Q.107 Which of the following is the Banker's Bank?

A. IDBI   **B.** RBI   **C.** SBI   **D.** UBI

Q.108 What is the largest Public Sector Bank in India?

A. Central Bank
B. SBI
C. Punjab National Bank
D. None of these

Q.109 In which year the Reserve Bank of India was taken over by the Government?

A. 1945   **B.** 1948   **C.** 1952   **D.** 1956

Q.110 In Capital Market SRO stands for_______.

A. Self-Regulatory Organisations
B. Small Revenue Operations
C. Securities Roll-back Operations
D. Securities Regulatory Organisations

Q.111 A project, which may not add to the existing profits, should be financed by _______.

A. debentures
B. preference share capital
C. equity capital
D. public deposits

Q.112 The management of the company is entrusted to _______.

A. Promoters   **B.** Employees
C. Shareholders   **D.** Board of Directors

Q.113 The ratio between cash in hand and total assets maintained by the banks is called

A. SBR (Statutory Bank Ratio).
B. SLR (Statutory Liquid Ratio).
C. CBR (Central Bank Reserve).
D. CLR (Central Liquid Reserve).

Q.114 What is 'Repo rate'?

A. Repo rate is the rate at which the RBI lends to State Government
B. Repo rate is the rate at which the International aid agencies lend to RBI
C. Repo rate is the rate at which the RBI lends to banks
D. Repo rate is the rate at which the banks lends to RBI

Q.115 What is the apex organisation of Industrial Finance in India?

A.   Industrial Finance Corporation

B.   Industrial Credit and Investment corporation of India

C.   Industrial Development Bank of India

D.   None of these

Q.116 Open market operations is a part of

A. Credit Policy.

B. Debit Policy.

C. Deposit Policy.

D. None of these

Q.117 Income tax in India was introduced by

A. William Jones.

B. James Wilson.

C. Nicholas Kaldor.

D. Mahavir Tyagi.

Q.118 National Food for Work programme aimed at intensifying the generation of supplementary wage employment was launched in

A. October 2004

B. September 2003

C. November 2004

D. January 2004

Q.119 Government has merged Annapurna Scheme with

A.   National Old Age Pension Scheme

B.   Ujjwala

C.   IRDP

D.   None of these

Q.120 Which statement is true about opening of account in the name of Pardanashin woman?

A.   Account Can be opened for literate and illiterate Pardanashin woman

B.   Account Can't be opened for either literate or illiterate Pardanashin woman

C.   Account Can be opened for literate Pardanashin woman

D.   Account Can be opened illiterate Pardanashin woman

// Smart Answer Sheet //

Correct Indicates percentage of students who answered questions correctly.

Skipped Indicates percentage of students who skipped questions.

Q.	Ans.	Correct / Skipped	Q.	Ans.	Correct / Skipped	Q.	Ans.	Correct / Skipped	Q.	Ans.	Correct / Skipped	Q.	Ans.	Correct / Skipped
1	A	39.34 % / 18.04 %	17	B	14.75 % / 40.58 %	33	C	37.3 % / 29.09 %	49	D	41.8 % / 40.99 %	65	B	32.38 % / 36.88 %
2	B	16.39 % / 40.17 %	18	D	17.21 % / 40.99 %	34	A	13.93 % / 41.81 %	50	D	34.02 % / 39.75 %	66	D	33.61 % / 40.98 %
3	C	34.84 % / 36.47 %	19	C	50.0 % / 16.39 %	35	D	53.28 % / 36.06 %	51	A	21.31 % / 37.3 %	67	C	36.07 % / 41.39 %
4	A	16.8 % / 42.22 %	20	A	18.44 % / 35.66 %	36	B	43.03 % / 36.89 %	52	B	26.23 % / 35.66 %	68	A	18.44 % / 41.81 %
5	C	42.21 % / 39.76 %	21	D	11.89 % / 33.6 %	37	B	39.75 % / 40.99 %	53	B	21.31 % / 41.39 %	69	B	40.57 % / 40.58 %
6	A	27.46 % / 39.34 %	22	A	39.75 % / 40.99 %	38	C	40.98 % / 40.17 %	54	C	14.75 % / 40.58 %	70	B	35.66 % / 41.39 %
7	B	46.72 % / 40.98 %	23	B	49.18 % / 24.59 %	39	B	44.67 % / 40.99 %	55	C	34.43 % / 37.7 %	71	C	34.43 % / 31.96 %
8	C	39.34 % / 40.99 %	24	B	41.39 % / 40.99 %	40	C	36.48 % / 41.8 %	56	D	49.18 % / 40.98 %	72	C	45.08 % / 36.48 %
9	D	12.7 % / 41.4 %	25	A	43.03 % / 40.99 %	41	C	32.79 % / 33.6 %	57	D	45.9 % / 40.99 %	73	A	41.39 % / 40.99 %
10	D	50.0 % / 40.16 %	26	B	29.51 % / 40.98 %	42	C	40.16 % / 41.4 %	58	A	32.38 % / 40.16 %	74	B	18.85 % / 40.58 %
11	C	31.97 % / 36.88 %	27	A	56.15 % / 32.78 %	43	D	41.8 % / 36.48 %	59	C	7.79 % / 38.11 %	75	D	29.92 % / 41.39 %
12	B	24.18 % / 40.57 %	28	A	28.69 % / 40.57 %	44	D	37.7 % / 40.99 %	60	C	28.69 % / 36.47 %	76	B	20.9 % / 39.35 %
13	B	33.61 % / 35.24 %	29	C	24.18 % / 34.02 %	45	B	30.74 % / 36.06 %	61	C	11.48 % / 40.98 %	77	C	32.38 % / 41.39 %
14	C	30.33 % / 40.98 %	30	C	54.51 % / 39.34 %	46	A	27.46 % / 40.98 %	62	A	45.9 % / 40.17 %	78	D	54.92 % / 40.57 %
15	C	9.84 % / 37.7 %	31	D	23.77 % / 37.71 %	47	C	38.11 % / 37.71 %	63	A	41.39 % / 38.12 %	79	C	50.41 % / 31.56 %
16	D	32.38 % / 36.88 %	32	A	22.54 % / 37.71 %	48	C	47.54 % / 40.98 %	64	B	48.77 % / 40.98 %	80	B	40.16 % / 36.48 %

Q.	Ans.	Correct / Skipped
81	A	29.1 % / 34.42 %
82	D	11.07 % / 40.57 %
83	C	22.54 % / 41.8 %
84	C	11.89 % / 39.75 %
85	A	24.18 % / 41.8 %
86	C	27.05 % / 40.57 %
87	C	27.87 % / 41.39 %
88	C	49.18 % / 40.98 %

Q.	Ans.	Correct / Skipped
89	A	41.8 % / 40.99 %
90	D	53.28 % / 40.98 %
91	D	52.05 % / 40.57 %
92	A	47.95 % / 40.98 %
93	A	45.08 % / 35.25 %
94	A	14.75 % / 42.63 %
95	B	31.15 % / 38.52 %
96	A	37.3 % / 39.34 %

Q.	Ans.	Correct / Skipped
97	C	36.89 % / 40.57 %
98	A	11.89 % / 40.57 %
99	D	20.49 % / 38.12 %
100	C	30.74 % / 36.88 %
101	A	48.36 % / 40.57 %
102	B	31.15 % / 40.98 %
103	C	22.54 % / 41.8 %
104	B	33.2 % / 39.34 %

Q.	Ans.	Correct / Skipped
105	C	31.97 % / 40.98 %
106	C	35.25 % / 40.98 %
107	B	58.61 % / 36.06 %
108	B	54.1 % / 40.98 %
109	B	30.33 % / 34.42 %
110	A	21.72 % / 40.98 %
111	B	27.46 % / 32.38 %
112	D	34.84 % / 40.57 %

Q.	Ans.	Correct / Skipped
113	B	52.46 % / 33.2 %
114	C	43.85 % / 41.4 %
115	C	29.51 % / 39.34 %
116	A	41.39 % / 40.58 %
117	B	29.92 % / 34.01 %
118	C	21.72 % / 42.21 %
119	A	31.56 % / 32.78 %
120	A	33.61 % / 36.47 %

Performance Analysis	
Avg. Score (%)	31.0%
Toppers Score (%)	95.0%
Your Score	

//Hints and Solutions//

1. The goods that form the subject of a contract of sale may be either existing goods, owned or possessed by the seller, or goods to be manufactured or acquired by the seller after the making of the contract of sale, in An Act for Codifying the Law Relating to the Sale of Goods called "future goods".

Hence, the correct option is (A).

2.

Category	Entities
Authorized Dealer – Category I	Commercial Banks, State Co-op Banks, Urban Co-op Banks
Authorized Dealer- Category II	Upgraded FFMCs, Coop Banks, Regional Rural Banks (RRBs), others
Authorized Dealer – Category III	Select Financial and other institutions

Hence, the correct option is (B).

3. According to section 106 of TPA, 1882, if there is an absence of a written contract or a local usage to the contrary then in the case, a lease of immovable property for manufacturing agriculture purpose will be valid till the time until it was a term and initiated by either of the party, by six months notice and if there is a lease any other purpose except agriculture or manufacturing then it will be terminated by 15 days notice.

Hence, the correct option is (C).

4. Meaning of pari passu charge – Pari-passu is a Latin phrase, which means "equal footing". "Pari Passu" charge means that when the borrower company goes into dissolution, the assets over which the charge has been created will be distributed in proportion to the creditors' (lenders) respective holdings.

In finance, the term pari-passu refers to loans, bonds, or classes of shares that have equal rights of payment or equal seniority. In addition, secondary issues of shares that have equal rights with existing shares rank pari-passu. Wills and trusts can assign an in pari-passu distribution where all the named parties share the assets equally.

Pari-passu can describe any instance where two or more items can claim equal rights as the other. Within the marketplace, all new shares within an offering have the same rights as those issued during a previous offering. In that sense, the shares are pari-passu.

Hence, the correct option is (A).

5. Banker's lien is an implied pledge Why?

Lien is one of the important rights enjoyed by a banker. A line means the right of the creditor to retain the goods and securities owned by the debtors until the debt due from him is repaid.

It confers upon the creditor the right to retain the security of the debtor and not the right to sell it.

Hence, the correct option is (C).

6. The person borrowing and transferring his interest in an immovable property to the lender is the mortgagor. The lender is the mortgagee and the funds lent against which the property is used as security is the mortgage money. A mortgage by deposit of title deed does not require registration.

Hence, the correct option is (A).

7. The lien is excluded if, to the knowledge of the banker at the time of deposit, the securities in question belong to a third party. But the lien is not excluded if the bank receives the securities in good faith and without knowledge that they in fact belong to a third party.

Hence, the correct option is (B).

8. Right of set-off is the right of the bank to combine the two accounts of the same person where one account which is in credit balance and the other account is in a debit balance in order to cover a loan default.

Hence, the correct option is (C).

9. A set-off clause is a legal clause that gives a lender the authority to seize a debtor's deposits when they default on a loan. A set-off clause can also refer to a settlement of mutual debt between a creditor and a debtor through offsetting transaction claims. This allows creditors to collect a greater amount than they usually could under bankruptcy proceedings.

Hence, the correct option is (D).

10. Garnishee Order is an order passed by an executing court directing or ordering a garnishee not to pay money to judgment debtor since the latter is indebted to the garnisher (decree holder). It is an Order of the court to attach money or Goods belonging to the judgment debtor in the hands of a third person.

Hence, the correct option is (D).

11. Similarly, as per the RTI Act, an appeal shall be disposed of within 30 days on the receipt of the appeal by the First Appellate Authority or within such extended period not exceeding a total of 45 days from the date of filing thereof, as the case may be, for reasons to be recorded in writing.

Hence, the correct option is (C).

12. At present, 39 Debts Recovery Tribunals (DRTs) and 5 Debts Recovery Appellate Tribunals (DRATs) are functioning across the country. Each DRT and DRAT is headed by a Presiding Officer and a Chairperson, respectively.

Hence, the correct option is (B).

13. The law provides that either side (department or party) if aggrieved by any order passed by the State Bench or Area Bench of the Tribunal may file an appeal to the High Court and the High Court may admit such appeal if it is satisfied that the case involves a substantial question of law.

Hence, the correct option is (B).

14. "A banking company cannot hold any immovable property, howsoever acquired, except for its own use, for any period exceeding seven years from the date of acquisition thereof. The company is permitted, within the period of 7 years, to deal or trade in any such property for facilitating its disposal".

Hence, the correct option is (C).

15. Companies Act, 2013. 141. (1) A person shall be eligible for appointment as an auditor of a company only if he is a chartered accountant: Provided that a firm whereof majority of partners practicing in India are qualified for appointment as aforesaid may be appointed by its firm name to be an auditor of a company.

Hence, the correct option is (C).

16. Duties of collecting bank - the duties of collecting bank are as follows: Duty of collecting bank is to open the bank account and follow up the reference. If the cheque is crossed to some other banker, then it's the duty of the bank to refuse to collect it. Duty to verify the instruments, defects in the instruments.

Hence, the correct option is (D).

17. The Consumer Protection Act, 1986, was enacted to provide a simpler and quicker redressal to consumer grievances. The Act seeks to promote and protect the interest of consumers against deficiencies and defects in goods or services.

Hence, the correct option is (B).

18. Under sub-section (3) of section 20, of The Recovery of Debts Due to Banks and Financial Institutions Act, 1993, an appeal has to be filed within 45 days from the date on which a copy of the order aggrieved has been passed or deemed to have been passed by the Tribunal is received.

Hence, the correct option is (D).

19. "For the purposes of this Act, "previous year" means the financial year immediately preceding the assessment year: Under Income Tax, the returns are filed by assessees after the end of the year/ period during which earnings are made and that period is called previous year/ financial year.

Hence, the correct option is (C).

20. Where an order under sub-section (1) has been made, the Reserve Bank may, by order in writing, appoint a suitable person in place of 8[the chairman or director], or chief executive officer or other officer or employee who has been removed from his office under that sub-section, with effect.

Hence, the correct option is (A).

21. As it is known and specifically provided, one cannot claim compensation for a breach of contract when the loss suffered is indirect and/or remote. However, there remains no such exception for a contract of indemnity. Much is left to the contractual freedom and will of the parties.

Hence, the correct option is (D).

22. A pledge or pawn is the delivery of chattels or choices in action by a debtor to his creditor as security for his debt or any other obligation. Whilst possession of the thing passes to the pledgee, the property in the thing (i.e. the legal ownership) remains with the pledgor.

Hence, the correct option is (A).

23. Tenure of Chairman of Banking Company

The whole time Chairman of a banking company can hold office for a period not exceeding five years provided he is eligible for reappointment.

Hence, the correct option is (B).

24. The guarantee is a legal term more comprehensive and of higher import than either warranty or "security". It most commonly designates a private transaction by means of which one person, to obtain some trust, confidence, or credit for another, engages to be answerable for him. It may also designate a treaty through which claims, rights, or possessions are secured. It is to be differentiated from the colloquial "personal guarantee" in that a Guarantee is a legal concept that produces an economic effect. A personal guarantee, by contrast, is often used to refer to a promise made by an individual that is supported by, or assured through, the word of the individual. In the same way, a guarantee produces a legal effect wherein one party affirms the promise of another (usually to pay) by promising to themselves pay if a default occurs.

Hence, the correct option is (B).

25. The initial public offering is underwritten by one or more investment banks, who also arrange for the shares to be listed on one or more stock exchanges. Through this process, colloquially known as floating, or going public, a privately held company is transformed into a public company.

Hence, the correct option is (A).

26. Section 30 of the Indian Partnership Act, provides that though a minor cannot be a partner in a firm, with the consent of all the partners, for the time being, he may be admitted to the benefits of the partnership by an agreement executed through his guardian with the other partners.

Hence, the correct option is (B).

27. The relationship between the banker and the customer is established by mutual agreement to open and operate the account. This relationship may be terminated at any time by either party by closing the accounts. In fact, the banker-customer relationship imposes an implied obligation on the banker not to close the account of the customer except in extraordinary cases supported by indisputable reasons.

In other words, the banker should carefully examine the issue before closing the customer's account and unless there are justifiable reasons, it should not close the accounts of the customer.

Hence, the correct option is (A).

28. Following are the pleadings that are filed in DRT by the parties. Original Application (O.A) refers to the claim filed by the bank or financial institution for recovery of debt from the borrower. Interlocutory Application (I.A) refers to the applications filed during the pendency of the case.

Hence, the correct option is (A).

29. The preferential payments shall be made by the official liquidator or adequate provision for such payments shall be made by him within **3 months** from the date of the winding-up order of the Bank.
Hence, the correct option is (C).

30. In a contract of indemnity, there are two parties i.e. indemnifier and indemnified. A contract of guarantee involves

three parties i.e. creditor, principal debtor, and surety. An indemnity is for reimbursement of a loss, while a guarantee is for the security of the creditor.

Hence, the correct option is (C).

31. Hearings Before the Committee on Banking, Housing, and Urban Affairs, the United States been granted to the Bank in the following described property If all information pertaining to a new or refinanced loan is not available on the date M. A delinquency and collection charge may be charged on each payment.

Under Section 131 of the NI Act, protection is not available to the paying bank.

Hence, the correct option is (D).

32. The Truth in Lending Act (TILA) is a Federal law that requires lenders to provide standardized information so that borrowers can compare loan terms. Lenders must provide information on what credit will cost the borrowers, when charges will be imposed, and what the borrower's rights are as a consumer.

Hence, the correct option is (A).

33. The Reserve Bank of India performs this function under the guidance of the **Board for Financial Supervision (BFS)**. The Board was constituted in November 1994 as a committee of the Central Board of Directors of the Reserve Bank of India. The primary objective of BFS is to undertake consolidated supervision of the financial sector comprising commercial banks, financial institutions, and non-banking finance companies.

Hence, the correct option is (C).

34. An adjudicating Authority can enquire contravention under FEMA only if the complaint is filed by Central Government. Adjudicating Authority has to endeavour to dispose of the complaints within one year from the date of receipt of the complaint.

Hence, the correct option is (A).

35. There was a need to have an effective system to recover the money from borrowers. This lead to the formation of Debt Recovery Tribunals (DRTs) after the passing of Recovery of Debts due to Banks and Financial Institutions Act (RDDBFI), 1993. DRTs handle the cases in relation to disputed loans above Rs.10 lakhs.

Hence, the correct option is (D).

36. When financial institutions and banks undertake activities related to banking like an investment, issue of debit and credit card, etc then it is known as universal banking.

Universal banks may offer credit, loans, deposits, asset management, investment advisory, payment processing, securities transactions, underwriting, and financial analysis.

Hence, the correct option is (B).

37. The loans with LTV ratios higher than 100% are called underwater mortgages.

The loan-to-value (LTV) ratio is a financial term used by lenders to express the ratio of a loan to the value of an asset purchased. The term is commonly used by banks and building societies to represent the ratio of the first mortgage line as a percentage of the total appraised value of the real property.

Hence, the correct option is (B).

38. A promissory note is a financial instrument that contains a written promise by one party (the note's issuer or maker) to pay another party (the note's payee) a definite sum of money, either on-demand or at a specified future date. In effect, promissory notes can enable anyone to be a lender.

Hence, the correct option is (C).

39. Attachment Order Issued by income-tax authorities: The credit balance in the account of a customer of a banker may be attached by the Income-Tax authorities if the former defaults in making payment of the tax due from him.

Hence, the correct option is (B).

40. The Reserve Bank of Australia released the world's first long-lasting and counterfeit resistant polymer (plastic) banknotes in 1988. **Australia** had completely switched to these banknotes.

Hence, the correct option is (C).

41. Bank of India was founded in 1906 in Mumbai. It became the first Indian bank to open a branch outside India in London in 1946 and the first to open a branch in continental Europe at Paris in 1974.

Hence, the correct option is (C).

42. Whoever fails to comply with any order made by either of the 3 forums, shall be punishable with imprisonment for a term which shall not be less than one month, but which may extend to three years, or with fine, which shall not be less than twenty-five thousand rupees, but which may extend to one lakh rupees, or with both.

Notwithstanding anything contained in the Code of Criminal Procedure, 1973, the three forums shall have the power of a Judicial Magistrate of First Class for the trial of offences under subsection (1) above, and on conferment of such powers, the said three forums, shall be deemed to be a Judicial Magistrate of First Class for the purposes of the Code of Criminal Procedure, 1973.

Hence, the correct option is (C).

43. One's complaint will not be considered if: One has not approached his bank for redressal of his grievance first. The institution complained against is not covered under the scheme. The subject matter of the complaint is not pertaining to the grounds of complaint specified under Clause 8 of the Banking Ombudsman Scheme.

Hence, the correct option is (D).

44. At the State Authority Level -

The Member Secretary of the State Legal Services Authority organizing the Lok Adalat would constitute benches of the Lok Adalat, each bench comprising of a sitting or retired judge of the High Court or a sitting or retired judicial officer and any one or both of- a member from the legal profession; a social worker engaged in the upliftment of the weaker sections and interested in the implementation of legal services schemes or programmes.

At High Court Level -

The Secretary of the High Court Legal Services Committee would constitute benches of the Lok Adalat, each bench comprising of a sitting or retired judge of the High Court and any one or both of- a member from the legal profession; a social worker engaged in the upliftment of the weaker sections and interested in the implementation of legal services schemes or programmes.

At District Level -

The Secretary of the District Legal Services Authority organizing the Lok Adalat would constitute benches of the Lok Adalat, each bench comprising of a sitting or retired judicial officer and any one or both of either a member from the legal profession; and/or a social worker engaged in the upliftment of the weaker sections and interested in the implementation of legal services schemes or programmes or a person engaged in para-legal activities of the area, preferably a woman.

Hence, the correct option is (D).

45. Constructive notice is the legal fiction that signifies that a person or entity should have known, as a reasonable person would have, of a legal action taken or to be taken, even if they have no actual knowledge of it.

Hence, the correct option is (A).

46. Consumer Protection Act provides for the establishment of Consumer Protection Councils at Centre, State and District levels. The purpose of these Councils is to review consumer-related policies of the government and suggest measures for further improvements for protecting and promoting the rights of the consumers. The composition of these councils is broad-based. The Minister Incharge of Consumer Affairs in the Centre is the Chairman of the Central Consumer Protection Council and it has other official and non-official members. The State Consumer Protection Council is headed by Minister In-charge of Consumer Affairs in the State and the District Consumer Protection Council is headed by the Collector of the District. These Councils are advisory in nature and their object is to protect the rights of the consumers enshrined under the Act.

Hence, the correct option is (A).

47. Yes, 75 percent of the amount determined by the tribunal is required to be deposited at the timing of filing the appeal.

In so far as appeals to the Tribunal is concerned, no appeal can be filed before the Tribunal unless the appellant has deposited in full, such part of the amount of tax, interest, fine, fee, and penalty arising from the impugned order, as is admitted by him, and a sum equal to 20% of the remaining amount of tax in dispute, in addition to the amount deposited before the AA, arising from the said order, in relation to which appeal has been filed.

Hence, the correct option is (C).

48. The SEBI Act frame regulations relating to the transfer of securities of listed companies, etc. The SEBI should have the power to inspect books of accounts, records of the listed companies. The rights issue with the right of renunciation is treated as a public issue.

Hence, the correct option is (C).

49. All statements which the Court permits or requires to be made before it by witnesses, in relation to matters of fact under inquiry, such statements are called oral evidence, [all documents including electronic records produced for the inspection of the Court], such documents are called documentary evidence.

Hence, the correct option is (D).

50. The new bank under Banking Companies (Acquisition & transfer of undertaking) Act 1970 stands for Nationalised Bank. An Act to provide for the acquisition and transfer of the undertakings of certain banking companies, having regard to their size, resources, coverage and organisation, in order to control the heights of the economy and to meet progressively, and serve better, the needs of the development of the economy in conformity with national policy and objectives and for matters connected therewith or incidental thereto.

Hence, the correct option is (D).

51. Tiwari committee was the first committee recommended for the establishment of special Recovery tribunals for Books and Financial Institution.

In 1991, the first Committee on Financial System headed by Shri M Narasimham considered setting up of the special tribunals with special powers for adjudication of such matters and speedy recovery as critical to the successful implementation of financial sector reforms.

Hence, the correct option is (A).

52. The main outcome of the FSLC's work was a draft Indian Financial Code. The main outcome of the Commission's work was a draft 'Indian Financial Code'. The Commission took a comprehensive, first-principles approach to the task, rooting its analysis and decisions in a conceptual analysis of financial regulation and review of the experience.

Hence, the correct option is (B).

53. When the board of a banking company is ordered to be reconstituted under Section 10A of the BR Act, directors will be removed by lots for the purpose of reconstitution.

The Board as per provisions of Section 10A of Banking Regulation Act, it is necessary to retire any Director or Directors, the Board may, by lots drawn in such manner as may be prescribed, decide which Director or Directors shall cease to hold office and such decision shall be binding on every Director of the Board.

Hence, the correct option is (B).

54. For the purpose of exposure norms, the meaning of 'Group' Commonality of Management, and effective control.

A group is a collection of individuals who have relations with one another that make them interdependent to some significant degree. As so defined, the term group refers to a class of social entities having in common the property of interdependence among their constituent members.

Hence, the correct option is (C).

55. Regulatory regime over banking companies means the regulation of control over banking companies. In India, banking companies are regulated by the Banking Regulation Act, 1949 and Reserve Bank of India Act, 1934.

Hence, the correct option is (C).

56. Banks are undertaking to trade in shares and securities and this activity is regulated by the Securities and Exchange Board of India.

Securities and Exchange Board of India (SEBI) is a statutory regulatory body entrusted with the responsibility to regulate the Indian capital markets. It monitors and regulates the securities market and protects the interests of the investors by enforcing certain rules and regulations.

Hence, the correct option is (D).

57. The first proviso explains that if two or more persons jointly hold any number of shares in a private company, those two or more persons will be deemed as one person only while counting the maximum limit of 200 members, irrespective of the number of shares held by them together or separately.

Hence, the correct option is (D).

58. This provision in the RBI Act is contained in Section 7 which says: The Central Government may from time to time give such directions to the Bank as it may, after consultation with the Governor of the Bank, consider necessary in the public interest.

Hence, the correct option is (A).

59. The Companies Act applies to the banking companies in relation to their registration and winding up.

The winding-up or liquidation of a company is the process by which a company's assets are collected and sold in order to pay its debts. When the winding-up has been completed, the company is formally dissolved and it ceases to exist. Broadly speaking, a company can be wound up in one of two ways.

Hence, the correct option is (C).

60. The Banking Regulation Act applies to cooperative banks as provided in the modification of Section 56.

The Reserve Bank regulates the banking functions of StCBs/DCCBs/UCBs under the provisions of Sections 22 and 23 of the Banking Regulation Act, 1949 (As Applicable to Co-operative Societies (AACS).

Hence, the correct option is (C).

61. Public Sector Banks (PSBs) are a major type of bank in India, where a majority stake (i.e. more than 50%) is held by the government. The shares of these banks are listed on stock exchanges. There are a total of 12 Public Sector Banks alongside 1 state-owned Payments Bank in India.

Hence, the correct option is (C).

62. The moral beliefs held by an individual are known as values. Moral values are usually communal and shared by the public in general, thus if there is no agreement among community members no moral values will be established.

Hence, the correct option is (A).

63. The word "ethics" is derived from the Greek word ethos (character). In philosophy, ethics defines what is good for the individual and for society and establishes the nature of duties that people owe themselves and one another.

Hence, the correct option is (A).

64. A banking company requires a license from RBI to undertake banking business as per the provision of Section 22 of the Banking Regulation Act.

For commencing banking business in India, every banking company is required to obtain a licence from the Reserve Bank of India, under the provisions of Section 22 of the Banking Regulation Act, 1949. No company can carry on banking business in India unless it holds a license issued by the Reserve Bank of India.

Hence, the correct option is (B).

65. Bank of Hindustan was established in 1770.

Bank of Hindustan is considered as among the first modern banks in colonial India. It was established by the agency house of Alexander and Company.

Hence, the correct option is (B).

66. Punjab National Bank is a PSU working under Central Government of India regulated by Reserve Bank of India Act, 1934 and Banking Regulation Act, 1949. Punjab National Bank was registered on 19 May 1894 under the Indian Companies Act, with its office in Anarkali Bazaar, Lahore, in present-day Pakistan. The founding board was drawn from different parts of India professing different faiths and of varying back-ground with, the common objective of creating a truly national bank that would further the economic interest of the country. PNB's founders included several leaders of the Swadeshi movement such as Dyal Singh Majithia and Lala Harkishen Lal, Lala Lalchand, Kali Prasanna Roy, E. C. Jessawala, Prabhu Dayal, Bakshi Jaishi Ram, and Lala Dholan Dass. The bank opened for business on 12th April 1895 in Lahore.

Hence, the correct option is (D).

67. Section 12 of the banking regulation act 1949 regulates the Shareholding in Banking Companies in India. No shareholder of a banking company can exercise voting rights more than 10% of the total voting rights of all the shareholders of the banking company.

Hence, the correct option is (C).

68. The interests and rights of customers are given top priority in the vendor model. A number of vendors produce and sell products that are designed to support credit-risk measurement and management functions within financial institutions. Such products may comprise risk measurement models, data, or systems developed by external commercial entities.

Hence, the correct option is (A).

69. Drawee is a legal and banking term used to describe the party that has been directed by the depositor to pay a certain sum of money to the person presenting the check or draft. A typical example is if you are cashing a paycheck. The bank that

cashes your check is the drawee, your employer who wrote the check is the drawer, and you are the payee.

Hence, the correct option is (B).

70. The oldest form of business organization is the sole proprietorship. When the ownership and management of a business are in control of one individual, the form of business is called sole proprietorship.

Hence, the correct option is (B).

71. The first Indian bank to have been started solely with Indian capital investment is **Punjab National Bank**. The first Indian bank to open an overseas branch is Bank of India. It established a branch in London in 1946. The oldest existing **Public Sector** Bank in India is **Allahabad Bank.**

Hence, the correct option is (C).

72. A partnership may come into existence by an express or implied agreement only.

The partnership comes into existence as a result of an agreement among the partners. The agreement can be either oral or written. The partnership act does not require that the agreement must be in writing.

Hence, the correct option is (C).

73. A Partnership Firm is nothing but an organization of two or more people having a mutual understanding to run a business and earned profit. Partnership firms are governed by the Indian Partnership Act, 1932 in India. Individuals are known as partners and collectively as partnership firms.

Hence, the correct option is (A).

74. The most important advantage of a joint-stock company form of business organization is that members can conveniently transfer their shares. The shares of a company are transferable. Also, in the case of a listed public company they can also be sold in the market and be converted to cash.

Hence, the correct option is (B).

75. Letter of Credit where in addition to advance payment, the beneficiary is entitled to payment of storage charges is called Green clause credit.

This is a normal documentary letter of credit, which provides a secured form of credit in that exporters can draw an agreed percentage of the value of the goods to be shipped against the presentation of warehouse receipts as collateral.

Hence, the correct option is (D).

76. Equality in Votes Co-operative society is governed by the principle of 'one man one vote'. Each member is entitled to equal voting rights irrespective of the amount of capital contributed by a member.

Hence, the correct option is (B).

77. Section 5(b) of the Banking Regulation Act, 1949, provides that "banking" means the accepting, for the purpose of lending or investment, of deposits of money from the public, repayable on demand or otherwise, and withdrawable by cheque, draft, and order or otherwise.

Hence, the correct option is (C).

78. The function of a Bank is to collect deposits from the public and lend those deposits for the development of Agriculture, Industry, Trade, and Commerce. Bank pays interest at lower rates to the depositors and receives interest on loans and advances from them at higher rates.

Hence, the correct option is (D).

79. In case of safe custody of articles relation between Bank and Customer are Bank bailor and Customer bailee.

When a banker accepts items like securities or documents for safe custody or maintains escrow accounts of the customers, the relation between the banker and customer is a Trustee and the Beneficiary (Trustier). In the above cases also the relation between the bank and the customer is between the principal and the agent.

Hence, the correct option is (C).

80. The line is a/an right of the creditor to retain possession.

A lien is the right of a creditor in possession of goods, securities, or any other assets belonging to the debtor to retain them until the debt is repaid, provided that there is no contract express or implied, to the contrary.

Hence, the correct option is (B).

81. Banks may change the composition of working capital by increasing the cash credit component beyond 20% or increase the loan component beyond 80%, as the case may be if they so desire.

The 'Loan System" was introduced to minimise the risks of cash and liquidity management on the part of the banking system, caused by volatile movements in cash credit component of working capital. In the current environment of short-term investment opportunities available to both corporates and banks, RBI has reviewed the guidelines relating to the 'Loan System'. Accordingly, it has been decided that banks will henceforth have the freedom to change the composition of working capital by increasing the cash credit component beyond 20% or to increase the 'Loan component' beyond 80% as the case may be, for working capital limits of Rs.10 crore and above, if they so desire. Banks are expected to appropriately price each of the two components of working capital finance, taking into account the impact of such decisions on their cash and liquidity management. The guidelines relating to the 'Loan System', as currently applicable are set out in the Annexure.

Hence, the correct option is (A).

82. Since 1967, the Freedom of Information Act (FOIA) has provided the public with the right to request access to records from any federal agency. It is often described as the law that keeps citizens in the know about their government.

Hence, the correct option is (D).

83. A minimum of ten members is required to form a cooperative society. The Co-operative Societies Act do not specify the maximum number of members for any co-operative society. However, after the formation of the society, the member may specify the maximum number of members.

Hence, the correct option is (C).

84. Co-operative and public companies are similar with respect to the maximum number of members.

The minimum number of members required to start a co-operative society is 10 and there is no maximum limit. But in a public company, the minimum member is seven and there is no maximum limit and in a private company the minimum number of member is 2 and the maximum limit is 50.

Hence, the correct option is (C).

85. The Certifying Authorities (CAs) issue digital signature certificates for electronic authentication of users. The Controller of Certifying Authorities (CCA) has been appointed by the Central Government under section 17 of the Act for purposes of the IT Act.

Hence, the correct option is (A).

86. On the admission of a new partner, it may happen, that the new partner pays goodwill to the old partners off the record of the firm i.e. privately. The amount paid privately as goodwill will not be recorded in the books of the firm. Example: X and Y are partners in a firm sharing profits and losses in the ratio of 3:2.

Very often the incoming partner is not in a position to bring anything in cash for goodwill. Under this circumstance, it becomes desirable to bring the goodwill at its full value by debiting the goodwill and crediting the old partners' Capital Account in their old profit sharing ratio.

This allows full credit to all the old partners for their interest in the overall goodwill. Goodwill Account then appears as an asset in the firm's Balance Sheet. It is not necessary that it should be allowed to stand there for an indefinite period.

After crediting the goodwill to the old partners, their capital accounts increase and thus the firm's status as regards the earning capacity descends from super earning to the normal earning one At this stage any share in partnership firm that is assigned to the incoming partner refers to the normal profit as against super profit.

Therefore, the newcomer cannot be asked for any extra payment because of none gains or sacrifices super profit. When the purpose is fulfilled the goodwill is written back to partners of the newly constituted firm in the new profit sharing ratio.

Hence, the correct option is (C).

87. Section 66C provides for punishment for Identity theft as Whoever, fraudulently or dishonestly make use of the electronic signature, password or any other unique identification feature of any other person, shall be punished with imprisonment of either description for a term which may extend to three years and shall also be liable to fine with may extend to rupees 1 lakh.

Hence, the correct option is (C).

88. Section 58 (a) of the transfer of property act, 1882, defines mortgage as, "A mortgage is the transfer of an interest in specific immovable property for the purpose of securing the payment of money advanced or to be advanced by way of loan, an existing or future debt, or the performance of an engagement which may give rise to a pecuniary liability."

Hence, the correct option is (C).

89. The person who gives the guarantee is called the 'surety', the person in respect of whose default the guarantee is given is called the 'principal debtor', and the person to whom the guarantee is given is called the 'creditor'. A guarantee may be either oral or written.

Hence, the correct option is (A).

90. The limit for the maximum number of members in a public company is unlimited.

In order for a company to be public, it should have a minimum of 7 members (maximum unlimited).

Hence, the correct option is (D).

91. One of your customers lost the Fixed Deposit Receipt issued by the bank. To obtain a duplicate FD he needs to furnish an Indemnity Bond.

Indemnity Bond a bond indemnifying an obligee against loss that arises as a result of a failure on the part of a principal to perform as required. For example, a lease bond guarantees that a tenant will make his/her rental payments.

Hence, the correct option is (D).

92. Minimum number of members: Minimum number of members required to form a private company is 2, whereas a Public Company requires at least 7 members.

Hence, the correct option is (A).

93. NABARD was established on the recommendations of the B. Sivaraman Committee (by Act 61, 1981 of Parliament) on 12 July 1982 to implement the National Bank for Agriculture and Rural Development Act 1981. It replaced the Agricultural Credit Department (ACD) and Rural Planning and Credit Cell (RPCC) of Reserve Bank of India, and Agricultural Refinance and Development Corporation (ARDC). It is one of the premier agencies providing developmental credit in rural areas. NABARD is India's specialized bank for Agriculture and Rural Development in India.

Hence, the correct option is (A).

94. The Reserve Bank held 72.5% of the equity in NABARD amounting to Rs. 1450 crore. The remaining shareholding of Rs. 550 crore was with the Government of India. The Union Cabinet in May 2008 approved the Reserve Bank's proposal to transfer its shareholding in NABARD to the Government of India.

Hence, the correct option is (A).

95. The decision to establish the National Housing Bank (NHB) as an apex level institution for housing finance was taken in the Union Budget 1987-88. Thus, NHB was set up on July 9, 1988, under the National Housing Bank Act, 1987, with its entire paid-up capital coming from the Reserve Bank of India (RBI).

Hence, the correct option is (B).

96. SBI acts as an agent to the RBI, where there are no branches of RBI available. Accordingly, there are many functions that are rendered by the SBI.

These are:

- Maintaining the currency
- Government's bank
- Bank's banker
- Acts as a clearinghouse
- Maintaining the currency

Hence, the correct option is (A).

97. A partnership firm cannot raise funds by debentures. A common source of funding for a new or expanding partnership is the pockets, deep or otherwise, of the partners themselves. Known as self-funding or bootstrapping, consider how much of your own financial resources you can put in toward your business, and ask your partners to do the same. Sources can include savings, stocks and bonds, and even retirement account funds.

Hence, the correct option is (C).

98. Issue of equity shares is not used for medium-term financing. Financing is the process of providing funds for business activities, making purchases, or investing. Financial institutions such as banks are in the business of providing capital to businesses, consumers, and investors to help them achieve their goals.

Hence, the correct option is (A).

99. Debentures prove a burden on the finances of the company when the company is not earning profits. Debenture puts a permanent burden on the earnings of a company. Therefore, there is a greater risk when the earnings of the company fluctuate.

Hence, the correct option is (D).

100. Cooperative Banks: All-State, Central and Primary cooperative banks, also called urban cooperative banks, functioning in States / Union Territories which have amended the local Cooperative Societies Act empowering the Reserve Bank of India (RBI) to order the Registrar of Cooperative Societies of the State / Union Territory to wind up a cooperative bank or to supersede its committee of management and requiring the Registrar not to take any action regarding winding up, amalgamation or reconstruction of a co-operative bank without prior sanction in writing from the RBI are covered under the Deposit Insurance Scheme. At present all co-operative banks are covered by the DICGC.

Hence, the correct option is (C).

101. CBS stands for Core Banking Solutions. Core Banking Solutions or CBS is a commonly used word in banking these days. It has expanded the scope of banking in a major way by letting the banks to develop a centralized system that allows their customers to operate their bank accounts and avail themselves of any facility irrespective of the bank branch. In technical words, "Core Banking is a banking service provided by a group of networked bank branches where customers may access their bank accounts and perform basic transactions from any of the member branches."

Hence, the correct option is (A).

102. Varada Grameena Bank is a Regional Rural Bank (RRB) named after the Wardha River which is one of the biggest rivers in the Vidarbha region in India. It is one of those banks which were amalgamated and newly opened. It has been serving Kumta in Karnataka, providing excellent bank service to those in need.

Hence, the correct option is (B).

103. Scheduled Banks in India refer to those banks which have been included in the II Schedule of Reserve Bank of India Act, 1934. RBI, in turn, includes only those banks in this Schedule that satisfy the criteria laid down vide section 42 of the Bank of India Act. Banks not under this Schedule are called Non-Scheduled Banks.

Hence, the correct option is (C).

104. The selection of the Bank's common seal to be used as the emblem of the Bank on currency notes, cheques and publications, was an issue that had to be taken up at an early stage of the Bank's formation.

The general ideas on the seal were as follows:-

1. The seal should emphasize the Governmental status of the Bank, but not too closely;
2. It should have something Indian in the design;
3. It should be simple, artistic, and heraldically correct; and
4. The design should be such that it could be used without substantial alteration for letter heading, etc.

For this purpose, various seals, medals, and coins were examined. The East India Company Double Mohur, with the sketch of the Lion and Palm Tree, was found most suitable; however, it was decided to replace the lion with the tiger, the latter being regarded as the more characteristic animal of India.

Hence, the correct option is (B).

105. As per the companies act, 2013, preference share capital is defined as instruments that have the preferential right with respect to dividend payment (fixed/ on a percentage basis) and repayment of capital during winding up of the company.

Hence, the correct option is (C).

106. The government through the Banking Companies (Acquisition and Transfer of Undertakings) Ordinance, 1969 and nationalized the 14 largest commercial banks on 19 July 1969. These lenders held over 80 percent of bank deposits in the country. Soon, the parliament passed the Banking Companies (Acquisition and Transfer of Undertaking) Bill, and it received presidential approval on 9 August 1969.

Hence, the correct option is (C).

107. In India, the Reserve Bank Of India or RBI is known as the banker's bank. It is so-called because it acts as a bank for all the commercial banks in India. RBI holds their cash reserves, lends them short -term funds, and provides them the central clearing and remittances facilities.

Hence, the correct option is (B).

108. State Bank of India is the largest bank of India and has the largest market share with around 23%. The origin of the State Bank of India goes back to 1955 when the Government of India acquired the then Imperial Bank and renamed it.

SBI has been ranked 216th in the 2018 Fortune Global 500 list of biggest corporations in the world. The corporation has 2,57,252 employees.

Hence, the correct option is (B).

109. The Reserve Bank of India was nationalized with effect from 1st January 1949 on the basis of the Reserve Bank of India (Transfer to Public Ownership) Act, 1948. All shares in the capital of the Bank were deemed transferred to the Central Government on payment of suitable compensation.

Hence, the correct option is (B).

110. Self-Regulatory Organisations.
A self-regulatory organization is an organization that exercises some degree of regulatory authority over an industry or profession. The regulatory authority could exist in place of government regulation or applied in addition to government regulation.

Hence, the correct option is (A).

111. A project, which may not add to the existing profits, should be financed by preference share capital. Preference shares share in a company that is owned by people who have the right to receive part of the company's profits before the holders of ordinary shares are paid.

Hence, the correct option is (B).

112. The management of the company is entrusted to the Board of Directors. A "Managing Director" means a Director who, by virtue of Articles of Association of a Company or an agreement with the company or a resolution passed in its general meeting, or by its Board of Directors, is entrusted with substantial powers of management of affairs of the company.

Hence, the correct option is (D).

113. The banks are required to maintain a certain ratio between their cash in the hand and total assets, this is called Statutory Liquid Ratio (SLR). The Reserve Bank of India (RBI) has the authority to increase this ratio by up to 40%. An increase in the ratio constricts the ability of the bank to inject money into the economy.

Hence, the correct option is (B).

114. Repo rate is the rate at which the central bank of a country (Reserve Bank of India in case of India) lends money to commercial banks in the event of any shortfall of funds. Repo rate is used by monetary authorities to control inflation.

Hence, the correct option is (C).

115. The Industrial Development Bank of India (IDBI) was established in 1964 as an apex financial institution to provide credit and other financial facilities for the development of the fledgeling Indian industry.

Hence, the correct option is (C).

116. Open Market Operations refer to the purchase and sale of the Government securities (G-Secs) by RBI from/to market. The objective of Open Market Operations is to adjust the rupee liquidity conditions in the economy on a durable basis. When RBI sells government security in the markets, the banks purchase them. When the banks purchase Government securities, they have a reduced ability to lend to the industrial houses or other commercial sectors. This reduced surplus cash contracts the rupee liquidity and consequently credit creation/credit supply. When RBI purchases the securities, the commercial banks find them with more surplus cash and this would create more credit in the system. Thus, in the case of excess liquidity, RBI resorts to sale of G-secs to suck out rupee from system. Similarly, when there is a liquidity crunch in the economy, RBI buys securities from the market, thereby releasing liquidity.

Hence, the correct option is (A).

117. The 19th century saw the establishment of British rule in India. Following the Mutiny of 1857, the British government faced an acute financial crisis. To fill up the treasury, the first Income-tax Act was introduced in February 1860 by James Wilson, who became British-India's first Finance Minister.

Hence, the correct option is (b).

118. Unsourced material may be challenged and removed. The National Food for Work Programme(NFWP), 2004 was launched by the minister of rural development, the central government on 14 November 2004 in 150 of the most backward districts of India with the objective of generating supplementary wage employment.

Hence, the correct option is (C).

119. The Annapurna Scheme has been launched with effect from 1st April 2000. It aims at providing food security to meet the requirement of those senior citizens who, though eligible, have remained uncovered under the National Old Age Pension Scheme (NOAPS). Both the schemes have been merged for better implementation.

Hence, the correct option is (A).

120. A Pardanashin lady is one who remains in complete seclusion and does not transact with people other than members of her family. Though Pardanashin lady is legally competent to enter into a contract, she may be able to able to avoid it on the pretext of undue influence and the onus of proving of influence is on the bank. Therefore, the bank should take extra care in this regards. Signature of Pardanashin lady should be attested by her guardian if she is unmarried and by her husband if she is married. The signature may be attested by any other member of the family also. If she is illiterate she will not be issued cheque book and for every payment, she will have to give the discharge in the presence of an independent witness. However, in the case of literate Woman, cheque book will be issued and payment will be made on the basis of recorded signatures.

Hence, the correct option is (A).

// Notes //

// Notes //